transformation journal

A ONE YEAR JOURNEY

THROUGH THE BIBLE

Edited by
Sue Nilson Kibbey
&
Carolyn Slaughter

Abingdon Press
Nashville

TRANSFORMATION JOURNAL

Copyright © 2007 Ginghamsburg Church

All rights reserved.

Library of Congress Cataloging-in-Publication Data

Transformation journal : a one year journey through the Bible / edited by Sue Nilson Kibbey & Carolyn Slaughter.
p. cm.   ISBN-13: 978-0-687-64215-1   ISBN-10: 0-687-64215-9   1. Bible--Meditations. 2. Devotional calendars.
I. Kibbey, Sue Nilson. II. Slaughter, Carolyn, 1949-

  BS491.5.T73 2007   242'.2--dc22   2006101697

07 08 09 10 11 12 13 14 15 16—10 09 08 07 06 05 04 03 02 01

PRINTED IN CHINA

introduction

This life *Transformation Journal* (TJ) is designed, created, and written with the passionate desire to help you grow in your relationship with God, through every book of the Bible.

As you use this daily journal, you will be introduced to the key people and stories that God has used to communicate love, demonstrate care, and offer provision. You will journey through the Bible by reading selected Scriptures, observing God's truths, and applying them to your life. By the end of one year, you will have traced God's loving hand throughout the Bible's pages, and you will deeply understand the unconditional love brought to us personally through God's son, Jesus Christ.

Spending a full week reading and reflecting upon each book of the Bible, you will gain a chance to develop the habit of a daily spiritual routine, an occasion to increase your knowledge of truth from Scripture, and an opportunity for God to engage and renew your mind and heart.

This journal was created and written by Ginghamsburg's TJ staff team (Sue Nilson Kibbey, Carolyn Slaughter, Dwayne Wilson, Jodi Long, and Kevin Applegate) and the Transformations team (Dottie Brown, Heather Cleary, Kate Johnsen, Donna McGraw, Kim Miller, David Phipps, Lisa Sowry, Bill Williams, Brad Wise and Dwayne Wilson). The *Transformation Journal* design is by Brad Wise with Tracey Verbeke.

COMPONENTS OF THIS JOURNAL

The *Transformation Journal* is arranged in sections for ease of use. Each week is designed to begin on Sunday and end on Saturday. Take a look at the first week and you'll see the following:

- A description of that week's book of the Bible, including background and overview information to help you understand its "big picture"
- A "Focus Point" plus Scripture readings for each day
- Space for personal study of each day's Scripture using the "S.O.N." method (see next section for guidelines), allowing you to record your insights, thoughts, and prayers
- Journal/reflection questions to help you further unpack the meaning of the Scripture you've read and the implications for your faith
- Transformations—an original reflective essay written on the week's Scripture

The best time to use this journal is when you are at your best! If you're a morning person, do your Bible reading and journal/reflection time in the morning. If you're an evening person, do it at night. Invest time with God during the best part of your day, every day. The bottom line is that God deserves your best. Note: If you find that you've fallen behind in your daily use of the TJ, just pick up with today's reading and resume your momentum.

A cell group (small group) guide with directions for how to use the *Transformation Journal* in your group has been included in these pages.

HOW TO USE THE S.O.N. METHOD OF JOURNALING

1) Begin with prayer, asking God to open your heart and mind to new truths, to let you see today's Scripture through God's eyes, and to help you understand it with the heart and spirit of Jesus.

2) S = SCRIPTURE. Carefully read the "Focus Point" and the Scripture for the day.

3) O = OBSERVATIONS. Reread the Scripture, writing down any particular observations you make about what is happening, questions or ideas you have about what you are reading, and insights into what God might be doing or saying. Try to avoid isolating any single verse or using it as a "proof text" for something you believe, but instead observe God's bigger intentions of love and grace. What do you notice?

4) N = NAME THE APPLICATIONS. What did you learn from your observations that you can apply to how you live your life today? What bigger principles does God want you to understand? What spiritual truths from today's Scripture challenge you to grow? What specific steps might God want you to take today in your attitude or your actions? Write them in your TJ.

5) Look at, ponder, and respond to the journal reflection questions that may take you even deeper into understanding the Scriptures you just read.

6) Close your time with God in prayer, asking God to show you how to apply what you've learned for life transformation. Write out your prayer in the TJ if you wish.

7) Meet with your cell group (small group) on a regular basis to discuss and interact together on the Scriptures you've read and what life applications you've made through the use of this *Transformation Journal*.

CELL GROUP GUIDE

Cell groups (small groups) are designed for investigating the Bible together as well as encouraging one's spiritual growth and relationship with Jesus (accountability). The following will help guide your cell group's meeting time as you use the *Transformation Journal* together.

GROUP RULES

1. A cell group practices confidentiality, which means what is shared in the group remains in the group.

2. A cell group is a safe place for people, where there is no judgment or ridicule for sharing thoughts, feelings, or past behaviors.

3. A cell group honors time, by starting and ending the group on time.

GATHER THE PEOPLE

Ask, "What was one God-moment you experienced this week?" and invite each person in the group to answer.

BIBLE STUDY

1. Choose and read one or more of the primary Scriptures for the week as a group.

2. Have each person share his or her response to one of this week's journal questions and the related Scripture.

3. Share personal stories about what God is currently transforming or changing in your life.

CARING TIME

1. Ask each person to share prayer requests, as well as blessings from the week.

2. Pray together as a group, acknowledging God's goodness and praying for the individual requests that were shared.

3. Pray that God brings others into your lives whom you may add to your cell group to increase your outreach.

orientation to the Old Testament

The exciting reality in following Jesus is that our lives become a progression of changes initiated and empowered by the presence of the Holy Spirit, gradually transforming us into the image of Christ. We use the Bible (also known as God's word) for education and learning to deepen our knowledge and understanding of God and God's ways. But this miraculous book is much more than a source of information. As we interact with God's word, we get to know God and learn what God wants for our lives. The sixty-six books of the Bible are "God-breathed," or written by human writers who were inspired by the Holy Spirit (as described in 2 Timothy 3:16), and are the source of God's teaching, correcting, training, and equipping us for life transformation.

The Bible is divided into two parts: the Old Testament, which covers the ancient time period from Creation to approximately 150 BC, and the New Testament, which includes the stories of Jesus and the early Christian church to approximately AD 100. The Old Testament (for Protestants) is made up of thirty-nine books that are grouped into categories, or sections. These sections are arranged in the following order: five books of the Law (Genesis through Deuteronomy, also known as the Pentateuch or the Torah), twelve history books (Joshua through Esther), five poetry or wisdom books (Job through Song of Songs), five books by the major prophets (Isaiah through Daniel), and twelve books by the minor prophets (Hosea through Malachi, also known as the Book of the Twelve). This *Transformation Journal* is designed as an overview of the entire Bible, and you'll find the study pages for the Old Testament books grouped according to these sections.

At least five great themes originate in the Old Testament books and continue through the New Testament. Your understanding of these particular themes will enrich your study, your devotional time in God's word, and your discernment of God's plan and purpose.

1) SIN

According to the Bible, the first sin was an act in which the first humans, created by God to share God's perfect nature and live in relationship with God, deliberately and knowingly chose to corrupt that relationship. Sin is the underlying human attitude that rebels against God and causes us to miss the mark of what God intended for us to be. Sin manifests itself in behavior harmful to others or ourselves. The initial choice of sin made by our spiritual ancestors in the garden has been handed down to us as our spiritual DNA, creating within all humans a natural bent to go our way rather than God's. Left unchecked, sin results in our eternal separation from God. Other words used in the Bible that mean "sin" include transgression, iniquity, trespass, disobedience, unrighteousness, lawlessness, and ungodliness.

2) SACRIFICIAL SYSTEM

Sin comes with the price tag of guilt and separation from God. People in the Old Testament used a sacrificial system in which they gave offerings to God to restore their relationship with God and make the community whole. Conscious of their sin and their separation from God, humans killed an animal on the altar to remove their sin and restore the community to God. Only a perfect, unblemished animal was worthy as a sacrifice to God. The sacrificial system was formalized in the centuries after the Temple was built by Solomon and included multiple types of offerings, such as the sin offering, burnt offering, peace offering, and others.

3) COVENANT

The theme of covenant (a binding agreement, or sometimes an unconditional promise) runs through the entire Bible and is established in Genesis 15. God made an agreement with Abraham that Abraham and his descendants would be God's representatives of faith to the world. However, Abraham and all humans since have been unable to live in total obedience to God and properly fulfill our part of the covenant. But through Jesus' death on the cross, God forgave Abraham's (everyone's) failure to abide by the covenant. Jesus, the perfect, unblemished Lamb of God, fulfilled the sacrificial requirements once and for all. Jesus called this the new covenant, the new unbreakable promise through which our relationship with God is restored for all eternity.

4) BLESSINGS OF OBEDIENCE

God's Law was given to Moses at Mount Sinai on behalf of the Israelites. It was to provide guidance and to shape God's followers into a people who would reflect God's character. For the Israelites, obedience to God brought blessings of land plus prosperous undertakings in farming and herding; it also meant victory during times of conflict and oppression. Disobedience brought a disciplinary response from God and withdrawal of the blessings of prosperity and military triumph. Like the Israelites of old, all generations (including ours) have struggled with ongoing obedience, but God's promise holds true: Daily obedience brings with it spiritual blessings from God.

5) WORSHIP

The Old Testament contains several Hebrew words that express worship offered to God. For example, *shakhah* means "to bow down," thereby to physically express respect and honor to God. This behavior is what we traditionally think of as worship. Another Hebrew word, *avadh* is also translated as worship, with a primary meaning "to serve." Thus worship that honors, respects, and shows reverence for God is expressed in the totality of life—not only in a powerful worship celebration but also in every aspect as we live out a vibrant, joyous, obedient relationship with God by serving God every moment of every day.

As you explore the characters, stories, and themes of the Old Testament, may you grasp the reality of God's covenant love, be challenged to walk in obedience every day, return God's love through a lifestyle of worship, and sense the transformation of heart and character that God is making in you.

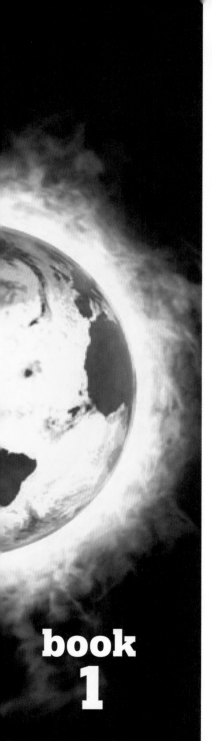

genesis

book of beginnings

book 1

Genesis, the first book of the Bible, is part of a group of five books (Genesis, Exodus, Leviticus, Numbers, and Deuteronomy) collectively known as the Pentateuch, the Book of the Law, the Torah, and the Law of Moses. These five books are among the world's most ancient writings. Moses obviously was not an eyewitness to the events contained in Genesis, which had been transmitted orally for thousands of years. Yet in Exodus 17:14 God tells Moses to write events down as they happen, especially as the commandments are revealed. This underscores why Moses is identified with the entire Book of the Law.

The word *genesis* means "origin" or "beginning." The book of Genesis tells the origin of the universe. In the beginning God already was, and in Genesis God is shown to be the creative force behind all that has come into existence. Genesis records the beginning of the cosmos, plants and animals, man and woman, marriage, evil, language, nations, the Israelite people, life, death, and salvation. It also records the history of Israel's generations through great stories and characters: Adam and Eve, Noah, Abraham and Sarah, Isaac and Rebecca, Jacob and Rachel, and Joseph, among others. What originated in Genesis became the framework for God's unfolding story through the rest of the Bible.

Genesis is divided into two sections. Genesis 1–11 includes the accounts of creation, humanity's rebellion against God, and God's response to disobedience. These events affirm that we live in a personal universe with a God who walks with people and cares about the quality of their relationship with God. Genesis 12–50 covers the story of one family. This section introduces Abraham and his descendents and records the beginning of salvation history, or God's continued efforts to reconnect with rebellious people. God's plan and purpose for all of human history is unveiled through the call and covenant God entered into with Abraham: to be a blessing to all people. The beauty of the Bible is that the story doesn't end with Genesis but is woven throughout its entirety. What begins in Genesis (God's loving creation of man and woman, God's longing to walk continually with humanity, and God's willing sacrifices to accomplish God's purpose) is fully developed through the other sixty-five biblical books.

Genesis' great stories of ordinary people and their interactions with God allow us enlightening insight into ourselves. As we recognize our own strengths and weaknesses in these characters, we catch a glimpse of how much God longs to be in relationship with us—and how far God is willing to go to be in connection with us.

The desire of God's heart is to walk daily with you in intimate relationship, just as God did with Adam and Eve. May the reality of God's love and provision for you sink deeply into your soul through your time in Scripture and reflection this week.

CREATION

_____

_____

_____

_____

_____

_____

_____

_____

_____

Genesis 1 gives us insight into who God is and what God is about. God existed before any design of time and space was implemented. These verses describe the birth of a world that reveals a God of order, purpose, and love, who entrusts the care of every part of creation to men and women, who are made in the very image of their Creator. From the beginning, and especially on the Sabbath (when God rested on the seventh day), we are called to worship this Creator.

GENESIS 1:1–2:3; JOHN 1:1-3

• What does it mean to be created in God's image?

• How does the awareness of being created in God's image affect how you care for all of God's creation—including yourself? What needs to change to make you a better caretaker?

mon.

ADAM, EVE, AND THE FALL

_____

_____

_____

_____

_____

_____

_____

_____

_____

God's deepest desire is to be in relationship with the people God created. Yet one small moment of rebellion shattered God's perfect oneness with humanity. Sin brings drastic consequences to our relationship with God and with others. But God lovingly pursued fallen humanity and set in motion the plan to overcome the effects of rebellion—a plan that culminates in the offer of complete forgiveness through God's Son, Jesus.

GENESIS 2:4–3; ROMANS 5:12-21

• What consequences resulted from Adam and Eve violating God's boundaries?

• God sets limits to protect us and provide for us. What boundary has God set that you struggle to stay within? What are potential consequences of crossing that line?

NOAH AND THE FLOOD

Early in Genesis, we see that all of humanity must deal with the realities of life, death, and sin. As we progress through the book, we see that morality—right vs. wrong—matters to God. The story of the Flood brings two new themes: God will judge sin, and God rescues from judgment those who live in obedience to God. God protected Noah and his family, and still protects those who faithfully follow God today.

GENESIS 6:9–8; 9:8-17

• What qualified Noah to be the remnant of humanity to be saved?

• God asked Noah to stand radically apart from the world, at the risk of ridicule and rejection. What is something difficult and risky God is asking you to do?

MORE SCRIPTURE
2 Peter 3:1-14—Creation and the promise of the Lord

ABRAHAM AND THE COVENANT

Covenant (a binding agreement) is a major biblical theme. God called Abraham to step out in faith and follow. Through the covenant, God promised that Abraham would be the father of a great nation.

GENESIS 12:1-7; 17:1-27; HEBREWS 11:8-19

• What did God promise Abraham in Genesis 12? How would Abraham be blessed and be a blessing?

• Ishmael was the son born as Abraham tried to carry out God's promise on his own terms (Genesis 16). It was important to Abraham for his son to live under God's blessing, and he completed the rite of covenant with him (17:26). Who is your Ishmael—the one you want to bring into God's covenant through Jesus?

thurs.

ISAAC AND HIS BLESSING

_____

_____

_____

_____

_____

_____

_____

_____

_____

_____

Isaac, the child born to Abraham and Sarah in their old age, was the first descendent to whom the covenant was confirmed. Isaac tended toward passivity, which at times led to compromise and dishonesty. Isaac teaches us much about God working in spite of and through our weaknesses.

GENESIS 26:1-6; 27:1–28:5; ROMANS 9:1-16

• How do you explain Isaac falling for Rebekah and Jacob's scheme? Which member of the family do you think was most in the wrong?

• When, like Jacob, have you attempted to sidestep God's plan or another person to get things done your way? What happened?

MORE SCRIPTURE

Genesis 21–28—Isaac's entire story

fri.

JACOB WRESTLES WITH GOD

_____

_____

_____

_____

_____

_____

_____

_____

_____

_____

Jacob, whose name means "cheat," grabbed things for himself early in life. But over the length of his lifetime Jacob experienced transformation and is now best remembered for grabbing onto and wrestling with God until God touched and blessed him.

GENESIS 32:3–33:4

• Twenty years had passed since Jacob and Esau were together. What was Jacob probably feeling about facing Esau? What preparations did he make?

• In the Bible, a name change marked a significant change in a person's life. What name would represent who you are as a result of your walk with God so far?

MORE SCRIPTURE

Genesis 25–50—Jacob's entire story

JOSEPH, AN ADMIRABLE MAN

Joseph grew to be a man of great faith and admirable character. His life marked a major turning point in Israel's history as his family moved from Canaan to Egypt to escape the effects of famine. New Testament and early Christian writers sometimes understood his story as an analogy to Jesus' story. Joseph, like Jesus, demonstrated forgiveness in the face of betrayal and lived sacrificially for the benefit of others.

GENESIS 37:1-36; 45:3-12; 50:15-26

• What purpose did Joseph play in the continuation of God's covenant?

• What is the one thing from Joseph's story that is most helpful in your present circumstances?

MORE SCRIPTURE
Genesis 37–50—Joseph's entire story

notes

AND PRAYER NEEDS

transformations

Rhinos and Donkeys

Downtown there's a homeless man named Rick. Rick is famous because for twenty years he's been building a time machine. If cardboard were waterproof and broken flashlights were truly laser beams, Rick would be long gone. For a quarter, he'll take a handwritten note to a loved one for you. You tell him the person's name and hair color, and Rick will find him or her in either the future or the past. He's going to both. People come from all over to talk to Rick and fill out a note. They gladly hand him a quarter and walk away laughing every time.

Outside of town there's a man named Noah. Noah is famous because for nearly one hundred years he's been building an ark. If the world would just flood like Noah keeps promising, he'd be long gone. You could board his boat along with thousands of animal couples for absolutely no cost. "Saving yourself is free," Noah tells everyone. Unfortunately, no one believes a boat full of crazy people and loosely caged, sharp-toothed animals is a good idea. They walk away laughing every time.

Imagine trying to convince people who were living in a desert that the earth was going to flood and that a floating zoo was their only hope. That makes as much sense as Rick's time machine. Imagine gathering thousands of tons of wood and then having to keep the goats and beavers from eating all of it. Imagine working for one hundred years on something and hearing nothing but ridicule. No one outside of Noah's family thought he was sane. If they did, they would've been on the boat. And nowhere in the Bible do we see God encouraging Noah by saying, "Trust me, Noah, it's going to rain like rhinos and donkeys, keep building." Amazingly, despite unimaginable mocking and self-doubt, Noah kept building. His faith saved his family and the future of all living things.

When I was a kid, my parents took me to a fair. The air was thick from fried foods and animal barns. I wanted badly to go on the Tilt-A-Whirl, but my dad told me those rides were for fools. So we bought tickets for the sensible and educational elephant ride. For an extra dollar you could feed it peanuts right out of your hand. I touched the elephant's skin while my dad paid. It was like rubbery concrete. On top I could see the parking lot as I felt the elephant's weight between my heels. I checked my pockets to see if I had enough money to ride forever.

In heaven I imagine Noah has a line of people waiting to speak with him. People with stories about washing their dog. People like me who wonder what he did with all that manure. There's so much I have to ask. At that first meeting, however, I'll show uncharacteristic restraint and just thank Noah for his crazy amount of faith. Because of him, I got to ride an elephant.

exodus

book of freedom

book 2

Exodus is a book of great adventure that revolves around one gifted leader, two main events, and three great themes.

The story of Moses dominates Exodus: his birth as a slave; his adoption, education, and upbringing as the Prince of Egypt; forty years spent as a shepherd in the wilderness; his call by God to lead the Israelites out of slavery and into the Promised Land; his leadership mistakes and triumphs; and the construction of the Tabernacle. Moses' life as told in the book of Exodus is a reminder that God is directly involved in the lives of people. It demonstrates God's extraordinary power unleashed through the obedient life of an ordinary, surrendered servant.

Moses led the Israelites through two foundational events in their history as the people of God: the Exodus and the giving of the Law at Mount Sinai. Several centuries earlier, Jacob (Israel) and his eleven sons had settled in Egypt to avoid the famine in their homeland. Jacob's twelfth son, Joseph, who had been providentially sent ahead and promoted to second-in-command of Egypt, made provision for his adopted country and his family to survive. Over hundreds of years, the population of Israelites in Egypt grew exponentially, posing a threat to the Egyptians through their sheer numbers. The Egyptians responded by making the Israelites their slaves. The Israelites' miraculous escape from the slavery and oppression of Egypt into the wilderness of Sinai under Moses' leadership is the subject of Exodus 1–18.

At Mount Sinai, God gave Moses the Ten Commandments to guide people on how to live together and how to worship God. This covenant of the Law was founded on the promises that God gave to Abraham centuries before (Genesis 15), but it was dependent upon the people's loyalty and obedience to God alone. Even with God's miraculous interventions within recent memory, the Israelites struggled to steer clear of idol worship. Their life journey shows God as the One who offers mercy, grace, and restoration, even when God's people prove to be disloyal and disobedient.

Three themes in the book of Exodus are presumed in the New Testament revelation of God:

- God as savior: God liberated people from slavery and oppression in Egypt as Jesus would liberate people from oppression and slavery to sin.
- God as revealer: The Law revealed who God is and how to worship God. Jesus, God in the flesh, is the ultimate revelation of God.
- God as indweller: After the Tabernacle was constructed, God departed the mountain and moved in among the people. The Holy Spirit, within every follower of Jesus, moves and empowers us to be everything God created us to be.

As you study Exodus this week, may you personally experience the power of our extraordinary God unleashed as you surrender yourself to God's use.

13

sun.

DIFFICULT CONDITIONS

_____
_____
_____
_____
_____
_____
_____
_____
_____
_____

Pharaoh and the Egyptians tried to oppress the Israelites and wear them down, but the Israelites continued to multiply and grow stronger. By limiting the number of males, the Egyptians could limit the number of men who might become warriors and fight against Egypt.

EXODUS 1:1–2:10

• How did the midwives respond when they were told to kill the firstborn sons?

• Have you ever been burdened or mistreated? If so, did it make you stronger and develop Christ-like character in you? What changes did it bring?

mon.

LIFE OF MOSES

_____
_____
_____
_____
_____
_____
_____
_____
_____
_____

God encountered Moses in the presence of a burning bush. Within this encounter God commanded Moses to declare to Pharaoh to free the Israelites.

EXODUS 2:11–4:17

• God expected great things from Moses, yet Moses doubted his own abilities. Why do you think Moses questioned God?

• When God commands you to do great things, do you ever doubt or question your abilities? What do you think God expects of you?

DELIVERANCE

God used the event of the Passover to engineer Israel's deliverance out of the hands of Egyptian bondage. The Passover became an annual celebration that reminded the Israelites of the faithfulness and protection of the Lord who delivered them out of the slavery of Egypt.

EXODUS 11:1–12:42

• What in the story of the Passover reminds you that God's plans and timing are perfect?

• Too often we forget what God has done for us in the past. How can we use past experiences in our lives to bring about faith and hope?

MORE SCRIPTURE
Exodus 6:29–10:29—The plagues God sent upon the Egyptians

THE TEN COMMANDMENTS

God encountered Moses on Mount Sinai in order to give the people of Israel specific commands for how they should conduct their lives. Through this encounter, the Israelites learned the promises of God and the importance of obedience in their relationship with God.

EXODUS 19:1–20:20

• Why do you think God chose to appear in a dense cloud before the people?

• God promised to bless those who obey. So why is it so difficult for us to commit fully to God? What is currently hindering you from standing on the promises of God?

MORE SCRIPTURE
Exodus 13:17–14:31—Crossing the Red Sea

Exodus 16—God providing manna and quail

LAW OF INSTRUCTIONS

_____

_____

_____

_____

_____

_____

_____

_____

_____

God gave specific instructions on how the Israelites should treat one another. God calls all who follow Christ to live lives of justice and mercy.

EXODUS 23:1-13; LUKE 10:25-37

• Since the beginning, God has been concerned with fairness and respect among all people. What in today's Scripture reminds you that this is one of God's big priorities?

• Has there been a time in your life when you have either experienced or witnessed injustice? What does Christ call us to do when we are faced with issues of injustice?

THE COVENANT CONFIRMED

_____

_____

_____

_____

_____

_____

_____

_____

_____

The covenant between God and the Israelites was a mutual agreement, freely entered into by both parties. The covenant was affirmed with blood sacrificed (called the "blood of the covenant") and vows taken. This was a formal agreement as the people of Israel vowed to obey God and God vowed to love and care for God's people.

EXODUS 24; HEBREWS 9:11-28

• Why was the covenant between God and the people so important?

• The covenant between God and Israel was confirmed by the people's pledge, "We will do everything the Lord has said." Have there been times in your life when you have made a vow to God? How successful have you been in keeping your vows?

The Lord gave Moses instructions on how to construct the Tabernacle, the portable place of worship that traveled with the Israelites. Moses followed every detail and did everything that the Lord required for furnishing the Tabernacle. Every item within the Tabernacle had a purpose, and through the Tabernacle God's presence was always with the Israelites.

EXODUS 40; 1 CORINTHIANS 3:16-17

• Name the specific furnishings used within the Tabernacle. What was the significance of each?

• The apostle Paul considers our bodies as temples. What things reside within us that bring God glory?

MORE SCRIPTURE

Exodus 32—Israel's disobedience and the golden calf

GOD'S GLORY

notes

AND PRAYER NEEDS

transformations

No Place Like Home

"There's no place like home," a distraught teenaged girl named Dorothy once said, tightly clutching her restless canine companion. The Israelites undoubtedly felt the same way as they faced the possibility of leaving the only country they'd ever known. Despite the bondage and abuse they had endured as slaves, Egypt was home—their habitat of comfortable dysfunction. And as long as they were willing to live as slaves to the needs of their oppressors, they felt safe and comfortable.

The emotions the word "home" evokes in the human psyche are incredibly deep. It's impossible not to have those emotions, whether positive or negative. We all have a place inside us that stores all our childhood relationships, environments, and experiences, creating a memory bank in our hearts. We call that place "home." There's no place like home.

Fifteen years ago during a weekly therapy session, I expressed to my counselor "George" my frustration that many of the painful experiences of my childhood continued to resurface in my adult life, bringing back a lot of the same old reactions and feelings inside. "How can I be finding myself in this recurring nightmare?" I inquired, "I thought that once I left the house of my childhood, the pain would go away." George wisely pointed out that even though my beliefs were trying to move forward in faith, I was returning "home" in my behaviors and responses because home was what I knew. Home was familiar. Home felt painfully normal, safe, and secure.

Exodus is a going out, a departure. A departure from all that is familiar, all that feels normal, safe, and secure. A departure from all the comforts of home. And each one of us is called to a grand Exodus, the adventure of leaving all that feels familiar and safe, regardless of how dysfunctional and unhealthy Egypt might have been. The exodus of a battered wife leaving a roof over her head and three meals a day for her children. The exodus of an alcoholic leaving his lifelong relationship with the bottle to face the real world with sobriety. The exodus of the CEO who must come clean in all his business practices, facing the possible desert of diminished income. The exodus of the codependent who must wean herself away from the constant approval of others.

Exodus is never easy, however, and during its initial stages the Promised Land of freedom, health, and prosperity is still just a promise. It would be so easy to click our heels three times and slip back home to Kansas, to Egypt, or to bondage of any sort. "There's no place like home," Evil whispers.

Faith forges towards the Promised Land, however, and new thoughts, new behaviors, new experiences, and new feelings begin to create a new reality for those who determine to embark on the Exodus journey. Jesus goes before us to this Promised Land and is preparing a place for us there that sounds rather incredible. No dysfunction, no abuse. Food, shelter, and freedom from brokenness: life in the presence of God. A Promised Land that takes all we've ever known, redeems it, and recreates it into all we could ever hope for. There really is no place like home.

leviticus

set apart for God

book 3

Countless persons have set out to read the Bible in its entirety and, after reading Genesis and Exodus, become bogged down in Leviticus. The lists of instructions cause many to feel like they are lost in a jungle without an experienced guide to show the way. But if you look closer, you'll find that the restrictions, dietary guidelines, and sacrifices are actually a well-articulated road map leading to an important purpose clearly named by God in Leviticus 20:26: "You are to be holy to me because I, the LORD, am holy, and I have set you apart from the nations to be my own."

This book is the message God gave to Moses as he and the people of Israel were camped at the foot of Mount Sinai after fleeing the slavery of Egypt. Having just built a Tabernacle to worship God, they were waiting for instructions to proceed toward the Promised Land that would be their new home. God spoke to Moses with these careful and specific instructions, clearly defining the ways they were to be a people set apart.

The core message of Leviticus urges us to understand God's holiness and God's call for us to be holy (whole and complete in our relationship to God) as God's people. In Leviticus, the Hebrew word for "clean" occurs seventy-four times, and the word for "unclean" occurs one hundred and thirty-two times. The Israelites understood persons, animals, land, and time as either "clean" or "unclean." One of the benefits we can gain from this book is the ability to discern the same in our own lives. A second lesson is the truth that God is present in the ordinary aspects of our lives. With God's all-pervasive presence come God's expectations for how we will honor God through our thoughts and behavior. Third, this book illustrates the theme of sacrifice. The concept of restitution for sinfulness, coming clean and becoming clean in God's eyes, forms the framework of our Christian understanding of Jesus' death and resurrection that came later. Lastly, Leviticus provides a powerful reminder of the importance of worship (giving full focus to interacting with God), of demonstrating obedience, of celebrating God's blessings, and of giving a tithe (tenth) back to God in thankfulness.

Through Leviticus, we gain a picture of the relationship that God longs to have with each of us in all aspects of our living. And as followers of Jesus, we can see how Christ himself came to embody the holiness, the presence, the sacrifice, and the celebration of that relationship with us. Though many of the regulations listed in this book may not apply to our current spiritual relationship with God through Christ, keep in mind the principle of God's desire for obedience, which is powerfully represented by the Law found in Genesis through Deuteronomy. For us to live holy lives, living out God's purposes in everything we do, we accept Christ's death and resurrection for us, and we celebrate this sacrifice with God through worship.

OFFERINGS TO GOD

_____

_____

_____

_____

_____

_____

_____

_____

_____

_____

Leviticus explains the significance of how we are to relate to God and to one another. Different types of sacrificial offerings are described in Leviticus 1–7. The burnt offering symbolized commitment and surrender to God. The guilt offering provided restitution for sin.

LEVITICUS 1:1-17; 5:14-19

• What details seem important to God in these readings about offerings? What is the symbolism of people bringing only "perfect" animals as offerings?

• What does it mean to you for Christ to have become your final "guilt offering" before God?

MORE SCRIPTURE

Isaiah 53:7-12—Identifying the Suffering Servant as the ultimate guilt offering

2 Corinthians 2:14-16—Our lives lived for Christ as a burnt offering

THE ROLE OF THE PRIEST

_____

_____

_____

_____

_____

_____

_____

_____

_____

_____

God's design (described in Leviticus 8–10) was for Moses to establish an order of priests who would represent God to the people and the people to God. Moses' brother Aaron and his sons were chosen as the first priests for the ministry of helping the people offer sacrifices. God's rules for how the priests were to handle the fire and the offerings were strict. When two of Aaron's sons broke the rules, God's reaction was swift.

LEVITICUS 10; HEBREWS 4:14–5:10

• What, according to the book of Hebrews, made Jesus the greatest priest of all? How did Jesus differ from Aaron and his sons?

• What was the result in a time when you had the right action but the wrong motivation behind it? What did God help you to learn from it?

CLEAN BEFORE GOD

Leviticus 11–15 describes practical instructions for how to live a holy life before God. These chapters were a handbook for the priests to follow, helping the people stay pure. In matters as specific as food, sickness, even sexual intimacy and childbirth, God's people have always been called to honor God in every way.

LEVITICUS 11:26-47; ACTS 10:9-48

• After Jesus' death and resurrection, God gave Peter a vision explaining that the sacrificial offering of Jesus was for all people. What happened after Peter announced this good news?

• Read Leviticus 11:45. This reminder occurs eight times in this book. What does the phrase "brought you up out of Egypt" bring to mind? What "Egypt" do you need to remember God delivered you from?

"SCAPEGOATING" OUR SIN

The "Day of Atonement" (known in the Jewish tradition as Yom Kippur) was celebrated annually to cleanse the priest and people from their sins and to purify the altar and Tabernacle of God. Leviticus 16–17 describes its rituals. Especially important about the Day of Atonement was the use of the scapegoat sent out alive into the wilderness to bear the sins of the people of Israel.

LEVITICUS 16; HEBREWS 10:1-14

• How was Jesus the ultimate scapegoat for the sins of the world?

• Understanding that Christ has been the scapegoat for your sins brings the opportunity for you to live a new, forgiven life. For what do you need to ask God's forgiveness? What freedom of renewed obedience to God can you now practice?

SOCIAL CONCERNS

_____

_____

_____

_____

_____

_____

_____

_____

_____

_____

_____

Leviticus 17–26 is often referred to as the "Holiness Code." These chapters summarize God's laws that have to do with living together as God's people in holy community. A major aspect of living out this communal holiness involves how we treat others. Today's reading is a summary of God's instructions on this topic.

LEVITICUS 19:1-18; MARK 12:28-34

• Leviticus 19:18 sounds similar to what we today refer to as the "Golden Rule." How does the Golden Rule relate to how God treats us?

• What out of today's Scripture readings are the most important instructions for you? What will you specifically do or change in response?

THE BLESSINGS OF OBEDIENCE

_____

_____

_____

_____

_____

_____

_____

_____

_____

_____

God used Leviticus to explain clearly and specifically the blessings that obedience in a relationship with God brings. God also outlined the consequences for rebellious refusal to obey.

LEVITICUS 26:1-26, 40-46

• God wanted to leave no question in the minds of the people how important their obedience was. What does this passage identify as the rewards for obedience to God?

• In Leviticus 26:6, God named "peace in the land" as one of the benefits of godly obedience. As a result of an act of your obedience, has God ever blessed you with a sense of peace? What choices could you make now that would bring you even more of God's peace?

"FIRST FRUITS" BELONG TO GOD

The final chapter of Leviticus describes offerings promised to the Lord as symbols of special thanksgiving. Instead of giving the actual item to God, it was possible instead to give its financial equivalent. God made it clear that our "first fruits" and tithes (ten percent) from our blessings of livelihood already belong to and are due to God.

LEVITICUS 27; MATTHEW 6:25-34

• Leviticus 27 describes different monetary valuations of people. What is Jesus' standard of individual human value?

• What of your best or "first fruits" can you dedicate to God? Evaluate your talents, income, and time. Write a letter to God describing your offerings.

MORE SCRIPTURE

1 Corinthians 15:20-28—Jesus as God's "first fruits"

notes
AND PRAYER NEEDS

Turn the page for this week's Transformations Reflection.

transformations

Do-it-yourself

I'm a "do-it-yourself" kind of guy. So when I decided that I needed some new lights in the house, it was natural for me to do it myself. I went to the store and picked up the necessary supplies. As I worked, I gained a sense of satisfaction. How thankful I was that I had the skills to do what was needed! I believed I was doing a pretty good job, and I was saving a lot of money. The new lights were almost installed when it hit me: Was I supposed to get a permit to do this? The inner battle began.

A little voice inside me said, "You're almost done. It's none of their business. You know the work is done properly. They will just take your money and rubber stamp 'APPROVED' on your work. Besides, no one will know if you don't tell." Gradually, I convinced myself that I would not check on a permit. Like the voice said, no one would know if I never said anything to anyone. Besides, hadn't I done everything correctly anyway?

That night I settled down to have my daily Scripture study and prayer time. I was in the process of reading through the Bible in a year, and my portion for the evening was a section from the book of Leviticus. The words seemed to jump from the page as I was reminded that when in any way I try to hide who I am or what I have done, I move myself into separation from a holy God who calls me to truthful and obedient living. The image came to my mind that making less than completely honest choices was like stepping from light into darkness. I realized that hiding my electrical work was going to hinder my fellowship with God. I could feel the darkness settling in my spirit. I knew I needed to ask about a permit.

Holiness means being set apart for God, doing what is right in God's eyes. Included in God's kind of holiness is ethical purity. Hiding from a permit was just a little thing, but I knew it had big spiritual consequences. I had almost chosen to hide in the darkness and separate myself from God. What a lesson this became about how easily any small decision, however casual it may be, can lead to spiritual separation from the God I love and serve.

Yes, I did check on the need for a permit. It turned out that I didn't need one after all. But what a good lesson came from the process! It taught me that as I stay open and obedient to God, my everyday decisions are aligned so that godly holiness and integrity can be seen in my life. I want to remember that God calls me to holy living in all my actions, large and small. Each choice is a chance either to stay in God's light or to find myself in darkness. I'm committed to the kind of close fellowship with God that only holy obedience can bring.

numbers

the journey

book 4

The book of Numbers is named for its census of the Israelite people. On two separate occasions, God commissioned Moses to establish a count of the people. The Israelites had only known captivity, and the census provided order and structure for managing the people. The first census was taken at Mt. Sinai soon after they fled Egypt and crossed the Red Sea. The second was taken thirty-nine years later in the Plains of Moab just before the Israelites crossed the Jordan River to enter Canaan, the land God promised to Abraham and his descendents.

Though named from the census-taking, the book is actually an account of the Israelites' journey from Mt. Sinai to the Promised Land—through the desert for forty years and finally ending on the Plains of Moab. Numbers records several milestones in the journey: the dedication of the altar and the Levites (the priestly tribe), the march of the tribes through the desert, the murmuring and disbelief of the people, the rebellion of the people, and the conquest of the Midianites across the Jordan River from Canaan. Numbers also contains various laws that impacted the lives of the Israelites.

The account of this journey reveals the special nature of the relationship between God and God's chosen people. Because they were God's people, they were expected to commit to God's leadership and place their faith in God's promise. Unfortunately, the Israelites constructed a pattern of behavior revealed in a cycle of sin, judgment, and repentance.

The people complained about God's provisions and Moses' leadership, failed to trust God's strength in acquiring their Promised Land, and rebelled against the God who had delivered them. As they wandered in the desert, we see the hard discipline of a life of deprivation. God was raising a nation, and it was on this journey that the law given through Moses would be put to the test as the foundation for that nation's moral, social, and spiritual behavior.

God used physical signs for direction: earth-shaking forms of judgment and miraculous acts of redemption and provision. God's interaction with the Israelites was direct and clear. God blesses people when they are faithful but punishes when they are not. The disobedience of God's people provided the backdrop to their forty years of wandering in the desert.

This week we read about the importance of trusting in God. As the journey unfolds, you will read about the requirements God placed on God's people—the same kind of obedience God requires today. The obedience God requires of us is based on faith, not on physical signs and wonders. We will see how God can be brought to wrath when God's people lack faith and disobey, but we will also see how God wants us to love and trust as God provides a way for us. God still provides the Holy Spirit to guide our thinking and living today.

sun.

GOD CHOSE YOU

_____

_____

_____

_____

_____

_____

_____

_____

_____

Abraham was the father of a great nation, a chosen nation. As the census was taken, God's promise to greatly increase Abraham's family was realized. It is from this nation and lineage that Jesus would come into the world and make a way for anyone to become one of God's chosen people and part of God's royal priesthood. Just as God chose Aaron and his sons to serve the nation of Israel, God has chosen us to be God's people and serve others.

NUMBERS 3:1-16; 1 PETER 2:9-12

• What was the job given to the Levites? What does Peter urge Christians to do?

• What does it mean to you to be a "priest"? How are you declaring the praises of God?

mon.

DEEPER COMMITMENT

_____

_____

_____

_____

_____

_____

_____

_____

_____

_____

Instructions regarding the Nazirite vow are listed among various laws given in the book of Numbers. This vow was to be taken by those who wanted to take the next step with God. It was a sign of separation from the general population to be used for God's purposes. The Nazirite rituals established outward, physical signs of a deeper commitment with God. God still wants to draw persons into a deeper spiritual commitment today.

NUMBERS 6:1-21; EPHESIANS 4:22-32

• What were the three requirements of the vow of the Nazirite? What aspects of the vow are interesting to you?

• As followers of Christ, we are called to be set apart. How are you setting yourself apart for God? How do those actions affect those around you?

FOLLOW GOD'S LEAD

God used an awesome physical sign to lead God's people to their Promised Land. God's glory physically surrounded the Tabernacle. Today we may not have physical signs to point us in the right direction, but we still discern God's leadership through a spiritual relationship with God. God has provided us with the internal presence of the Holy Spirit to guide us.

NUMBERS 9:15-23; 2 CORINTHIANS 5:7

• How did God lead his people once they were freed from Egypt? According to Paul's letter to the church in Corinth, what should Christians live by?

• Describe a situation when it was hard to know where God was leading you. Write a prayer asking God to allow the Holy Spirit to help you in your journey.

GOD'S PROMISE FOR YOU

God was ready to fulfill the covenant promise to Abraham to give Abraham's descendants land (Genesis 12). God led the Israelites through the desert to the Promised Land, but the people had to choose to take hold of God's promise and actually move forward into the land. Fear and negativity can rob you of God's promises, so don't let overwhelming situations blind you to the possibilities God has for you.

NUMBERS 13

• What reports did the spies bring back?

• How does the faith of Caleb inspire you toward your own faith in God's promise?

ACTING IN FAITH, NOT FEAR

_____
_____
_____
_____
_____
_____
_____
_____
_____
_____

Numbers 14 contains the response of the people to the report given by the spies Moses sent to scout out the Promised Land. The Israelites forgot how God had provided their deliverance from Egypt and how God's presence had been with them on their journey. The consequences of faithless decisions can be costly, drastic, and detrimental.

NUMBERS 14

• How did the people respond to the reports from the spies? What were the consequences of their response?

• God does not want us to react out of fear but to act out of faith. What type of approach do you commonly have in tough situations? What can you do to act in faith rather than react in fear?

A DANGEROUS PLACE

_____
_____
_____
_____
_____
_____
_____
_____
_____
_____

After missing the opportunity to enter the Promised Land, the Israelites struggled to accept the leadership of Moses and God. They focused on themselves rather than God, and the resulting distrust led them to a dangerous place: rebellion. The writer of Hebrews encourages followers of Christ to place their faith in God and God's leadership rather than acting like those who rebelled against God and Moses.

NUMBERS 16; HEBREWS 3:7–4:1

• What effects did the rebellious attitude of a small minority have on the entire community?

• What influences you to complain and tempts you to rebel against God? How can you be sure to listen to God and not be motivated by others or by your own desires?

INDIVIDUAL ACCOUNTABILITY

The cycle of sin, judgment, and repentance challenged Moses' leadership. Regardless of how God provided for the people, Moses had to answer their complaints, plead with God for mercy on their behalf, and deal with their rebellious attitudes. This story reveals Moses' frailty, which cost him a great price.

NUMBERS 20:1-13; 27:12-23

• Why did Moses strike the rock rather than speak to it like God commanded? What was the consequence?

• Moses acted out of frustration and was held personally accountable. To whom are you accountable? How can you prevent yourself from acting out of frustration?

MORE SCRIPTURE
Numbers 33—The stages in Israel's journey

notes
AND PRAYER NEEDS

Turn the page for this week's Transformations Reflection.

transformations

The Walk of My Dreams

Buddy loves a good walk. He's crazy about experiencing the outdoors from the end of a three-foot leash. Toward the end of a summer evening, all I have to do is whisper, or even spell out, the word w-a-l-k and Buddy goes ballistic, aware that his nightly excursion is about to commence. His walks are clearly the highlight of his otherwise predictable dog days. For Buddy, every walk holds the potential of being The Walk of His Dreams. In his dog brain, we are always headed for the Promised Land, wherever that is.

As Buddy's walking companion, however, I found myself growing more and more frustrated. Buddy was assuming the role of a dog on a mission and would forge ahead of me, pulling and jerking on the leash, leaving my arm quite sore and my patience quite short. I tried everything I could think of to solve the problem of this forty pounds of fur-coated muscle lording it over me: two kinds of harnesses, three different leashes. I tried treats, commands, and punishments. I checked out books on dog discipline from the library. I obsessed over how to communicate to this canine creature that his nightly thrill would be cut off completely unless he could learn to walk with me, not ahead of me. Buddy, however, remained oblivious.

Out of the blue one day, a friend told me a tip she'd learned in "dog school." "When your dog begins to pull on the leash, just stop and wait a few seconds before stepping out again. Repeat as often as necessary, and soon he'll get the idea that pulling doesn't work. He'll begin to walk next to you, sensing your lead."

Much to my amazement, the "stop" method worked. Buddy learned that he could walk much farther and longer if he would watch my steps and let me take the lead. We began mutually to enjoy our walks together. Dogs were never meant to lead people, after all.

The book of Numbers tells the story of chosen people who were on a big walk. Anxious to get to the Promised Land, they pulled, cajoled, and jerked in every direction, oblivious of the God who desired to lead them on The Walk of Their Dreams. It took them forty years to go just two hundred and fifty miles, and most of that time was spent wandering around in a big circle. People were never meant to lead God, after all.

True confessions: I'm a lot like Buddy—and the Israelites. Every day I wake up ready to experience The Walk of My Dreams. My mind engages and my body is ready to roll, and I can get totally carried away out in front, pulling and cajoling, oblivious of the God who could lead me if I'd just stop to wait for God's wise direction. I'm learning, though. And when I do stop and take that time each morning, my walk goes further, and my influence extends longer. The Promised Land is in sight. Each day I sense my Creator taking the lead, and I realize this is The Walk of My Dreams.

book 5

"You shall have no other gods before me" is a command that claims the authenticity of God's identity—the one true, living God. If, as God's people, we could keep this first commandment, we would be able to keep the rest. However, when we place ourselves, others, and even objects before God, we sin.

Moses knew the importance of keeping this first commandment. The book of Deuteronomy contains several sermons Moses gave to the Israelite people before God led them across the Jordan River into Canaan, their Promised Land. This was a time of change for the people. They had finished their long journey from captivity to the Promised Land, and Moses was about to pass leadership to Joshua. Knowing that his time was almost over, Moses was inspired by God to leave a legacy for the Israelites. He knew they would have to stay focused on God to have victory in the new land.

Moses' sermons place great emphasis on commitment to God and contain additional instructions about the law they had already received. Deuteronomy actually means "second law." Moses gave expanded instruction on how to keep laws given by God. Moses wanted to ensure that the people understood what was important for godly success in their continued life together.

Moses encouraged the people to remember all they had experienced during the forty years since they had left Egypt and how God had led them thus far. Emphasizing the importance of relationship between the Israelites and God, Moses reminded the people that they were to love and serve only the one true, living God. Moses warned them to drive out the other nations inhabiting the Promised Land so they would be able to keep focused on God and not be led astray by other gods and worship practices. Moses gave instructions to the people on how to obey and worship God.

The words recorded in this book had a significant impact on the teachings in the New Testament. Jesus quoted Deuteronomy on two separate occasions. When tempted by Satan, Jesus used Scripture from Deuteronomy to remind Satan of the law and that God was the ultimate authority. When confronted by an "expert in the law" asking him to identify God's greatest commandment, Jesus responded with, "Love the Lord your God with all your heart and with all your soul and with all your strength and with all your mind," words given to the Israelites through Moses' sermons in Deuteronomy.

Deuteronomy is the last book of the Pentateuch, and it ends with the death of Moses. From a baby left floating on the Nile River to a son of Pharaoh, from a runaway murderer to successful shepherd, from a humble servant to a man who knew the face of God, Moses' colorful earthly journey came to an end. The book of Deuteronomy cites the legacy that Moses left for his people—to love, obey, and worship the one true, living God.

THE ONE TRUE GOD

_____
_____
_____
_____
_____
_____
_____
_____
_____
_____

After leading the people for over forty years, Moses knew all too well how they were prone to fall short of trusting God. For this reason, Moses encouraged them to remember the miracles God had performed in front of them. He knew they would have to be firm in their faith in God to be successful in the land of Canaan.

DEUTERONOMY 4:1-40

• What words of advice did Moses give to the people?

• What "idols" are you distracted with, and what can you do about them?

mon.

LOVE THE LORD

_____
_____
_____
_____
_____
_____
_____
_____
_____
_____

Moses encouraged the Israelites to love God. He reminded them of their origin, a choice made by God based in a loving relationship between God and Abraham. This loving relationship continued in God's relationship with God's people and, through Christ, has been extended to all people today.

DEUTERONOMY 6; LUKE 10:25-28

• According to Deuteronomy 6, what actions demonstrate love for God and what actions do not?

• What spiritual legacy can you leave if you practice Deuteronomy 6:6-7? How can you love the Lord your God with all your heart, soul, and strength?

In Deuteronomy 4, we read about God having a holy jealousy. God is heartbroken and angered when people follow other gods or their own selfish ways. When people do not place their faith in God, they position themselves for failure. Moses warned the people against accepting anything other than what God had provided, and encouraged them to purify their new land. We, too, must purify ourselves.

DEUTERONOMY 7;
2 CORINTHIANS 6:14–7:1

• Why was it so important to completely drive out the other nations? What reasons did God have for choosing the Israelites (Deuteronomy 7:7-9)?

• What responsibilities do we have as the "temple of God"? How can you be separated for God's purposes yet also be a light in the world?

While Moses was away on Mount Sinai receiving the Ten Commandments, the people collected gold and fashioned it into an idol to be worshiped. Moses knew God's desire for God's people to be faithful; he insisted the people must serve God and nothing else.

DEUTERONOMY 9:7-29;
MATTHEW 6:19-24

• What pattern of behavior is illustrated in the story of the golden calf? What would have happened to the people if Moses had not pleaded with God?

• When have you tried to serve two masters? How will you serve only God today?

MORE SCRIPTURE
Exodus 32—Detailed reading on the golden calf

WORSHIP THE LORD

_____

_____

_____

_____

_____

_____

_____

_____

_____

_____

Worship is not just singing songs and speaking praise; it is much broader and more comprehensive. Worship is characterized by acts of respect and submission to our object of worship. Our thoughts, attitudes, and actions reveal who or what we worship. Moses encouraged God's people to faithfully worship God alone. We are called to this same faithfulness of worship today.

DEUTERONOMY 12; ROMANS 12:1-8

• Why was worship important to the Israelites? What role did possessions play in their worship?

• Why is it important for you to worship the Lord? What everyday actions express your worship of God?

fri.

CELEBRATE WHAT GOD HAS DONE

_____

_____

_____

_____

_____

_____

_____

_____

_____

_____

As part of their worship, the people were commanded to remember God through celebration. They were to celebrate the Passover in remembrance of their deliverance from Egypt. The Feast of Weeks and the Feast of Tabernacles were also celebrations honoring God. In the letter to the Romans, who were Gentiles (those outside the original covenant between God and Abraham), Paul urged all followers of Jesus to praise God and celebrate their relationship through Christ.

DEUTERONOMY 16:1-17; ROMANS 15:1-13

• What did the Feast of Weeks and the Feast of Tabernacles celebrate? What promises do we all have from the Romans passage?

• What blessings from God can you celebrate in your life?

INDIVIDUAL ACCOUNTABILITY

Moses is among the great people of faith listed in the Bible. From a baby released in a basket on the Nile to the leader of the nation of Israel, Moses' life was filled with awesome God experiences. Today's passage reveals the Lord's care for Moses. Although Moses was not allowed to enter the Promised Land, Moses, who had met God face to face, was counted as God's friend.

DEUTERONOMY 34; PHILIPPIANS 3:12-21

• What was special about the death and burial of Moses? Who received the legacy that God gave through Moses?

• What have you learned this week from Moses' last words to his people?

notes

AND PRAYER NEEDS

Turn the page for this week's Transformations Reflection.

transformations

Master of the Universe

I hate the birthday song. I really do. I'd rather endure the criticism of Carly Simon singing, "You're so vain," over and over again. My wife, however, loves the birthday song. She loves the presents, loves the candles, loves it all. Every time we gather around a glowing cake to remind people it's their birthday, she gives me the stink eye as I stare at the ceiling fan. I don't enjoy the stink eye, so I decided to get to the bottom of my hatred. After retracing years of birthday pasts, I think I've figured it out. It's my mom's fault.

When I was in third grade, I was down the street at the ultimate birthday party. Everyone was there. We ate oatmeal pies for hors d'oeuvres and got presents just for coming. I gave my best friend Matt the perfect gift, and he told me so. After cake, we played Capture the Flag without caring about grass stains. The party ended with everyone piling in Matt's van and going to watch the most important movie of our lives, *He-Man: Master of the Universe*.

I ran down to my house to get money from my mom. I told her the great news and said I didn't even need money for popcorn. I was stuffed. She said I couldn't go. I melted right in front of her. My life ended. I walked back down to Matt's and told a van full of my favorite friends I couldn't go. As they drove off pretending to stab each other with He-Man swords, I think I almost cried.

At the time, my mom's reasoning for ruining my life was a PG-13 issue. I later found out it was much deeper. My mom really took to heart Moses' teaching about there being no other gods. There was one true Master of the universe, and it wasn't He-Man. I'm not sure if she thought I'd get that concept confused because I was still young enough to believe rabbits lived in magicians' top hats. Regardless, she was unwilling to compromise her belief. She knew how important it was to me and how badly I wanted to go. But, she also knew how badly God desires us to follow only God—not any other person or thing.

Today my mom will admit that it wouldn't have killed me to see that movie. She won't admit that she killed the joy of birthdays for me. And nor should she if I'm being honest. I have a great deal of respect for her as a result of that day. She showed me that faith is not circumstantial. We serve one God, and my family took that so seriously that if the ultimate birthday party was ruined as a result, then so be it. My mom knew firsthand that if I experienced compromise as a kid, I'd experience compromise as an adult when things like paychecks, power trips, and materialism became my reality too.

Sure, singing the He-Man theme song and fake stabbing my friends in Matt's van would've been great. And yes, I would now love to sing "Happy Birthday" with genuine gusto. But I won't. I will, however, look at that "life-ending" birthday experience and realize it was the exact opposite.

joshua

into the Promised Land

A forty-year mistake. That's what the Israelites experienced after they followed Moses out of slavery in Egypt and began their journey to the Promised Land. Their disobedience cost them forty extra years of wandering in the wilderness while they struggled to learn to be faithful to the God who had claimed them as God's own people. Only after a whole new generation of Israelites had been born and had grown up within the weary band of sojourners did God anoint a new leader to help them complete their journey. This book is named after that leader, Joshua, and it records the stories of the Israelites' miraculous entry into the land of Canaan as well as the battles and victories that were necessary to settle the land.

Joshua and his friend Caleb were the only two original Israelites who had been enslaved back in Egypt. They had witnessed the miracles and survived the travel through all forty years until the people of Israel arrived and entered Canaan. As two of the twelve spies sent to check out the Promised Land forty years before, they were the only two who had brought back an optimistic perspective. Before his death, Moses anointed Joshua as his successor. And Joshua demonstrated total obedience to God as well as exceptional military strategy as he helped his people possess their new homeland. He was no longer a young spy who had been sent out to assess the new land but was instead God's leader, filled with the Spirit and prepared for a monumental task such as this.

The early chapters of the book of Joshua are filled with accounts of the capture of key cities and towns in Canaan. These chapters also include stories detailing several military defeats of the Israelites, always related to their refusal to follow God's direction. The second part explains how Joshua divided land and directed each of the tribes of Israel to their allotment upon which to settle. The final segment records Joshua's farewell to the people, his last plea reminding them to stay faithful to God, and his death.

As the writers of the book of Joshua see it, the battles waged by the Israelites to gradually claim and inhabit various parts of Canaan were not only about gaining property for themselves. The Israelites' victories were also divine victories because the power of Israel's deity, Yahweh, was often in conflict with the power of other deities, such as Ba'al or Dagon, that other tribes and towns worshiped. In the book of Joshua, the Israelite tribes understood that their responsibility was to establish worship of the one true Lord (Yahweh) everywhere they settled.

As you'll read this week, the Israelites miraculously and obediently crossed the Jordan River in order to enter their Promised Land at last. As followers of Jesus today, the example of crossing the river reminds us that we all need to cross over from old practices in order to pursue the promises that God has prepared for each of us.

book 6

sun.

GOD'S MESSAGE TO JOSHUA

_____

_____

_____

_____

_____

_____

_____

_____

_____

Joshua assumed the role of leading the Israelites into the Promised Land, and sent two spies to scout out the land. With the assistance of Rahab, the spies returned with the assurance that God would deliver Jericho into their hands.

JOSHUA 1:1–2:24

• God reassured Joshua that God would be with him wherever he went (1:9). How did Joshua respond to this overwhelming command?

• How do you respond to life challenges that seem overwhelming?

mon.

ISRAEL CROSSES THE JORDAN

_____

_____

_____

_____

_____

_____

_____

_____

_____

_____

Joshua led the Israelites across the Jordan River into Canaan after God miraculously dried up the river. The people set a memorial made of twelve stones, one from each of the twelve tribes, on the west bank of the Jordan to remind later generations that the Lord miraculously allowed them to cross over.

JOSHUA 3:1–4:18

• Joshua commanded the people to build a memorial as a reminder of crossing over the Jordan. Why do you think Joshua was so persistent in establishing this memorial?

• What do you use in your life as a memorial or daily reminder of what God has brought you through?

THE FALL OF JERICHO

As Joshua began the campaign of possessing the Promised Land, he prepared to lead the Israelites' attack on the fortified walls of Jericho. As a result of the Israelites' persistence and obedience, the walls came down.

JOSHUA 6

• The walls were symbolic of Jericho's strength, and after they were destroyed the city was vulnerable. How did God command Joshua and the Israelites to bring the walls down?

• Too often, we build walls in our lives due to the fear of vulnerability. What "walls" have you built that are preventing God from totally consuming your life?

THE ISRAELITES DEFEAT AI

Following the conquest and occupation of Jericho, the disobedient act of one man, Achan, caused God's disfavor and the removal of God's protection in battle. Israel was soundly defeated at Ai. After the people of Israel had been cleansed from Achan's sin, they prepared again for battle against Ai. This time, through the clever use of an ambush, the Israelites defeated Ai.

JOSHUA 8:1-35

• After Ai defeated the Israelites the first time (7:12), what did Joshua and the Israelites do differently in the second battle to accomplish victory?

• Name a time God gave you a second chance after you experienced defeat. What was the key to success the second time around?

thurs.

JOSHUA DEFEATS THE KINGS

_____

_____

_____

_____

_____

_____

_____

_____

_____

_____

God empowered Israel to fight seven successful battles and gain control over all of southern Canaan. Even though the northern Canaanite kings decided to partner together to stop Joshua, God was with Joshua and the Israelites once again.

JOSHUA 10:1–11:23

• The Israelites ultimately defeated the Amorites, but how did Joshua secure the victory?

• Name a time when you witnessed God radically change a situation. Why is it so difficult at times for us to believe in miracles?

fri.

JOSHUA DIVIDES THE LAND

_____

_____

_____

_____

_____

_____

_____

_____

_____

_____

Even though the Israelites essentially controlled Canaan (11:23), there was still much land to be settled. Though the land was not fully under Israelite control, God told Joshua to begin dividing the land among the tribes.

JOSHUA 13:1-7; 21:43-45; HEBREWS 11:29-40; 12:1-2

• Despite much opposition, the Israelites finally possessed all of the land that was promised. In the end, why was no one able to stand against Joshua and the Israelites (21:44-45)?

• Has God ever made you a promise that seemed like it would never be fulfilled? Name a promise from God for which you are currently waiting.

THE DEATH OF JOSHUA

In Joshua's farewell address to the Israelite leaders, he urged them to remember all they had seen God do for them. Joshua also warned that the God who had faithfully blessed them for their obedience would also faithfully punish them for disobeying. Joshua challenged them to choose whom they would serve and established his own loyalty to God: "As for me and my family, we will serve the Lord."

JOSHUA 23:1-16; 24:14-31

• Joshua warned the people of God's impending judgment on them for disobeying. Why was it so easy for the Israelites to commit the same old sins?

• Even though we serve a God of grace, why is it so easy for us to disobey? What is the most obvious factor causing you to continue the same old sinful habits?

notes

AND PRAYER NEEDS

Turn the page for this week's Transformations Reflection.

transformations

Paparazzi down by the River

I have an uncle who thinks he's one of the paparazzi. Only, he hounds his relatives instead of famous people. He interrupts family hikes to gather around the perfect stump for a group photo. He makes you "do that again," if you do something cute and he doesn't capture said cuteness. At family functions he puts his camera down only to eat and drink. Even then it's hanging from his neck.

Paparazzi-uncles did not yet exist when Joshua and the Israelites crossed the Jordan because there were no cameras at that time! Preserving memories, therefore, was harder than just saying "cheese."

So after crossing the Jordan River, before going any further, God had Joshua and the Israelites build a memorial. The people took twelve stones and put them by the river to remind the future generations of God's power. They weren't going to rely on word-of-mouth to remember such a remarkable event. My uncle does the same thing with his pictures. I say he "hounds" us; he says he's a "historian."

This story in Joshua made me wonder why I'm relying solely on memory to remember God's power in my life. I've already forgotten things from last week. In fact, I can remember things about as well as I can polka. Not well.

The Israelites were the same as I am. God knew that even though an entire river had been dried up for them, they wouldn't remember. They'd get bogged down with day-to-day things and simply forget. And if they didn't tell their kids and grandkids about God's power, there wouldn't be a library, a photo album, the internet, or the History Channel to do it for them. The future of their faith rested in those twelve stones.

Where is the future of my faith resting? When times get tough, where's proof that I'm not believing in vain? I need proof that God will answer my prayers now, just like God did in the past. I need something I can show my friend when he asks me why I believe in God. I need a memorial.

So here's what I've decided: I'm going to scribble notes, round up pictures, and put them all in a journal. I'll need to buy tape. I'll also need to take more pictures—like one of the house my wife and I just bought. I'll write about the prayers that were answered in ways only God could've dreamed. I'll get that stump picture from my uncle so I can remember why everyone was laughing. I'll need a picture of my beautiful wife and my crazy dog so I can write that God has blessed me with two girls who love me beyond reason and more than they really should.

My life is touched and directed by God every single day. My memory alone cannot be trusted to preserve that miracle.

judges

God's deliverers

book 7

Included in the pages of Judges are a series of colorful stories—some inspiring, others rivaling the contents of sensational, modern-day tabloid newspapers. If this book of the Bible were summarized by one overall message, it would be that spiritual compromise always leads to conflict and chaos. Judges contains the account of the difficult segment of history that followed Joshua's death, illustrating the people of Israel's struggle to stay obedient to God.

After Joshua's death, the Israelite tribes were to take full possession of their long-awaited Promised Land. Joshua's last words to them had contained instructions to stay faithful to the one true God and remain obedient to God's laws and purpose. Some of the stories of Israel's efforts to triumph over the locals already living in the land reveal obedience and attention to God's direction. Others show self-serving decisions and a lack of faith. The stories portray idol worship, disarray, and disobedience on the part of the tribes.

The title of this book refers to a series of military leaders, champions whom God raised up to help refocus and lead the people. These "judges" (the Hebrew word can also be translated "rulers" or "deliverers") were ordinary individuals upon whom God's Spirit came for particular tasks or for leadership in war. Each judge led the tribes for a given time period, restoring obedience to God's law and engineering efforts to further settle the Promised Land. Yet as one judge followed another, most of the tribes turned from God back to disobedience and idol worship. The book of Judges features a distinct pattern, repeated at least seven times: the people rebelled against God, exhibited sinful behavior and disobedience, suffered defeat and loss of property, then repented and cried out to God for forgiveness and redemption—and God forgave and restored the relationship with the people yet again.

As you read stories from Judges during the next several days, notice how subtly and effectively the results of one disobedient decision after another gradually led both individuals and entire tribes of Israelites not only to estrangement from God but also to negative influence upon others by their example. Notice also how God allowed them the consequences of their choices but always responded when the people asked for forgiveness and committed to spiritual faithfulness once again.

God is equally faithful to us, asking only for our heart's complete obedience to love and minister to the needs of broken and suffering people. If you, like the Israelites, have fallen away into meeting your own needs and have entered into a season of disloyalty and disobedience, you, too, can ask God for forgiveness and restored relationship. God provides empowerment for faithful daily living through the Holy Spirit. As followers of Jesus we receive this not just for certain tasks of ministry, but for every moment of obedient service.

JUDGES: CYCLE OF FAITHFULNESS

_____
_____
_____
_____
_____
_____
_____
_____
_____
_____
_____

Today's Scripture from Judges offers a summary of the entire book. Only one generation after Joshua's death, the people of Israel had already forgotten God's faithfulness, provision, and laws.

JUDGES 2:6-23; PSALM 1

• Describe the cycle of faithfulness/unfaithfulness of the Israelites in the time after Joshua died. What were the results of the faithful times? The unfaithful times?

• According to Psalm 1, what are the consequences of godly obedience? What does it mean to you that God desires your "leaves not to wither" (1:3)?

THE FIRST THREE JUDGES

_____
_____
_____
_____
_____
_____
_____
_____
_____
_____

The first three "judges," or military champions, to lead Israelite tribes were individuals whom God raised up and empowered for specific purposes. God provided judges to lead the people in response to their cry for God to forgive their unfaithfulness.

JUDGES 3:7-31

• What unique empowerment did each of these three judges seem to receive? What followed each of the military victories by these three judges?

• When has God seemed to empower you (or someone you know) for a special task or purpose? Describe or explain. What was the result, and what did you learn?

DEBORAH AND BARAK

Accomplishing God's work is usually a team project, done by faithful followers who are willing to trust God and one another. When one of God's leaders refuses his or her mission, God may move the task to another who is willing.

JUDGES 4–5

• Deborah is the only female judge for the people of Israel documented in the Bible. What different leadership responsibilities did she fulfill in this passage?

• Deborah and Barak chose to tell their people the story of God's amazing faithfulness through a song. In what ways are you uniquely equipped to tell stories of God's faithfulness to you?

GIDEON—FROM FEAR TO FAITH

God called a reluctant, timid peasant named Gideon to become one of Israel's most influential judges. Even the least among us can be God's heroes if we are willing to step out in obedience.

JUDGES 6–7

• On what occasions did Gideon respond in obedience to God's instructions? What range of emotions did he display?

• Gideon requested physical signs from God before he would obey. Followers of Jesus, however, live a life guided by faith rather than by signs. Read Hebrews 11:1-2 and John 14:26-27. What instructions do these verses offer you?

MORE SCRIPTURE

Judges 8—Gideon's final victory, then spiritual downslide

JEPHTHAH—THE PRICE OF PRIDEFULNESS

_____

_____

_____

_____

_____

_____

_____

_____

_____

Even a questionable personal history (according to the world's standards) doesn't stop God from using a willing, faithful leader for great purposes. The judge Jephthah was one such leader, but his own pride became his devastating personal downfall.

JUDGES 11:1–12:7

• Who initially put Jephthah into leadership? How was his leadership clearly confirmed by God?

• God didn't require a vow from Jephthah in order to be victorious in battle, and the results of Jephthah's prideful decision to make one anyway had disastrous results. Have you ever made a promise to God you did not need to make or were unable to keep? What happened? What did you learn?

SAMSON AND DELILAH

_____

_____

_____

_____

_____

_____

_____

_____

_____

Samson's adult life was filled with both heroic feats and moral compromise. His blatant violation of God's law eventually brought about his defeat. But as an analogy to the pattern of the Israelite tribes, Samson turned from his wayward behavior back to God and received empowerment one last time to accomplish a victory.

JUDGES 16

• Samson possessed physical strength but lacked moral strength. What reasons do you think Samson as a judge (leader of Israel) used to justify his behavior?

• Are you in spiritual compromise of any kind right now? What needs to happen for you to realign yourself with God's desires for your life?

MORE SCRIPTURE

Judges 13–15—The earlier chapters of Samson's story

MICAH'S IDOLS

The two-episode story of Micah's idols gives a clear illustration of what unravels when God's word is not honored: Worship of God turns into worship of our own making—our own idols. Eventually we take others with us into the facade of our false gods and bring them down spiritually as well.

JUDGES 17–18

• From today's Scripture, list the examples of each person or group who chose their own version of counterfeit worship rather than the true worship of God. How did one person's decisions influence the next?

• According to Judges 18:30, even Moses' grandson became involved in idol worship. What helps you avoid getting lulled into distractions that could sabotage your faith?

_____
_____
_____
_____
_____
_____
_____
_____
_____

notes

AND PRAYER NEEDS

_____
_____
_____
_____
_____
_____
_____
_____
_____
_____

Turn the page for this week's Transformations Reflection.

transformations

Broken Promise

A convent full of nuns owned the land and woods that surrounded my neighborhood as a kid. There was a small log cabin always left unlocked in the corner of the nuns' woods. We were convinced, however, that an escaped convict owned it. We believed this convict had weapons, like axes and shovels, inside the tool shed. The guns were somewhere; we just never found them. He was a sneaky convict.

We spent many afternoons spying on the cabin. After a while that got boring, and we decided we needed our own log cabin. That meant we needed to cut down trees. Unfortunately, our fathers weren't keen on our borrowing their saws, so we borrowed the convict's.

We'd get tools out of his shed in the morning and return them in the afternoon. We efficiently cut down eight trees by sawing and singing like the chorus line in *Paul Bunyan* the musical. On the fourth day of construction, someone suggested we go swimming. It was hot, and we desperately needed a cannonball contest. So we took off for home, forgetting to return the convict's tools.

That night after dinner we reconvened at my house. Our parents were out walking dogs and mowing lawns. A blue pick-up drove by and stopped out in front. The driver got out and pulled a rake from the truck bed—panic time! There was a quick conversation between the adults, and my dad took the rake from the driver. The parents started toward us. Super panic time!

My dad glared at me with his laser eyes and said, "Father Casserta says he found my rake along with eight of his trees cut down. You boys know anything about this?"

Our pounding hearts screamed no while our turncoat mouths whispered, "Yes."

"He's missing some tools and wants them returned right now. We'll talk about this when you get back." To my dad, *talking* meant *spanking*. Running back out to the woods, we were certain we were all going to jail—right after we got spanked to death. I prayed desperately as we ran, "God, I swear if you help us, I'll never cuss again, I won't steal any more tools, and I'll be perfect God. I promise. Just please help us."

I've spent my life breaking that childhood promise even though we didn't die or go to jail. Fortunately, God expects my dependence and that I make progress in my acts of faith and works of mercy. God promises that if I truly depend on Jesus, then I will make progress in my attempts to be like Christ. Christianity is about progressively striving toward perfection. God knows that I'll never become perfect, but God also knows that I'm no longer the kind of person who steals from convicts to purposefully kill trees owned by nuns. I'm making progress.

ruth

one family's faith

Nestled within the Old Testament narrative is a four-chapter book that gives personal insight into the period covered during the time of Israel's judges. The book of Judges describes Israelite tribes moving further and further from God and consequently experiencing God's judgment. The book of Ruth is written in the style of a short story, illustrating the experiences of one family and giving insight into what life was like for individuals of faith within Israel at this time.

Three major themes emerge from the book of Ruth:

• The providence of God:

Romans 8:28 tells us God causes all things to work together for the ultimate good for those who love God and are called according to God's purpose. Providence is God's intervention and work in all situations for the welfare of people. Even in the worst of times—like the disobedience, idolatry, and violence of the time of the judges—God is still at work, using unconditional love and grace to bring about God's ultimate purpose. Within this setting, God was powerfully working in the lives of faithful individuals like Ruth to bring redemption to all people.

• An all-inclusive God:

Ruth had much stacked against her. She had no husband in a culture where women were dependent on their connection to a man; she had no children in a culture that gave worth to women through childbearing; as a Moabite, she was a foreigner in the closed Israelite faith community and thereby at a distinct social disadvantage. And yet Ruth, the "outsider," is the one whose faithfulness God used to redeem Naomi and her. As grandparents of King David, Ruth, the foreigner from an enemy tribe, and Boaz, the descendant of a prostitute, were in the direct ancestral line of the Messiah and at the very heart of God's plan of deliverance.

• Family love and loyalty:

This is the story of relationships based in "khesed," the Hebrew word for loyalty or faithfulness birthed out of devotion and sacrificial commitment. *Khesed* describes God's relationship to the nation of Israel and the demonstration of covenant love and commitment to God's people, even during cycles of disobedience. Within this book, the main characters reflect *khesed* to one another. Ruth risked her chances for future marriage and happiness to follow Naomi. Boaz honored his family responsibility to care for Ruth and Naomi. Love, loyalty, and commitment were the thread leading to God's redemption of all humanity through Boaz and Ruth's lineage.

We are patterned for faith through significant relationships with people who love us and provide safe space for us. Ruth's connection with Naomi culminated in her declaration of faith in Ruth 1:16. The connection among Naomi, Ruth, and Boaz is a positive statement about the importance of relationships in fulfilling God's purpose in our lives and the world.

book 8

sun.

A SIGNIFICANT RELATIONSHIP

_____

_____

_____

_____

_____

_____

_____

_____

_____

_____

Forced into a foreign land because of famine, Naomi's sons eventually married women of Moab, traditionally an enemy nation of Israel that served gods other than Israel's one true God. Naomi's daughter-in-law Ruth left her people, along with their deities and culture, to identify with Naomi, Naomi's people, and Naomi's Lord. People come to God through intimate, significant relationships.

RUTH 1:1-22

• Describe the different attitudes presented by Ruth (1:16-17) and Naomi (1:20-21). Which attitude most closely mirrors your attitude toward God?

• Who is like Ruth to you—loyal and positive even in difficult situations? For whom could you be like Ruth?

mon.

BOAZ, GOD'S PROVISION

_____

_____

_____

_____

_____

_____

_____

_____

_____

_____

God always works physically and spiritually through people to provide for the needy, powerless, and disenfranchised. Although Ruth had stepped out and joined God's community, she still saw herself as a "foreigner." Boaz, as God's representative, was vital in protecting Ruth physically and helping her realize her new spiritual identity.

RUTH 2:1-13;
DEUTERONOMY 24:19-22

• In what specific ways can you identify Boaz's provision for Ruth, both physically and spiritually?

• When you are feeling physically and/or spiritually depleted, what steps could you take to respond proactively like Ruth?

The kinsman/redeemer played an important role in the Israelite family system. This close relative did financially for family members what they could not do for themselves, such as buying back family land or enslaved family members. He also had the option of marrying a widow within the family in order to provide an heir for his dead relative.

RUTH 2:14–23

• In what ways did Boaz, as kinsman/redeemer, show exceptional kindness to Ruth?

• What acts of exceptional kindness could you do for someone today?

MORE SCRIPTURE

Deuteronomy 25:5-10 and Leviticus 25:25—More on the role of the kinsman/redeemer

The customs of ancient Israel sometimes seem foreign to us and have a much different meaning than we would assign to them. Ruth, following Naomi's instruction, approached Boaz with a request. By sharing part of his covering, Ruth identified Boaz as her kinsman/redeemer and protector and let him know he could marry her.

RUTH 3:1-18

• What insight into Boaz's character does Naomi give in 3:18?

• Ruth handled her desperate predicament by boldly approaching someone with the power to sustain her life. What request do you need to take boldly to God?

BOAZ CLAIMS RUTH

_____

_____

_____

_____

_____

_____

_____

_____

_____

_____

The true next of kin to Ruth's husband passed the responsibilities of kinsman/redeemer to Boaz, perhaps in fear of a possible dispute over inheritance issues between his current family and any offspring with Ruth. Boaz was willing to take responsibility for the expense and care of a family and Naomi's land while receiving nothing in return.

RUTH 4:1-12

• What character attributes do you admire in Boaz?

• Important women in Israel's history and the lineage of the Messiah are described in Ruth 4:11-12. What women have played an important role in your personal and spiritual development? What could you do this week to thank them?

MORE SCRIPTURE

Genesis 38:1-30—The story of Tamar and Judah, mentioned in Ruth 4

THE GENEALOGY OF DAVID

_____

_____

_____

_____

_____

_____

_____

_____

_____

_____

The bloodline of Jesus came through King David and included kings and commoners, Gentiles and Jews, broken and whole persons. God was working for centuries to establish the Messiah; God's hand was in every event along the way, often without people seeing the long-term results. Our choices today will affect generations to come, perhaps without our ever seeing the long-term results.

RUTH 4:13-22; MATTHEW 1:1-17

• For what did Boaz become "famous throughout Israel" (Ruth 4:14)?

• In what events in your life can you identify God's hand? What choices are you making today that will leave a positive heritage for future generations?

Acting in faith, Ruth trusted in a kinsman/redeemer. The role of kinsman/redeemer was ultimately fulfilled for all people in Jesus, who came to buy us back from slavery to sin and reinstate us to God's family. By acting in faith we trust Jesus to be our kinsman/redeemer.

EPHESIANS 1:3-14; GALATIANS 3:10-14

• Ruth received the blessings of a loving relationship, children, and financial provision as a result of her "redemption" by Boaz. In the Ephesians passage, what are the spiritual blessings we receive when Christ redeems us?

• Which of those blessings do you value most?

JESUS, OUR KINSMAN/REDEEMER

_____

_____

_____

_____

_____

_____

_____

_____

_____

_____

notes
AND PRAYER NEEDS

_____

_____

_____

_____

_____

_____

_____

_____

_____

_____

Turn the page for this week's Transformations Essay.

transformations

Decisions, Decisions...

She didn't have a lot going for her that day on the road. Not by today's standards anyway. Dolly Parton would've had a heyday with this woman's story. It had all the notes of a sad country song: no man, no home, no money, no hope. Her past felt painful, and her future looked dim. All she had to her name while walking down the desert road that day was one simple possession: a choice—the power to make a decision, declaring what she alone wanted to do. Not her sister-in-law's choice, not her mother-in-law's choice, but her choice. And on that day, at that moment in time, a choice was all she had.

Have you ever been there? A relationship gone south, a house turned empty, a financial deal that hit the fan? Maybe you've discovered that hurt has taken over the place where hope once lived. Life's challenges can close in on us when we least expect them and convince us that we have no options. There is a name for people without options; we call them victims.

Ruth was no victim, however. She embraced her choice firmly that day on the road. Ruth declared aloud to Naomi the response that would change everything about the course of her life. "Where you go, I will go," she had decided, "and where you stay, I will stay. Your people will be my people and your God my God. Where you die, I will die, and there I will be buried." Little did Ruth know that this one decision would position her to be in the lineage of the Messiah— God's miracle yet to be birthed.

We romanticize Ruth's words and know them today as vows spoken between couples in love. Ruth envisioned no such fantasy. She spoke this promise to her mother-in-law, demonstrating a decision made with nothing to gain that we can see. It's hard to know why Ruth chose to do the difficult thing that day, but she did, and God blessed her for it. In time, Ruth found a husband to provide for her, a community to support her, a son to fill Naomi's empty arms, and the favor of the God she had chosen to follow that day on the road—all because of a choice. God's best miracles often begin with just one choice.

Our lives are full of decisions, some seemingly insignificant and mundane: Cheerios or Chex? Jeans or khakis? Paper or plastic? Other decisions represent a much larger fork in the road of life. There are no small decisions, however, only small life-pictures. God has given each of us the awesome ability to affect daily the outcome of our own lives, to choose our own direction.

God offers us life, provision, relationship, and favor, but you get to decide. Who knows? You might be positioned to birth the next miracle of God.

1 samuel

a dynasty begins

If only God's people could see how frequently God protects us from what we want by giving us instead what we need! In 1 Samuel, God gave the people exactly what they wanted: an earthly king. But though they got what they wanted, it ended up being exactly what they did not need. The Israelites' desire for a human king revealed their lack of trust in God and caused years of frustration for God's people. This week, you'll read about the struggles and trials during the time of the kings that God anointed.

This book was named after Samuel, one of the most honorable leaders Israel would know. He was one of the last judges, a priest born from the tribe of Levi, and a prophet to the Israelite tribes. From birth to death, Samuel was surrendered to the cause and mission of God. Through Samuel, God provided a voice to lead the people; but, as Samuel grew older, they didn't trust God's provision, and they asked God for an earthly king.

Despite God's warning, the Israelites were granted their desire, and Saul was anointed the first king of Israel. With their new king, Israel suffered misguided leadership. Saul did not do what God commanded him to do. His selfish motives even led him to seek counsel from a spiritual medium rather than from God. Saul's decisions had disastrous consequences for his relationships: he lost favor with God, almost killed his own son, and rejected David, the servant who respected him.

But God did not abandon the people. While Saul was still king, God was already preparing someone else to lead the people of Israel. Though David was just a boy, his faith in God's provision won victories in his personal life and eventually for his nation. As a shepherd boy, an armor bearer, and a warrior, David found favor in God's eyes, enabling him to overcome Israel's enemies.

With God's direction, Samuel anointed David as king while Saul was still in power, and David became known as the king loved by God. Because of his victories, David became famous among the people and despised by Saul, who became jealous to the point of attempting murder. The struggle between David and Saul completes the book of 1 Samuel, setting the stage for the reign of David and the other kings of Israel.

Although this book contains wonderful stories about Israel's leaders and individuals such as Hannah (Samuel's mother) and Jonathan (Saul's son and David's best friend), 1 Samuel is not just about human relationships. It is about Israel's relationship with God. In spite of the Israelites' lack of faith in their heavenly king, God provided deliverance. It is a story of God giving people what they asked for as well as preparing them for what they ultimately needed.

book 9

PERSONAL DESIRE AND SURRENDER

_____
_____
_____
_____
_____
_____
_____
_____
_____
_____

Sometimes in life we want something so badly we make rash promises to God. In her desperation, Hannah made a difficult promise, and God gave Hannah the desire of her heart. In faithfulness to her promise, Hannah surrendered her life dream to God and trusted the outcome. God does not just serve up our wants; God works with those who depend on God and seek to do God's will.

1 SAMUEL 1:1–2:11

• What life difficulties did Hannah face? What was Hannah's attitude when she acted on her promise?

• What are you passionately longing for? Does your "want" honor God? If so, how can you surrender it to God for God's best outcome?

PRAYING FOR OTHERS

_____
_____
_____
_____
_____
_____
_____
_____
_____
_____

It was the God-appointed responsibility of Israel's priests, prophets, and kings to pray for the people. God used Samuel's prayer of faith on behalf of the Israelites to deliver them from the Philistines. God still answers prayer today and calls each of us to pray for others' needs.

1 SAMUEL 7:2-17; JAMES 5:13-16

• What did the Israelites ask Samuel to do, and why? What were the results?

• For whom in your life could you be faithfully praying? What specific requests will you pray for them today?

The people of Israel struggled to trust God as king and pushed for their own human solution. God wanted the Israelites to trust and rely on God alone. We sacrifice God's intended future blessing when we recklessly ask God to satisfy our desires now rather than trust God to provide for our needs.

1 SAMUEL 8

• Why did the Israelites believe they needed a king? List the consequences of having an earthly king, as stated by God through Samuel.

• What kings or substitutes for God's leadership have you chosen to follow? In what areas of life do you need to trust God's leadership more?

MORE SCRIPTURE
1 Samuel 9–10—The story of Samuel anointing Saul as Israel's first king

Saul's position as king resulted from the people's lack of patience and trust in God. Saul's leadership was compromised from the beginning, and today's passage reveals the consequences of taking matters into one's own hands. God does not want ritualistic sacrifice. God wants us to be obedient.

1 SAMUEL 13:1-15; 15:1-35

• Why did God "regret" that God had made Saul king? What were the results of Saul's disobedience?

• God wanted Saul's obedience, not his ritualistic sacrifice. What does Saul's experience teach you about your relationship with God?

GOD'S ANOINTING BRINGS POWER

_____

_____

_____

_____

_____

_____

_____

_____

_____

_____

Through Samuel, God had anointed Saul as king. Being anointed meant Saul had been set apart and empowered to serve God. Following his disobedience, Saul became vulnerable to evil spirits. Although in name Saul was still Israel's king, God was preparing another (David) to replace Saul. Even in negative circumstances, God prepares a way for God's people.

1 SAMUEL 16:1-23

• What difficulties did Samuel have to go through to anoint Israel's new king? What did God tell Samuel to look for?

• As God looks at your heart, what qualities do you think would please God? What qualities do you think God would want to transform?

 fri.

THERE MAY BE GIANTS

_____

_____

_____

_____

_____

_____

_____

_____

_____

God's promise of provision does not eliminate obstacles in our walk with God. However, God does provide deliverance as we face those challenges with determination and confidence in God, as David did. We will overcome the "giants" in our lives as we trust in God's power and provision.

1 SAMUEL 17

• What characteristics did David demonstrate in this trial? What benefits did David's faith bring to his community?

• What "giants" are you facing right now? What actions can you take that will model David's character as you address these obstacles?

David had tremendous success in battle, and Saul grew jealous of David. Eventually, Saul's selfish leadership led him to extremes as he sought to physically destroy David, the one he perceived as a threat to his power and position. David, however, reflected God's character in how he responded to Saul.

1 SAMUEL 26; MATTHEW 5:38-48

• How did David honor God in this passage? How did David's action affect Saul?

• When and with whom is it most challenging for you to apply Jesus' teaching in Matthew 5? How should you respond rather than react to this person?

MORE SCRIPTURE
1 Samuel 28; 31—The rest of Saul's story

RIGHT RESPONSES

notes
AND PRAYER NEEDS

Turn the page for this week's Transformations Reflection.

transformations

Giant Battles

I enjoy wearing t-shirts and jeans more than a certain character named Sam enjoys eating green eggs and ham. I wear this combination as a tribute to everything good and pure about our culture. And yes, Sam, I would wear them in a box.

Unfortunately, not everyone appreciates my tribute. My wife says I sometimes look like a homeless person. If I happen to dress up for work, my colleagues say things like, "Wow, look at you! Did your wife dress you?" Their words are like tiny daggers. Sadly, I'm forced to answer, "No, but she bought it. I'll tell her you like it."

In college I reached a point where I could no longer tolerate the criticism of my wardrobe. One morning I said to myself, "It is time. I will abandon my tribute to cool culture and purchase collared shirts. I will be respected. My homework will be completed with excellence, and my professors will notice. I will go to parties, and my peers will notice. Goodbye Captain Casual, hello Señor Style."

So I made it happen with Christmas gifts and T.J. Maxx. Six new dress shirts with starched collars hung at attention in my closet. I wore them, and a few people (my roommates) noticed. But after one month, I still felt uncomfortable and out of whack with the pointy, poking collars. Collared shirts didn't get my homework done any faster nor were they the talk of any party. So I returned to my post as Captain Casual.

In the story of David and Goliath, we find some analogy for choosing comfort and avoiding the unnatural.

David showed up in his t-shirt and jeans, wanting to fight Goliath. Saul showed up and covered David in armor. Tiny David clinked around in a grown-up-sized metal suit until he told Saul he wanted his comfortable, normal clothes. David knew the add-on, protective stuff was unnatural and would paralyze him on the battlefield. He knew his natural, God-given talents were enough to solve his giant problem.

I say we buck the system and quit buying unnatural, add-on stuff. I say we battle our giants head-on. Let's start believing that we can do all things through Christ. God has given us the natural resources, abilities, and protection to overcome anything.

So if you'll excuse me, I have a load of cotton and denim armor in the dryer that needs to be folded for this week's challenges.

2 samuel

trial and triumph

Although named after the prophet Samuel, the book of 2 Samuel is the story of King David as an adult. Originally one book together with 1 Samuel, the stories of these two books are interrelated and share the themes of Israel's rejection of God as sovereign leader and the emergence and development of Israel's human kings. These books contain a study of leaders and the nature of leadership—both powerful and weak, inspired and flawed.

Saul, Israel's first king, died at the end of 1 Samuel. After Saul's death, David became the man chosen by God to create a dynasty (house) of spiritual leadership, and his tribe of Judah finally acknowledged him as king. David prevailed in battles and was recognized as king of all Israel seven and a half years later.

Although never reaching the size and scope of Egypt or Rome, Israel was one of the larger sovereign territories during David's time, and David was one of the strongest rulers of his day. Scripture reflects his multifaceted leadership skills:

• The twelve tribes were integrated into one unified nation.

• From a system of regional judges ruling different tribes and territories, David changed Israel's government to a monarchy with one strong, spiritual leader.

• Under David's leadership, the Israelites were no longer subject to neighboring territories.

• David's top priority was worship, and he centralized worship in Jerusalem. He was instrumental in organizing the people who served during public worship and wrote many psalms that inspire people to worship even today.

David's leadership also illustrates the importance of congruence between public and private life. Second Samuel 9–24 records the story of his personal choices: adultery, murder, passive parenting, and the resulting destructive behavior of his children. David's story demonstrates the reality of human leadership: even one chosen and set apart by God is capable of sin. David's compromise jeopardized his family, his nation, and his own relationship with God. This event was a turning point in his life, and David became an example of the redemption and restoration available to anyone who is repentant and truly seeks an intimate relationship with God.

This extraordinary man was most of all a man of the Spirit. Despite his shortcomings, David was the one God entrusted to establish the bloodline of the Messiah (2 Samuel 7), the coming king who would set God's people free eternally. The New Testament writers pointedly connect Jesus with David's lineage, and as Christians we affirm the long-promised Messiah as Jesus.

David's leadership inspires us through his courage, his character in the face of his enemies, and his wholehearted love for God. As you read and meditate on David's life, may his example lead you to a deeper love for God.

sun.

A STRUGGLE WITHIN

_____

_____

_____

_____

_____

_____

_____

_____

_____

_____

Even though Saul had died, David still faced the opposition of those loyal to Saul. David reigned over the tribe of Judah, while those loyal to Saul governed the other tribes. In today's reading we see the bitterness of a divided kingdom and the turmoil the Israelites faced within their own people.

2 SAMUEL 2:1–3:1

•The kingdom struggled under the leadership of two conflicting kings. Whom did the Saul loyalists crown as their king? What happened to those men?

•The nation of Israel faced many internal struggles. What internal struggles are you dealing with today? Write a prayer to God asking for help.

mon.

COMPASSION IS THE BEST MEDICINE

_____

_____

_____

_____

_____

_____

_____

_____

_____

_____

David struggled to honor Saul, the king he had served, and Saul's son Jonathan, the friend he loved. David showed kindness to Mephibosheth as an act of reconciliation. Just as David granted Mephibosheth full access to the king's table, God invites us fully into God's presence and to the "table of life."

2 SAMUEL 9:1-13

•How did Mephibosheth refer to himself and give insight into his self-concept? What did David do to honor Jonathan and serve Mephibosheth?

•As Christians, how are we like Mephibosheth? How can we be like King David and show compassion to others?

MORE SCRIPTURE
1 Samuel 20—David's and Jonathan's friendship

COMPROMISE AND CONSEQUENCE

While his own army went off to war, David decided to stay behind, neglecting his responsibility as king to his people and his God. His decisions had significant consequences. When we act on our sinful desires, we compromise what God has given us and suffer the consequences.

2 SAMUEL 11:1–12:25

•What compromises did David make? What were the consequences of his decisions?

•How have you made compromises in your life? What changes can you make to honor God today?

FAMILY CONSPIRACY

The dysfunction in David's family led to the death of David's son Amnon at the hand of his brother, Absalom. Following his murderous act, Absalom fled Jerusalem, lived in exile, and eventually developed a plot to unseat his father as king of Israel. In today's reading, we have part one of Absalom's challenge to David's throne.

2 SAMUEL 15

•How did Absalom betray his father? How did David respond to Absalom's betrayal?

•When we sin, we betray the love God has for us. What can you do to honor God's love rather than betray it?

MORE SCRIPTURE
2 Samuel 13–14—The destructive relationship between David's children

thurs.

WHAT IS YOUR MOTIVE?

_____
_____
_____
_____
_____
_____
_____
_____
_____
_____

In this second part to Absalom's challenge for the throne, Absalom gave cause for both him and his father to rally their troops. A unique circumstance and an overzealous response brought Absalom to a premature death. Despite Absalom's conspiracy against his father, David's compassion and love for his son never wavered.

2 SAMUEL 18:1–19:15; JAMES 2:12-13

•Absalom, Joab, and David each had different motives. What were these motives? Which of them honored God?

•What are your primary motivations? How does mercy impact the way you treat others?

fri.

JEALOUS LOSER

_____
_____
_____
_____
_____
_____
_____
_____
_____
_____

King David appointed military leader Amasa to lead his army into the next battle, rather than his previous leader, Joab (who had killed his son Absalom). Jealousy led Joab to extreme attempts to regain his position. Giving in to jealousy has the potential to bring about attacks on other people and eventually the destruction of your spirit.

2 SAMUEL 20:1-26; PROVERBS 27:4

•As a result of his jealousy, what did Joab do? What did his action gain him?

•Joab may have secured his position but at great cost to his example of leadership. When do you tend to become jealous? What do you have to gain in those situations? What do you have to lose?

VICTORY IN LIFE

David fought many battles, and he found victory in war and in his life. As the king appointed by God, he was able to outlast Saul and his loyalists, restore his relationship with God after compromising, and establish his throne to be passed on to his son Solomon. Today's reading is David's song of praise.

2 SAMUEL 22

•What was David singing about? Whom does David honor with his song?

•What battles have you won with God's help? Write out a song of praise for what God has done for you personally.

notes

AND PRAYER NEEDS

Turn the page for this week's Transformations Reflection.

transformations

A Gift of Grace

Some things are so undeserved, so unnaturally generous, that they can only be described as a gift—a gift of grace.

I would turn ten years old that week, finally making it into the double digits. It was my special year, and my parents had granted my perfect birthday wish: the three of us going out to eat at The Lincoln Lodge, my favorite seafood extravaganza. Eating out with my parents was an unprecedented delicacy for my short life. We weren't poor, but I could've counted my childhood restaurant experiences on one hand—clearly a luxury. To go without my four siblings running up the tab sent me over the top.

In those days, our after-school recreation generally consisted of bikes with banana seats, kickball, and an occasional game of foursquare. Being the fourth child, I had developed a competitive streak and always tried to perfect these childhood activities beyond the norm for my age. Then, late in my ninth year of life, Linda's sister got a skateboard.

Skateboarding became my little vice. I didn't talk about it at home, fearing someone would try and stop me. When my dad saw neighborhood kids skating, he told me, "A skateboard is a piece of wood with screws underneath and a nut on top. You are absolutely forbidden to be the nut on top."

The plot thickened. I would not give it up. I loved the thrill of starting at the top of Linda's driveway, gliding all the way down. Going straight out into the street was a little risky, so I practiced the best methods for turning sharper so I could hit the sidewalk. And hit the sidewalk I did—feet flying, skateboard shooting one direction, and I the other. Landing on my shoulder I did a forward roll and to this day I can feel the crack of that bone, that one little collarbone that had to be x-rayed, diagnosed, and set. I was busted.

What I knew that day on my way to the hospital was that my dad wasn't into forgiving or forgetting. I held my arm, whimpering, "Forget my birthday. I'll be lucky if I'm allowed to live." My mom knew better than to say it wasn't so.

That night my dad came home from work and didn't disown me—first miracle. He must've thought I looked pitiful, all seventy-five pounds of me, and calmly asked, "Do you think you can still eat some perch?"

Sitting in The Lincoln Lodge that night was all I'd hoped for—the smells, the servers, the silver—all stating that this was one fine table, very fine. And so this girl found herself eating at her parent's table, and she was crippled in one arm.

Sitting in the king's palace every day was all he'd hoped for—the smells, the servants, the silver—all claiming that this was one fine table, very fine. It was David's table, a spread so sumptuous, each day's invitation was nothing short of a miracle. And Mephibosheth always ate at the king's table, and he was crippled in both legs.

1 kings

story of Israel's kings

book 11

First Kings serves as a sequel to 1 and 2 Samuel, continuing the story of Israel's kings. The people had asked God for a human king (1 Samuel 8:1-22). God knew they were rejecting their relationship with the one true God, and warned them of the dire consequences they would experience under human control. Then God gave them what they wanted. Israel's kings, beginning with Saul and David, were meant to lead the people in obedience to all God's commands, but as humans they struggled with this godly responsibility.

Once part of a single book with 2 Kings, the two books were divided early on to create two shorter, easier-to-handle books. The first eleven chapters of 1 Kings tell the story of Solomon, Israel's third king and David's son, who reigned over a united kingdom during a time of unparalleled world prominence. It was a time of economic prosperity and peace with neighboring countries as well as the beginning of Israel's literary age. As a young man, Solomon followed his father's pattern of seeking guidance from God and received the greatest gift God could give: divine wisdom to govern.

But this golden age had a dark side. Unfortunately, this man of wisdom was unable to manage wisely his personal and spiritual life. Solomon eventually led Israel into ongoing spiritual compromise. Solomon used marriages to form political alliances with other countries in order to maintain peace and increase the country's prosperity. After he built the Temple in Jerusalem to provide a permanent place of worship and honor for the one true God, he set up altars to his wives' gods throughout the countryside and frequented them regularly.

God's judgment of Solomon's behavior was severe; it led to the division of Israel into two kingdoms following Solomon's death, and the slide of God's people into spiritual apathy and disobedience. Israel, the Northern Kingdom with its capital in Samaria, had nineteen kings who were each unfaithful to God. Judah, the Southern Kingdom with its capital in Jerusalem, had twenty kings, only half of whom stayed somewhat faithful to God. The line of kings ruling these two nations is the subject of the last eleven chapters of 1 Kings. They transferred Solomon's spiritual DNA of compromise and disobedience to the following generations. The result was the rise of God's prophets, beginning with Elijah, who would confront and challenge people to return to God.

As you explore the deeds and relationships of kings this week, note the importance of godly character, the need for spiritual wisdom, and the consequences of obedience and disobedience in the lives of those who belong to God. As you do, may the power of God in you overcome any tendency to compromise and reduce God to second place in your life.

SOLOMON BECOMES KING

_____

_____

_____

_____

_____

_____

_____

_____

_____

As David neared death, his son Adonijah would have been next in line for the throne in a human system of royalty. David's older sons (Amnon and Absalom) had been killed earlier, leaving Adonijah the heir apparent. Adonijah deceptively tried to seize the throne, although God had identified Solomon as the future king (1 Chronicles 1:29-30).

1 KINGS 1:1–2:12

•David was a powerful and godly leader, but he fell short of greatness as a parent. What weaknesses in parenting can you identify from this Scripture passage? What were the results in the lives of his children?

•Despite his failures, David knew God personally and passed on wise counsel to Solomon. What is the most important piece of spiritual advice you could give to others?

SOLOMON'S WISDOM

_____

_____

_____

_____

_____

_____

_____

_____

_____

_____

Solomon asked God not for riches or fame but for wisdom—the ability to apply knowledge and assess the right thing to do in a situation. As a result of God's gift of wisdom, Solomon and Israel experienced prosperity like no other time in history.

1 KINGS 3:1-28; 4:29-34

•At the beginning of his reign, whose interests did Solomon have at heart? What priorities did he want to be about during his time as king?

•In what area do you, like Solomon, feel overwhelmed and not know what to do (1 Kings 3:7)? Write a prayer expressing your need for wisdom and the discernment of what actions to take.

MORE SCRIPTURE
James 1:5—Ask for wisdom

SOLOMON BUILDS THE TEMPLE

Solomon's father David wanted to build a temple to honor God, but God said no because God wanted a peacemaker, not a warrior, to build God's dwelling place. The Temple housed the ark of the covenant, which contained the tablets of the law and signified God's presence.

1 KINGS 6:1-37; 9:1-9;
1 CORINTHIANS 3:16-17

•Look back at 1 Kings 2:2-4 from your reading on Monday. Compare what David said to Solomon and what God says to Solomon in 1 Kings 9:1-9. How important is obedience to God?

•Solomon honored God with excellence in every aspect of building the Temple. How are you honoring God by how you treat God's temple—your body?

SOLOMON'S DOWNFALL

With prosperity came temptation for Solomon to depend on his own wisdom rather than God's. He maintained peace in the territories through political alliances sealed with marriage to women from foreign nations. Solomon lived out half-hearted commitment by integrating spiritual idolatry with worship of God.

1 KINGS 10:23–11:13

•Although the wisest man who ever lived, Solomon had weaknesses. What weakness do you identify in these verses? What consequences did Israel experience as a result?

•Take a personal spiritual inventory. In what area(s) can you identify half-hearted commitment? What results in your life point you to that assessment?

MORE SCRIPTURE

1 Kings 11:41–12:20—The kingdom is divided

ELIJAH, GOD'S PROPHET

_____

_____

_____

_____

_____

_____

_____

_____

_____

_____

_____

Following Solomon, the separate kingdoms of Israel and Judah had a long line of ineffective and unfaithful kings who led the people into idol worship. Ahab was among the worst. In the midst of this moral and spiritual vacuum, God raised up prophets to confront the kings and people to turn back to God. Elijah was the first in the line of prophets who would address these rulers over the next three hundred years.

1 KINGS 16:29–17:24

•What did God do through Elijah to show that God (Yahweh) was greater than Baal, the god whom people believed brought rain and plentiful harvest? How did God physically provide for Elijah during this time?

•What has your experience of God's provision been during times of spiritual drought? In what ways do you expect God to come through for you?

ELIJAH AND THE PROPHETS OF BAAL

_____

_____

_____

_____

_____

_____

_____

_____

_____

_____

Elijah is among the most well known of Israel's prophets. Both the Old and New Testaments refer to him because of the actions he took as he challenged the people of God to forsake false gods and take a stand for the God of Israel. Today's reading is a dramatic example of Elijah's outspoken commitment to God.

1 KINGS 18:1–45

•Elijah set up a contest to show who was truly the living God. At the end of the demonstration, how did the people respond? Do you think they were sincere? Why or why not?

•"How long will you waver between two opinions? If the LORD is God, follow him" (18:21). How does this question challenge you? What is your action step to stop wavering and fully follow God?

GOD PROVIDES FOR ELIJAH

Despite his great accomplishments and experience of God's supernatural intervention, Elijah ran in fear from queen Jezebel and fell into a period of depression. The great people whose stories are found in the Bible were human. They experienced the emotional ups and downs of life just as we do.

1 KINGS 19:1-21

•What do you think God said to Elijah in the whisper? Why do you think God did not speak dramatically in the earthquake, wind, and fire?

•Have you ever reached a point of wanting to give up like Elijah did? What happened? Where do you need God's encouragement now?

MORE SCRIPTURE

1 Kings 20–22—Stories of standoffs between kings and prophets

notes
AND PRAYER NEEDS

transformations

Godly Wisdom

When I finished my counseling degree, I began my career with excitement and confidence, believing I was well prepared. I had studied hard and read many helpful books and articles on counseling children. I thought I was ready for the challenges that were ahead. But I quickly found out that the issues and problems didn't necessarily fit into the textbook. All my head knowledge, however carefully learned, didn't always provide the answers for the children and families at my school. Knowledge alone was not enough. I needed something more.

In my daily devotional time during that beginner stage as a school counselor, I found myself humbled before God. Prayerfully I sought insight and assistance with so many issues at work. As I asked God for the skills I needed, God showed me three biblical qualities I should actively seek as a Christian counselor: wisdom, integrity, and compassion. I felt convicted to pursue those qualities with my whole heart, just like I knew King Solomon had done on behalf of the people he served so long ago. As I drove into the school parking lot every morning, I began the day with a special prayer asking to learn God's wisdom.

Over the years I learned the importance of living constantly in God's presence and asking for "God-sight" in each counseling situation. I know now it is impossible to guide others wisely, no matter how much book learning you have, without asking for and receiving the wisdom of God. One morning at work, I was asked to come outside the school building. I saw parents, teachers, and police standing around a car that contained one of my students who had angrily locked himself inside. As I walked over to the car, I felt at a loss as to how to handle the situation. With no other options in mind, I simply asked God to give me a wise sense of what to do.

In an instant, God's wisdom came. I asked the crowd surrounding the car to go inside the school building. When they were gone, I turned to the student locked in the car and said, "Johnny, I am really cold out here because I don't have my coat on. Could you lock me in the car with you so I won't be so cold?" He promptly unlocked the car and locked me in. I was then able to talk with him, find out why he was so upset, and figure out how to help resolve the situation.

Where did that and many other ideas come from throughout my counseling career? When I have consistently and intentionally pursued godly wisdom, God's guidance has not only helped me to know what to do but has also given me the courage to do it. God's voice has become more and more familiar to me over the years. I am committed to asking for and keeping God's wisdom before me in everything.

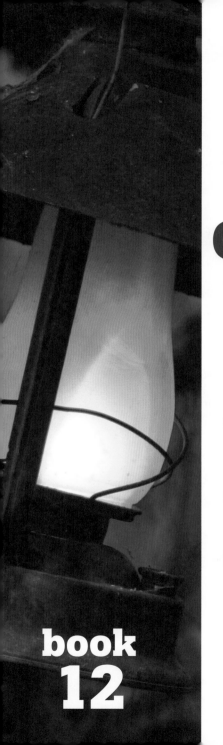

2 kings

the dynasty begins

book 12

The books of 1 and 2 Kings provide a historical landscape upon which to understand a primary truth: unfaithfulness to God's covenant love for humanity always leads to downfall. First Kings begins with God's promises and the hopefulness of God's people, and 2 Kings ends showing the results of their disobedience: defeat and ruin.

Second Kings describes the decline of the two kingdoms: the Northern Kingdom, called Israel (comprised of ten of the tribes), and the Southern Kingdom, called Judah (comprised of the other two tribes). Chapters 1–17 provide the stories of Israel's fall to the Assyrians, including the flagship city of Samaria. Chapters 18–23 tell the history of Judah, the southern kingdom that survived longer but ultimately fell to Babylon. Judah's key city, Jerusalem, was captured; the Temple was destroyed; and God's people were deported from their "Promised Land" into Babylonian exile.

When you read highlights from 2 Kings, you'll notice a common thread. As the reigning kings of each kingdom demonstrated either faithfulness or unfaithfulness to God, so went the blessing or the destruction of their people. The Northern Kingdom had nineteen kings and nine different dynasties from the time the tribes of Israel split into two kingdoms until its fall. All of the Northern kings were disobedient to God's desires, resulting in ongoing bloodshed and unrest. The Southern Kingdom had twenty kings in one long dynasty. It lasted longer before its fall because a few of these kings worked to restore faithfulness to God during their reigns. It was through the lineage of the southern kingdom of Judah that Jesus Christ eventually came, hundreds of years later.

Second Kings describes strong, prophetic individuals sent by God to challenge the wayward behavior of the kings and to bring spiritual direction and hope to the people. The two most prominent prophets described in this book are Elijah and his successor, Elisha. The early chapters describe Elijah's final season of life and the transference of God's Spirit to Elisha. God's further miraculous works through Elisha are shown to be many and varied. The purpose of Elijah, Elisha, and their fellow prophets was to keep reminding the kings and the people of God's covenant relationship of love that God had established with them long before. Proclaiming this truth was often a dangerous responsibility.

At the close of 2 Kings, both the northern kingdom of Israel and the southern kingdom of Judah had been defeated. The book has strong implications for our own lives: As we live faithfully to God's desires for us, we enjoy God's peace and spiritual blessings. And when we willfully choose disobedience, we step outside God's providential hand of love and care. God's relentless love allows us the consequences of our disobedience and still is ever ready to forgive and reconcile as we return our hearts to God.

PASSING THE MANTLE

_____
_____
_____
_____
_____
_____
_____
_____
_____
_____

At the end of the prophet Elijah's ministry, his student Elisha was next in line to carry on the prophetic message of God through God's powerful anointing of the Holy Spirit. After Elijah's departure, Elisha faithfully carried on the spiritual servant leadership he had seen and learned from his mentor.

2 KINGS 2

•Elijah instructed Elisha to keep his focus on his mentor until they parted ways, and in so doing Elisha was able to assume the mantle of leadership and carry on God's work. What potential distractions do you think Elisha might have had but resisted?

•As you diligently pursue spiritual growth, how might God use you in a special way? What could possibly distract you from your pursuit?

mon.

GOD'S MIRACULOUS PROVISIONS

_____
_____
_____
_____
_____
_____
_____
_____
_____
_____

Elijah's ministry was characterized by confrontational challenges to kings and leaders who had abandoned faithful obedience to God. Elisha's ministry had a different flavor: he worked among the people to demonstrate repeatedly God's abundant, miraculous ability to provide for their everyday needs.

2 KINGS 4; MARK 6:35-44

•God has the ability to transform and multiply everyday things into miraculous provision. What ordinary ingredients did Elisha use to bring God's extraordinary provision in the situations described?

•Jesus also used ordinary bread and fish to teach the people about God's ability to provide. What practical lessons for your own life and faith can you learn from these readings?

All through history, humanity has struggled with humility and obedience to God's direction. Naaman, highly successful by the world's standards, nearly missed God's miraculous provision by refusing to listen and obey. Gehazi, a servant of Elisha, allowed his own desires to become more important than his spiritual faithfulness.

2 KINGS 5

•God's path to healing requires humility and obedience. Both were a struggle for Naaman. What did it take for him to decide to humble himself and obey? What was the result?

•Gehazi stepped outside God's blessing when he selfishly tried to provide for his own needs, rather than rest in God's provision. In what area do you struggle with allowing God to provide, rather than taking control yourself?

FAMINE IN SAMARIA

Elisha's role as a prophet to the king of Israel offered pathways to peace. God blessed and provided for Israel through the king's willingness to be obedient to God's plans, no matter how desperate the circumstances.

2 KINGS 6:8–7:20

•God's help may be all around us (2 Kings 6:17), but unless our spiritual eyes are opened, we are unable to respond. What instances of blindness and eyes being opened are described in today's Scripture?

•Israel's king struggled to accept Elisha's "outside the box" answer when looking for God's solutions to famine. Where do you need to be open to God's miraculous solutions, rather than your own skeptical fears?

JOASH REPAIRS THE TEMPLE

_____

_____

_____

_____

_____

_____

_____

_____

_____

_____

King Solomon's spiritual compromise eventually allowed enemies to enter Jerusalem and plunder the Temple. The Temple continued to languish for over three hundred years until King Joash gave leadership to its restoration.

2 KINGS 11:21–12:16

•The Levite priests were supported through the people's offerings. When King Joash initiated change, why do you think it took a while for the priests to allocate some money for Temple repairs?

•Joash established a division of offering to cover both Temple repairs and the priests' financial support. Are you, like Joash, a solution finder, or are you often an obstacle to change? What adjustments do you need to make?

MORE SCRIPTURE
2 Kings 17:16-23—Fall of the northern kingdom of Israel, and its city of Samaria

KING HEZEKIAH AND HIS SONS

_____

_____

_____

_____

_____

_____

_____

_____

_____

_____

King Hezekiah pleaded for more years of life, and God miraculously answered his prayer. Hezekiah's pride during those years led him to build a relationship with an enemy king, and during that added time, he fathered Manasseh, who succeeded him as king. Manasseh had the longest reign of all the kings of Judah and was the most spiritually unfaithful leader of all. Manasseh's son carried on his disobedient legacy after him.

2 KINGS 20–21

•In what ways did Hezekiah compromise the responsibilities God expected of him? What could Hezekiah have done differently to change his legacy?

•Length of life is not as important as quality of life. How would you rate your own quality of spiritual life right now as a follower of Jesus?

King Josiah made sure the Temple was restored. The book of the Law (probably an early version of Deuteronomy) that had been lost for several generations was found. Josiah helped restore his people to spiritual obedience.

2 KINGS 22:1–23:3

•Despite Huldah's message that God's anger would eventually burn against the people's disobedience, what did King Josiah do to bring his kingdom back into faithfulness to God?

•How do you stay faithful to God? Name the activities and choices you can (or do) make to keep your heart, soul, and mind focused upon your relationship with God.

MORE SCRIPTURE

2 Kings 23:4-30—History of King Josiah's entire reign

2 Kings 25—The final fall of Jerusalem (the Southern Kingdom) and the Temple

JOSIAH FINDS THE BOOK OF THE LAW

notes

AND PRAYER NEEDS

transformations

Mentors Unaware

We told our kids we didn't want a party for our twenty-fifth wedding anniversary. Just a simple celebration, we said, small and meaningful. So that evening we were a little surprised when our grown children kidnapped us and blindfolded us with the very same bandanas we'd used to blindfold them in their early pin-the-tail-on-the-donkey days. Forcing us into our SUV, they drove while we rode some distance away from home, all the while being confined to asking only "yes/no" questions. "Are we going far?" "No." "Is it one of our favorite places?" "No." "Have we ever been there?" "No." "Why are you taking us someplace new on our anniversary? Can you afford this?" Silence.

Once out of the vehicle, we were guided through doorways and hallways, steps and funny smells. Next thing we knew, our blindfolds were removed and we found ourselves in the dark corner of a downtown pool hall. Now we were crazy confused!

What took place before our eyes in the next five minutes makes me smile even as I think about it today, several years later. Our kids each had a chosen character role and reenacted, line by line, the entire scenario of how their mom and dad had met. It was a story they'd heard over and over through their twenty or so years of life, a story of love at first sight that by God's grace had somehow made it through all the better, worst, richer, poorer, sickest, and occasionally healthy days of our lives. We'd met through a mutual friend's introduction in a student union "pool hall" on my husband's college campus.

Newsflash: Kids reenact the stories of the grown-up lives they see. It's the script they know best in the drama of life. The essence of mentorship is more than ensuring that our perfect wisdom is taught; it is trusting that our authentic stories are caught. Thankfully, our stories don't have to possess fairy tale endings to have redeeming quality; rather, those whom we mentor long to hear about our experiences of all kinds, to glean from our failures and what we would've done differently had we listened to God. A legacy is simply a string of stories whose imperfect characters embody Redemption's plan.

Elisha caught Elijah. Naaman's wife's mistress had seen Elisha in action. Joash had watched Jehoida the priest from between the bars of his playpen. Unfortunately, Manasseh had done the same, catching every good and evil act his father Hezekiah devised.

So tell a story today—one you're proud of, or one you're not. And invite Jesus into that story, whether he was there the first time or hadn't yet been welcomed in. Tell that younger person in your life what you learned from the good, the bad, and the ugly days of your lives, and then go look in the mirror. Somebody's gonna grow up to reenact the stories of your life, and whether in a pool hall or a palace, they'll know the script and will be playing the part of you. The redeemed you.

1 chronicles

a family history

book 13

First Chronicles points out the importance of family and tribal history. Written particularly for the Israelites who had just been delivered out of captivity in Babylon, 1 and 2 Chronicles give specific details about the reign of King David and summarize the period of time leading up to the destruction of Jerusalem and the Israelites' captivity in Babylon. During exile, the Israelites were stripped not only of their culture but also of their identity, both national and personal. Separated from their land and history, they were left wondering if the covenant God had made with their ancestors was still valid. First Chronicles ultimately traces the Israelites back to their connection to King David, and even more back to God.

The author of 1 Chronicles began to reconnect the Israelites to their ancestors by writing their genealogy as far back as Adam, the first human. This family history served to trace their covenantal relationship with God that had been handed down through the generations and to reassure the Israelites they had not lost that connection. The author dedicated the first nine chapters of 1 Chronicles to verifying that God was present with and active in the lives of the Israelites and to guaranteeing that God would continue to keep God's promises.

First Chronicles shares many similarities with another biblical book, 2 Samuel. Both books describe the same period of history, reminding the Israelites of their relationship with God and their connection with King David. Unlike 2 Samuel, which details many of David's weaknesses, 1 Chronicles highlights David's life from a more positive viewpoint and identifies his strengths:

• David was wholeheartedly devoted to God and became the model for Israel's priests and leaders. His personal devotion was inspirational as well as instrumental in teaching Israel the importance of worship.

• David identified the future site for God's Temple, although God did not grant him permission to build it. David's ability to prepare the people for its construction showed great leadership.

• David left a meaningful legacy for his son Solomon, who would eventually build the Temple. The Temple would represent not only a place of worship but also a sign of God's fulfilled covenant with the people.

As you read 1 Chronicles, you'll be reminded to contemplate and grasp the significance of your own family origins and how they have impacted your journey of faith. God has been present and active through past generations; now as then, God continues working to give us full assurance that we truly are God's chosen and adopted people.

sun.

ANCESTRY OF THE NATION

_____

_____

_____

_____

_____

_____

_____

_____

_____

_____

_____

The names recorded in the beginning of this chapter illustrated for the Israelites the importance of family lineage, all the way back to Adam. As you read through this list, be reminded that God's plans extend through generations of individuals. God has a unique purpose and plan for each of God's children individually.

1 CHRONICLES 1; PSALM 139

•Why do you think it was imperative to give such an extensive genealogy?

•Too often we feel that our lives aren't as important as those mentioned in the Bible. How does your life illustrate to others that you are significant to God?

mon.

PREPARATION FOR WORSHIP

_____

_____

_____

_____

_____

_____

_____

_____

The priests were completely responsible for all aspects of worship. This included their leadership in worship rituals and also the provision of everything needed for worship. No matter how menial the task, everything was to be done with a spirit of excellence. God expects us to approach worship with the same attitude of excellence.

1 CHRONICLES 9:14-34;
1 CORINTHIANS 12:12-31

•Every priest had a specific role in worship. Why do you think job duties were outlined in such detail?

•We, too, are called to give adequate preparation and detail to honoring God. What, if anything, do you need to change so God receives an honorable and excellent offering from you?

DAVID BECOMES KING

The life of David teaches us that despite obstacles, God's timing is always perfect. Even though Samuel anointed David at an early age, it took twenty years for him actually to become king. It was not until shortly after the death of Saul that David finally assumed the position and authority of king.

1 CHRONICLES 11

•David's military strength came from his team of mighty men. What characteristics of these men do the Scriptures describe?

•What "mighty" men or women surround you? Do you need to add or remove anyone to ensure that God's expectations are at work in your life?

THE ARK IS BROUGHT TO JERUSALEM

Years before, the Philistines had taken the Israelites' ark of the covenant, a wooden box containing the Ten Commandments and other sacred items. After suffering God's punishments, the Philistines voluntarily returned the ark, and David had it brought back to Jerusalem. It was the Levites' responsibility to carry the ark to its new location.

1 CHRONICLES 15:1–16:6

•David told the Levites (priests) to purify themselves before carrying the ark. Why do you think that was so important?

• Followers of Jesus are also called to be set apart and to live with pure hearts. How do you keep your heart pure?

MORE SCRIPTURE

1 Samuel 5–6—History of the ark with the Philistines

thurs.

GOD'S PROMISE TO DAVID

_____

_____

_____

_____

_____

_____

_____

_____

_____

_____

Nathan was a prophet of God sent periodically to call King David into accountability. This time Nathan's news radically changed David's hopes and plans. David's response revealed his true godly character.

1 CHRONICLES 17

•When God changed David's plans, how did David respond?

•Write a prayer to God expressing your own humility and trust in God's directions for your life dreams.

fri.

DAVID TAKES THE CENSUS

_____

_____

_____

_____

_____

_____

_____

_____

_____

_____

King David, feeling confident after his military victories, chose to focus on how numerous and strong his army was rather than rely on God's strength alone. Taking a census without specific instructions from God to do so was a reflection of David's arrogance and self-reliance. The results of one person's sin can negatively impact the lives of many innocent people.

1 CHRONICLES 21:1–22:1

•After David took the census, God gave him the option of choosing his own punishment. What did David choose?

•David acknowledged the cost of his disobedience in his response to Araunah. Have you ever committed a sin because of disobedience and pride? What were the consequences you faced?

DAVID'S FAREWELL ADDRESS

In his farewell address, David did what he did best. He blessed and encouraged his son Solomon as he transitioned power to Solomon. He cast vision to the people for the support of the Temple building project, personally offering generous support and challenging the people to do the same. And he humbly prayed to God with a sense of awe and wonder that ended with praise for God's provision.

1 CHRONICLES 28:1–29:20

•In 29:6-8, after David challenged the people to support Solomon, what was the people's response?

•In spite of many of his actions and yet because of his faithful heart, David had great influence throughout the nation. How does your own leadership influence others? What can you do to enhance your overall leadership ability?

notes

AND PRAYER NEEDS

transformations

A Gerbil Named Sam

Bill has a pet gerbil named Sam who lives in a 1,500 square foot, two-story house. Bill lives out back in a tent, even though he owns Sam and the house. While Sam lounges around watching Animal Planet on the big screen, Bill is outside trying to ignore the barking of his neighbor's dog.

Sam continues living the high life in the house while Bill camps in the backyard. Bill works day and night on making Sam's life even better, even though day and night Sam eats holes through perfectly good drywall.

I imagined the story of Bill and Sam, the gerbil, when trying to make sense of 1 Chronicles 17. King David felt anxious about the ark of the covenant living in a tent while he was living in a house of expensive cedar. David was uncomfortable that he was living larger than God. So he wanted to build a proper Temple for God. God didn't want a temple. God's ark was fine in the tent. And God chose to remain there while David built a dynasty.

Shouldn't the Creator of the universe have the best house on Earth? I imagine two explanations for why God prefers a more humble dwelling.

One, heaven is so plush that God needed to get out and camp for a while. Or two, God cares more about humans than we deserve. Let's go with reason number two. When Jesus came to Earth he could've built himself an air-conditioned RV. Instead, he slept in the sand and hiked through the hillside like everyone else. Jesus didn't want to live the high life; he wanted to live our life. God wasn't on Earth to live in a Temple. God was on Earth to dwell among the least of us in God's kingdom, even if that meant living in a tent.

I may never fully understand how the creation seems to be living better than the Creator. Yet these strange thoughts of Bill and his gerbil Sam humble me and make me want to turn off the television to help God with the kingdom.

book 14

2 chronicles

new way of life

The author of 2 Chronicles speaks to the people described in the last chapter of this book—those who were released from captivity in Babylon and allowed to return to their homeland of Israel. There had been a period of hundreds of years during which Israel, under a series of kings, slid spiritually as the people rejected worship of God in favor of idol worship. The Babylonians destroyed the city of Jerusalem and God's Temple in 586 BC, and the Israelites who survived were carried off into exile in Babylon. After seventy years in captivity, Persia conquered Babylon, and the Persian king allowed scattered groups of Israelites to return to Jerusalem.

Second Chronicles provided history needed by the groups of Israelites who were in the process of resettling Israel and rebuilding their Temple, city, and society. The author's goal was to inspire those groups of Israelites allowed to return to their homeland. The author pointed to Solomon and the glory days of Israel to remind the people of God's promises and provision. He also told of both good and evil kings as he challenged the Israelites to learn from their predecessors' experiences and encouraged them to not repeat those mistakes.

Though they cover the same period of history, 1 and 2 Chronicles are more in the factual style of a reporter than 1 and 2 Kings, which read like a colorful story. The chronicler also took a more positive approach than the writer of 1 and 2 Kings. He emphasized the wealth and power of Israel during the reign of Solomon and did not include the personal shortcomings of Solomon as described in 1 Kings. The author ignored the history of the unfaithful Northern Kingdom (Israel) and focused almost entirely on the kings of the Southern Kingdom (Judah), who demonstrated some faithfulness to God. Those kings (such as Hezekiah and Josiah) who helped refocus the people on God were given the most emphasis. The remnant of Judah released from Babylon was assured of its position as the chosen people of God.

Primary themes in 2 Chronicles include:

• The lives of those who have gone before provide lessons for today. By observing the history of Judah, we see how easy it is to slip backwards in our relationship with God if we are not consciously moving forward.

• Those who truly depend on God can count on God to intervene in even the most hopeless of circumstances. Those who humbly turn to God will be rescued.

• Even within cycles of sin and decline, nations and people still have a God-given purpose to fulfill.

Like the Israelites, we have the promise of God's guidance and provision. As God moves us from the captivity of spiritual, relational, or psychological issues, the end of our bondage becomes the beginning of a new way of life in God.

sun.

THE COMPLETION OF THE TEMPLE

_____

_____

_____

_____

_____

_____

_____

_____

By building a Temple and placing the ark of the covenant in it, the people of Israel centralized their place to worship the Lord. This location would help prevent the worship practices of popular religion from creeping into Israel's relationship with God because the Temple priests would be able to oversee all Temple worship.

2 CHRONICLES 5:1–6:11

•After the ark of the covenant was placed in the Temple, how did the people know God was not only present but also pleased?

•Solomon celebrated God's presence by praising God for the promises God had kept with the Israelites. What promises has God kept with you? List a few of them.

mon.

ISRAEL REBELS UNDER REHOBOAM

_____

_____

_____

_____

_____

_____

_____

_____

_____

Today's reading describes the splitting of the original twelve tribes of Israel into two kingdoms: the Northern Kingdom of ten tribes, which retained the name Israel, and the Southern Kingdom of two tribes, which was called Judah. King Rehoboam's dictatorship and lack of faithfulness to God triggered this division.

2 CHRONICLES 9:30–11:4

•Why do you think Solomon's son Rehoboam refused to listen to the wisdom of his father's elders about how to treat the people? To whom did he listen instead?

•The persons we choose as our counselors when making important decisions is crucial. How can you surround yourself with wise, godly perspective when you have big choices to make?

GOOD KING ASA

King Asa dedicated himself to faithfulness to God, both in peace and in battle. As God did for other kings, God sent a prophet to challenge Asa. The prophet Azariah urged King Asa to take radical steps and lead the people of the southern kingdom of Judah into spiritual renewal.

2 CHRONICLES 14:1–15:19

•What specific actions did King Asa take to bring honor to God? Which one do you think might have been the most difficult for him?

•What symbolic "foreign altars" or "Asherah poles" occupy the remote corners of your life, distracting you from fully devoting yourself to God? What would it take to remove them?

MORE SCRIPTURE

2 Chronicles 16—The latter part of King Asa's life

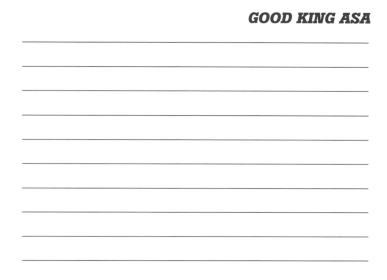

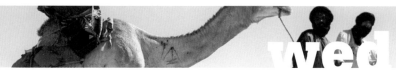

JEHOSHAPHAT ORGANIZES JUDGES

King Jehoshaphat dedicated himself to bringing justice and faithfulness to the people of Judah. His successful strategy was to accomplish this through "judges," who would make sure that God's law was obeyed, which brings righteous and fair verdicts in case of disputes.

2 CHRONICLES 19:1–20:30

•When crisis came, what did King Jehoshaphat and the people do? What were the results?

•Look again at 2 Chronicles 20:15. How would your attitude change in facing your current problems and struggles if you applied this perspective?

MORE SCRIPTURE

2 Chronicles 18—God delivers Jehoshaphat from an unhealthy alliance with wicked King Ahab, ruler of the Northern Kingdom

HEZEKIAH HONORS THE PASSOVER

_____

_____

_____

_____

_____

_____

_____

_____

_____

_____

King Hezekiah worked hard to reunite the Northern Kingdom and the Southern Kingdom for a huge celebration of the Passover at the Temple in Jerusalem. The celebration was so significant that it was extended in length—and the spiritual results of this united Passover were significant.

2 CHRONICLES 30:1–31:1

•After the Passover celebration ended, what actions did the Israelites take to demonstrate their devotion to God alone?

•What happened when King Hezekiah prayed for those who ate the Passover meal without purifying themselves first? What does this tell you about God's willingness always to receive you, just as you are, when you come to God?

MORE SCRIPTURE
2 Chronicles 34—King Josiah's reorganization

JOSIAH'S MISTAKE

_____

_____

_____

_____

_____

_____

_____

_____

_____

_____

Though King Josiah had made hugely successful efforts to help keep the Southern Kingdom's focus on allegiance to God alone, his resulting pride became his downfall.

2 CHRONICLES 35:16–36:1

•God used the king of Egypt as his mouthpiece to try to protect King Josiah. What do you think caused Josiah to ignore him?

•After you have successfully served on God's behalf, what makes you (like Josiah) vulnerable to spiritual defeat? What safeguards can you put in place to prevent such a slide?

Zedekiah was the last king of the southern kingdom of Judah before the nation finally fell to its enemy, the Babylonians. The people were deported from their promised land into captivity, and their precious Temple in Jerusalem (joyously built by King Solomon many generations before) was plundered and destroyed.

2 CHRONICLES 36:11-23

•How did King Zedekiah's hardness of heart towards God influence the spiritual life of his leaders and people? What did God send to try to get their attention?

•What type of influence would you say you are providing to the spiritual lives of those around you every day? What "messengers" has God sent you to help you improve your faithfulness?

THE LAST SOUTHERN KING AND THE FALL OF JERUSALEM

_____
_____
_____
_____
_____
_____
_____
_____
_____

notes
AND PRAYER NEEDS

_____
_____
_____
_____
_____
_____
_____
_____
_____
_____

Turn the page for this week's Transformations Reflection.

transformations

The Effects of Arguing

All of us must have certain needs met in order to live. We all need water, oxygen, food, and passion for something greater than ourselves. But I have a superfluous need that I wish I could get my sanitation workers to take away with my weekly garbage. I have the frustrating need to always be right. It's plagued me my whole life, following me like a stray dog—the kind of stray that walks a few feet behind; constantly disobeys my plea to, "Go away!"; and creates a ruckus at every "confrontation."

As a young child I got into an argument about God's strength. A kid actually tried telling me once that Skeletor (He-Man villain) could take God in a wrestling match. With self-righteous outrage I said, "That's the stupidest thing I've ever heard." He couldn't be convinced that it was impossible for a cartoon to take God. He was beyond reason. So, I told him to go home.

In the eighth grade I played basketball. Our coach was a college student who demanded but did not receive respect. One day in practice he diagrammed a play that even a wrestler would recognize as a mistake. So I raised my hairless arm and told the coach I didn't think his play would work. He didn't appreciate dissent from a 4'11" point guard. I spent the rest of the season on the bench keeping the water bottles organized.

When I was in college, I had a roommate who possessed the need to be right as ferociously as I did. We got into some doozies during our four years. I'll spare you the details of one in particular and summarize that we once argued about directions for ten minutes while driving around lost. At the nine-minute mark he screamed, "If you say one more word I'm gonna go off. You won't even get a punch in." He was serious. My other roommate begged me to stop. I grinned, took a dramatic pause, and said, "But I'm right, and you know it." That was it. He demanded the car to be stopped. He called me by names my mother did not give me, and then exploded out of the car. He had a forty-five-minute walk home, all up hill.

Unfortunately, like King Josiah, I have mastered the art of useless arguing. Josiah was an ally to the Babylonians, so he wasn't happy when he heard that Neco, king of Egypt, wanted to attack his Babylonian friends. Josiah hurried off to confront the Egyptians, who told Josiah they wanted nothing to do with him. Josiah also learned that God was the one who told Neco to attack the Babylonians in the first place. So by messing with the Egyptians, Josiah was actually messing with God. Josiah didn't listen and went to battle anyway, only to end up dying. In the end, pride and the "need to be right" killed Josiah.

Paul says in 2 Timothy, "Avoid foolish and ignorant arguments, knowing that they generate strife. A servant of the Lord must not quarrel but be gentle to all." I've tasted enough strife and hurt enough people to conclude by simply saying, "Amen, brother."

ezra

restoration of God's Temple

God is amazingly persistent to reach and restore people. The book of Ezra was named after a priest whom God used for those very purposes. Together with the book of Nehemiah, Ezra helps provide the continuing historical record of how the Israelites, exiled from their homeland following a crushing defeat, returned to Jerusalem after many years to rebuild.

Preceding the book of Ezra, 2 Chronicles records the victory of Babylon's King Nebuchadnezzar over the people of Israel, complete with physical destruction of their beloved Temple—a symbol of the spiritual destruction of their relationship with God. The Israelites were banished from the southern kingdom of Judah and exiled to Babylon for seventy years. The book of Ezra picks up at the point when a new king in their land of exile issued a decree allowing them to return home.

Chapters 1–6 reveal the transformation of God's people as they returned to Jerusalem and worked to restore their physical place of worship, which was initially a pile of rubble. God's Temple had for several hundred years been the center for the people's worship. But because of the exile, the priests had no longer been able to offer sacrifices there, consequently losing their structure for both worship and spiritual relationships. For these reasons, the Israelites were strongly motivated to restore the Temple.

No story of God's restoration would be complete without a description of how forces of evil are quick to challenge spiritual progress, and, sure enough, the faithful remnant of Israelites who returned to rebuild were nearly thwarted in their efforts. But God's prophets Haggai and Zechariah spoke powerful messages of truth and encouragement. So in spite of the opposition, the construction of the Temple was successfully completed.

In chapters 7–10, God called the priest Ezra to lead the people to restore their relationship with God. Though the Temple had been rebuilt, the people remained connected to practices of worshiping other gods, which was the reason for God's judgment seventy years before. God used Ezra's strong leadership and truthful call for repentance to move the hearts of God's people back towards faithfulness and obedience. The drastic steps that the people took to realign their lives with God's desires may surprise you—and will definitely remind you that nothing is more important than a right relationship with God.

Haggai and Zechariah, the prophets who encouraged the returning Israelites in their building efforts, each wrote during this time period a book of prophecy that we'll study later. For now, our focus from Ezra is on the loving, amazing God who longs for restoration in both our lives and our spirits. No exile is too long or too remote to keep us ultimately from returning to rebuild our spiritual "home" with God.

book
15

PREPARING FOR GOD'S PRESENCE

_____
_____
_____
_____
_____
_____
_____
_____
_____
_____

God's people prepared to return home, where they could rebuild the Temple. From the stories in the books of Samuel we know that the prophets did not initially support the idea of building a centralized place of worship. But God accommodated human needs, and after several centuries the Temple in Jerusalem became the center of Israelite worship. The exile taught some of the people that worshiping in one true place was not as important as worshiping one God in a true way.

EZRA 1–2

• What preparations did the Israelites make? What did they do once they arrived in Jerusalem?

• What preparations do you need to make to spend regular quality time with God? How will you spend that time?

mon.

REBUILDING

_____
_____
_____
_____
_____
_____
_____
_____
_____

Due to God's people's long absence from Jerusalem, the altar and the Temple lay in ruins. This prevented the people of Israel from being able to worship God and to make sacrifices as commanded in the Torah (the first five books of the Old Testament). Our lives can be like the Temple. When we allow things around us to negatively affect our choices, we need God's help to rebuild our lives.

EZRA 3

• What was rebuilt first? What evidence do you see that shows the character of the people who started the rebuilding process?

• When we return to God after poor choices, we usually need to have our lives rebuilt. What kind of construction is happening in your life right now?

OPPOSITION

Whenever God's people are working together, the power of evil seems to provoke us to quit. God's people were trying to rebuild their lives in Jerusalem. The Temple, which was the centerpiece of their lives socially and spiritually, needed to be rebuilt. But those opposed to God's people tried to stop the rebuilding process.

EZRA 4

• What opposition did the Israelites face in rebuilding the Temple? Why did people want to stop it?

• What opposition or distraction from God's work have you faced, or are you facing now? What can you do to ensure you will keep on faithfully working in the face of opposition?

DETERMINATION

The people opposed to rebuilding the Temple managed to stop the construction, but not for good. The people of God were determined to restore the Temple of the Lord and proceeded by faith, though the Persian king had not yet approved. Regardless of our circumstances, we will always have to overcome obstacles, especially in our spiritual lives. We must have determination if we are going to be overcomers.

EZRA 5–6

• Why did the people keep building, even though they had been told to stop?

• Describe your determination for God. How might you show more determination for growing in your faith?

EZRA'S FAITHFULNESS

_____

_____

_____

_____

_____

_____

_____

_____

_____

_____

_____

God's word gives us a moral code by which to live. Because Ezra was faithful to study, know, and apply God's word, God blessed him. As we seek to know God through God's word, the same relationship is made available to us.

EZRA 7

• What was granted to Ezra? How did Ezra honor God with this privilege?

• With what have you been blessed? How can you honor God with your blessings?

PETITIONS TO GOD

_____

_____

_____

_____

_____

_____

_____

_____

_____

_____

Ezra knew what trials the people might face as they were preparing to return to Jerusalem. In our lives today, we must be aware that we will face trials and will need to turn to God for protection and help.

EZRA 8:15-36

• What did Ezra have the people do before returning to Jerusalem? What did the people do when God answered their prayer?

• What requests do you take to God on an ongoing basis? How do you respond when you receive an answer from God?

DISREGARDING GOD

The people of Israel had been exiled to Babylon because they disregarded God's commands. But upon returning to their homeland, the people again disregarded God's commands, including their marriage practices. We know that God has clear expectations for Christians who follow Jesus, just as God had clear expectations for the exiles who returned from Persia. When we disregard God's expectations, we are in jeopardy of losing God's presence and guidance in our lives.

EZRA 9:1-15; 10:1-17

• Why did God command the Israelites not to intermarry? What did Ezra and the people do about their sin?

• What godly practices have you been disregarding? What must you do to restore your relationship with God?

AND PRAYER NEEDS

_____

_____

_____

_____

_____

_____

_____

_____

_____

_____

Turn the page for this week's Transformations Reflection.

transformations

Home Sweet Home

Just before I entered kindergarten, my family moved onto a dead-end street near an international airport. This was exciting for me because one of the landing patterns was directly over our house. I was fascinated by the wonder of the awesome machines that were always passing right over my roof. I can remember having to pause our conversations until the roaring jets finally landed. Some people in our neighborhood found this aggravating. Not me.

I left that house at the age of nineteen to serve in the Navy. I soon learned, however, that no matter how long I might have been away, there was always something special about returning to the comforts and warmth of home. Unfortunately, the opportunities for a literal homecoming did not last. A few years into my military service, the airport forced every family on our street, including my parents, to sell their homes. To my surprise, my next trip "home" to a different house was initially devastating.

I did not realize how quickly my adolescent history could be erased. The house was gone. The flower gardens I helped my mom build were gone. The rope swing my sisters and I swung on was gone. The fort at the rear of our property was gone. The driveway basketball court where I spent most of my summer days shooting hoops was gone. Everything was a pile of rubble. Every now and again I pass by the street and still experience a sense of loss.

After moving a few more times, however, I realized that "home" isn't just a place constructed of bricks and boards. Home isn't limited to a structure. Home is an experience that happens when I am with my family. I don't need to rebuild my old street in order to experience home. As a matter of fact, I like where I am now. I don't have to talk over those noisy planes anymore!

But because of my experiences, I can imagine how the Israelites felt when they finally returned to Judah, their homeland. As exiles, they faced insurmountable odds on their return. Their once familiar city, like my old house, was nothing more than a pile of rubble. Not a pile of old rope swings and basketball courts, but a pile of Temple courtyards, markets, and the community they had once known.

At first I thought it must have been difficult for God's people to restore their city. After all, they had to do a lot of rebuilding. Then I realized something. During their years away, the Israelites must've learned the same truths about "home" as I did when I was away. God's loving presence is not limited to the confines of a building. God is everywhere and always available, and as long as we seek God's ways, God will make sure that wherever we go is home.

nehemiah

servant leader

book 16

The book of Nehemiah is the story of a humble servant committed to a faithful relationship with God and God's people. Nehemiah gives us a clear picture of what it means to lead from a position of servanthood. Even though Nehemiah was an ordinary man, he had extraordinary faith that God could use to help restore the damaged walls in Jerusalem.

The books of Ezra, Nehemiah, and Esther relate overlapping accounts of the story of God's people. Ezra and Nehemiah tell of the reestablishment of the people of Judah after their long exile. The Israelites, long banished from their beloved city of Jerusalem, had finally been allowed to return. Under the priest Ezra's leadership, they had rebuilt their Temple, but the walls around the city of Jerusalem remained in rubble.

It was imperative for Nehemiah to begin a building campaign to restore Jerusalem's walls, which were significant in several ways. The walls were symbolic of Jerusalem's physical strength, and they provided identity and solidarity to a hopeless group of people. Rebuilding the walls not only restored the people's damaged identity but also reunited a broken community. The people ultimately began rebuilding the walls to restore the dignity and pride that had once resided within the community.

Some scholars have pointed out that the first six chapters of Nehemiah describe the reconstruction of Jerusalem's wall and the last seven chapters describe the reconstruction of the spiritual life of the Israelite people. Throughout the rebuilding project, Nehemiah demonstrated the qualities of careful and strategic leadership: planning ahead, involving people in rebuilding close to their homes and according to their skills, holding a focus that could not be distracted by negative people, and establishing a relentless commitment to God's mission.

The story of Nehemiah highlights his powerful prayer life and his willingness to sell out totally to God's mission. The book describes thirteen occasions of prayer, including an opening prayer and a closing prayer. Nehemiah probably recorded the quickest prayer in the Bible, as described in Nehemiah 2:4, when he prayed before answering the king's question, "What do you want?" He also recorded the longest, found in Nehemiah 9, when the people of Israel confessed their sins and asked for God's mercy, which is the centerpiece of the whole book.

Nehemiah was able to proceed with passion because he realized that this divine assignment wasn't about him but was about restoring Jerusalem to its former dignity. This week as you read Nehemiah, God may be currently calling you to a difficult servant task. Whether it is rebuilding the walls in your life that lie in rubble or assisting someone else in rebuilding his or her walls, know that God will give you the determination and courage to complete the task to which God has called you.

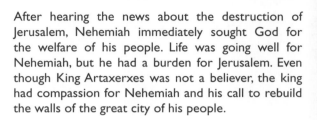

NEHEMIAH'S CALL

_____

_____

_____

_____

_____

_____

_____

_____

_____

_____

After hearing the news about the destruction of Jerusalem, Nehemiah immediately sought God for the welfare of his people. Life was going well for Nehemiah, but he had a burden for Jerusalem. Even though King Artaxerxes was not a believer, the king had compassion for Nehemiah and his call to rebuild the walls of the great city of his people.

NEHEMIAH 1:1–2:10

• Nehemiah felt compelled to go back to help rebuild the walls in Jerusalem. In Nehemiah's prayer, what did he ask God to grant (1:11)? What was the outcome of his prayer?

• God calls us not only to pray for ourselves but for one another. Have there been times in your life when you experienced a burden for someone else and prayed for him or her? What was the outcome?

BEGINNING TO REBUILD

_____

_____

_____

_____

_____

_____

_____

_____

_____

_____

_____

Before Nehemiah actually began to rebuild the walls of Jerusalem, he took a few men with him to assess the damage. After the assessment, Nehemiah challenged them to rebuild Jerusalem's wall and rid themselves of the disgraceful evidence of Israel's disobedience to God years before.

NEHEMIAH 2:11–3:32

• When Nehemiah first arrived in Jerusalem, he took an account of all the damage. What did he identify in 2:17-18? What was the response of the people?

• When you are faced with what seems to be an overwhelming situation, how do you usually respond? How does the faith of the people who were willing to rebuild Jerusalem's walls encourage you?

FACING OPPOSITION

Sanballat and Tobiah, governors of neighboring regions, were angry and felt threatened about the fact that Nehemiah had inspired and empowered the Jewish community to begin rebuilding. Sanballat and Tobiah plotted to sabotage their plans and began to stir up trouble.

NEHEMIAH 4

• Whenever we are called to do a great work for God, we are usually met with some form of opposition. What was Nehemiah's response when he heard the news?

• As a follower of Jesus, has there ever been a time in your life when you were attacked or ridiculed for pursuing your purpose? Did your response hinder your progress, or did it give you momentum?

NEHEMIAH AS GOVERNOR

As the people of Jerusalem continued to rebuild the walls, the effort began to take a toll on them. The building project brought out other issues that began to surface within the community.

NEHEMIAH 5

• As the Jewish community began to rebuild, the nobles and officials exploited them. How were these nobles taking advantage of the people? What was Nehemiah's response?

• Have you ever witnessed issues of injustice and exploitation? If so, did you speak up or remain silent?

THE POWER OF PRAYER

_____

_____

_____

_____

_____

_____

_____

_____

_____

The closer Nehemiah got to rebuilding the wall, the stronger opposition grew. The more he was faced with attacks, the more Nehemiah prayed.

NEHEMIAH 6:1–7:3

• When Nehemiah was faced with attacks from his enemies, for what did he pray? How did God answer?

• When you are faced with hardship, for what do you pray? How can you strengthen your current prayer life?

CELEBRATING GOD'S LAW

_____

_____

_____

_____

_____

_____

_____

_____

_____

After the walls were finally completed, the Israelites came together to hear God's law. Nehemiah and Ezra assembled the community to hear the word of God that would encourage and equip them for the next steps for their lives. The goal of the assembly was to remind the people of what God expected and, even more, from where God had brought them.

NEHEMIAH 7:73–8:18

• Why did the Israelites weep after hearing God's law read and explained? What was Nehemiah's response?

• When you are reminded about God's mercy in your life, how do you usually respond?

COMMITMENT TO OBEDIENCE

In a long prayer, the Israelites were reminded of all God's provisions for them through many generations. In Nehemiah 10:30-39, they bound themselves with specific vows to obey God's law.

NEHEMIAH 9:1-37; 10:28-39

• What are some of the characteristics of God's faithfulness named in Nehemiah's prayer?

• As you reflect on God's presence in your life, how would you describe God's faithfulness? Write out your own prayer.

notes

AND PRAYER NEEDS

transformations

Trust God and Pray

Twenty-two years ago, I was in my kitchen looking at a stack of bills with no way to pay them. My husband had been laid off from work and had used up his unemployment extension. We were to the end of our resources. We had no money, not much food left, and a baby to care for. I was scared, and felt very alone.

My mom had given me a Christian financial book that I had tossed aside almost as soon as I had received it. I dug it out now and blew off the dust. The first page stated that before anything else, before any rebuilding in any part of my life could take place, I needed to trust God. I never did get any farther in the book because after reading that statement, I put it down and got on my knees, right there in my living room. I didn't know if God cared about me, and I wasn't even sure God was listening. But I promised through prayer that I would trust God to provide the resources to restore what my family needed. When I opened my eyes, it seemed like the world outside looked different somehow. I didn't understand until later that a miracle had occurred, and the spiritual eyes of my heart had been opened in a whole new way.

Within a couple of hours after my prayer, there was a knock on my front door. A gentleman standing there introduced himself, saying that he had heard my husband Brad was looking for work and that he needed him. Brad went to work the next day for scale wage, no less—more than I asked for or ever imagined. That led to a job offer he accepted in another state. And that eventually provided the setting for Brad to become a Christian believer and to experience deliverance from his drug and alcohol addictions.

God had been busy arranging answers to prayers I didn't even know how to pray yet, and providing resources that exceeded human possibility. I learned, like Nehemiah did, that whatever my need is, there is one beginning step: trust God and pray. God can and will provide what you need, when you need it. Even when I felt isolated and without a resource to draw on, God was at work on our behalf beyond what I could have imagined, and God continues to be at work in our lives today.

esther

those who remained

book 17

Ezra, Nehemiah, and Esther describe events surrounding the return of God's people to their homeland in Judah following a seventy-year exile in Babylon. While Ezra and Nehemiah record the rebuilding efforts in Jerusalem, the book of Esther describes the threatening events happening among those who remained in the land of exile.

Despite the urging of God's prophets, most of the exiled Jews chose not to go back to their homeland. They had spread to every province of the Persian Empire, making their home among their captors yet distinguishing themselves from the general population by their refusal to obey all of the king's laws (Esther 3:8). The lifestyle of the Jews stood in direct contrast to the great wealth and elaborate lifestyle of the Persian court, which favored feasts for thousands of people and drinking parties that lasted for days. The Jews became the hated target of Haman, an important Persian official who schemed to have the entire Jewish race destroyed. The book of Esther features the story of two ordinary Jews who acted with integrity and courage to counter the threat and set the stage for God to deliver the people.

Although not specifically named in this book (a characteristic unique to the book of Esther), God's presence and intervention are apparent. We can relate to the ambiguity that we feel when trying to understand God's purposes in our lives and in our community. We too must discern God at work in our lives through events and persons we encounter each day.

Through the events and characters of this book, we are given valuable insight into God and God's relationship with people:

- God is at work, operating behind the scenes. Mordecai counseled Esther that mass murder would be prevented, with or without a specific person's participation. "For if you remain silent at this time, relief and deliverance for the Jews will arise from another place, but you…will perish" (Esther 4:14).

- Seemingly "random happenings" are not truly the result of coincidences or chance. Mordecai summed it up for Esther: "Who knows but that you have come to royal position for such a time as this?" (Esther 4:14). The story of Esther teaches us how to discern God's involvement and positioning of people and events and how to acknowledge our responsibility in those situations.

- Following a time of fasting and preparation, Esther acted as a woman of courage and conviction who was able to say, "I will go…and if I perish, I perish."

Just as God used Mordecai and Esther strategically to save people, God has plans to strategically use each of us. May the story of Esther inspire you to evaluate how and where God has positioned you to have influence for God and what your response will be.

QUEEN VASHTI'S BANISHMENT

_____
_____
_____
_____
_____
_____
_____
_____
_____

In Esther's day, women were viewed and treated in a far different way than we find today. Wives were required to obey the wishes of their husbands without question. We can only speculate as to why Queen Vashti refused her husband's command, but King Xerxes' resulting edict affected women across the empire. Respect among persons never results from legislation; it comes from valuing each other through the process of building a relationship.

ESTHER 1

• What motivated Xerxes to call for Vashti? What was the reasoning behind his resulting edict (1:15-18)?

• Decisions made in haste are often irrevocable. Have you ever made a hasty decision that reflected disrespect for another person? What could you do to make a better decision next time?

MORDECAI AND ESTHER

_____
_____
_____
_____
_____
_____
_____
_____
_____
_____

The Persian king had vast property holdings, including large numbers of women who were known as concubines. Though disturbing to present-day readers, King Xerxes would choose his next queen from this group gathered for his sexual pleasure. Through a series of events that some would consider coincidences, God purposefully placed both Esther and her cousin Mordecai in pivotal positions to protect the future of God's people.

ESTHER 2

• Why did Mordecai instruct Esther to keep her identity a secret?

• Have you, like Esther, ever kept your background and spiritual affiliation a secret? For what reason? What was the result?

Haman, second in command in the Persian Empire, was also a descendant of Agag, king of the Amalekites, the ancient enemies of Israel. He singled out Mordecai, a Jew, and forced him into a choice: either bow down to God's enemy or stay faithful in honoring the one true God. From this choice came a ripple effect that would affect all Jews and bring Esther to a point of decision.

ESTHER 3–4

• What was Esther risking? How did she process information from Mordecai and finally make her decision?

• Like Esther, God positions each one of us to exert influence upon others. Look at your current situation as a spouse, parent, family member, friend, or coworker. Where can you identify God positioning you to have influence "for such a time as this"?

HAMAN'S PLOT

_____

_____

_____

_____

_____

_____

_____

_____

Unbridled pride and its resulting hatred and bitterness led Haman to act out his prejudice toward an entire people group. Haman's public humiliation and downfall were sealed, and God's people were saved through Esther's willingness to risk her own well-being.

ESTHER 5–7; HEBREWS 12:14-15

• What "random" events can you identify in today's Scriptures that, when linked together, showed God's involvement on behalf of God's people?

• Hebrews 12:14-15 instructs us to demonstrate the grace of God to others and not allow pride and bitterness to take hold of and destroy us. What are you doing to deny pride and foster humility toward others?

ESTHER'S PLAN FOR HER PEOPLE

_____

_____

_____

_____

_____

_____

_____

_____

THE JEWS PROTECTED

_____
_____
_____
_____
_____
_____
_____
_____
_____

Edicts released by the Persian kings were not retractable; although Haman was executed, his plan went on. The announced attack against the Jews was to take place as planned. A second edict, written by Mordecai and Esther, countered the first and allowed the Jews to defend themselves against their enemies, giving them approximately nine months to prepare.

ESTHER 8:1–9:17

• In I Samuel 15, Saul disobeyed God by taking plunder from the Amalekites and not completely destroying them. How do the actions of the Jews in Esther 9 compare to Saul's actions? Why do you think they were so intentional in their actions?

• If you had warning of a life-changing event nine months in advance, how would you reorder your life to prepare? What part would you do this week?

THE FEAST OF PURIM

_____
_____
_____
_____
_____
_____
_____
_____
_____

Using a common way of making decisions in this time period, Haman cast "Pur" (lots) to decide what day to destroy all Jews within the Persian Empire. Because God intervened to save God's people and because events were so dramatically turned around, those days were set aside as annual feast days to commemorate what God had done. Jews worldwide still celebrate the Feast of Purim to acknowledge God's ongoing protection and intervention.

ESTHER 9:18–10:3

• Do you think Esther and Mordecai were purposefully trying to obey God, or were they unaware God was using them? Why do you think so?

• What do you do to commemorate and celebrate God's power and intervention in your life? To whom could you tell your story this week?

God faithfully takes care of those who trust God. As we saw in the book of Esther, God will get involved in the ordinary and extraordinary circumstances of life to protect, provide, and bring about God's desired outcome. As God's people, we are called to celebrate God's work in our lives through personal and community celebration and by giving gifts to those in need (Esther 9:22).

PSALM 145

• Make a list of all the reasons found in this psalm to praise God.

• What could you do for someone else as an expression of your thanksgiving to God?

THE PROVIDENCE OF GOD

_____

_____

_____

_____

_____

_____

_____

_____

_____

_____

AND PRAYER NEEDS

_____

_____

_____

_____

_____

_____

_____

_____

_____

_____

Turn the page for this week's Transformations Reflection.

transformations

"If I Perish, I Perish"

Let it never be said that God has a small imagination. God gets the all-time prize as Magnificent Creator. God thinks of everything—all the details and intricacies that render every human being totally unique and utterly useful for kingdom work. Sometimes we miss it and mistakenly flatline the world of possibilities. Or we claim, "There's nothing special about me." But our seeming humility is nothing more than veiled refusal to acknowledge the creative work of the God we name when really we should dare to uncover the Master-piece within us and watch the world explode towards a powerful redemption. Like Esther did.

On the outside, Esther was exceedingly beautiful. "The king was attracted to Esther more than to any of the other women" (Esther 2:17). On the inside, Esther was passionately courageous. But the secret ingredient that allowed God to use Esther so powerfully was her attitude that "it's not about me, " which projects a different kind of beauty. Beauty put this young woman's reputation on the map as a savior, laying down her life and all she could have selfishly gained, choosing instead to stand in the gap for her people. Her resolution, "If I perish, I perish" (Esther 4:16), demonstrated a deep belief that life was not about her. Those words launched Esther's risky endeavor, speaking out to save her people from certain death. Esther determined to rise to the task for which she'd been created, no matter how illegal or dangerous it appeared to be.

The world is still full of people needing to be saved from certain death. Our God is still the Magnificent Creator. And each one of us is still totally and uniquely gifted to be an utterly useful part of the plan. It may not happen automatically, for even Esther had some prep time (twelve months of makeover madness) to get ready for the task. But consider the possibilities…

What would it look like if you went back to school to hone that God-given talent within? What could be more powerful than getting the counseling you need to heal from the pain that holds you back? What might happen if you started that little business on a shoestring and temporarily ate a few more pb&j's to make the numbers work? What could happen?

Chances are, the world would change quite a bit. People might see your faith and feel your courage. People might be attracted to the beautiful life emerging within you. The world might begin to explode towards a more powerful redemption. And hey, what could it hurt? You will have made use of all the gifts you've been given. You're only going to get this one chance.

So go ahead. Identify your gifts, make a plan, and rise to the task for which you've been created. How bad can it be? And here's a little resolution to say on the days that look like the risk is just too great: "If I perish, I perish."

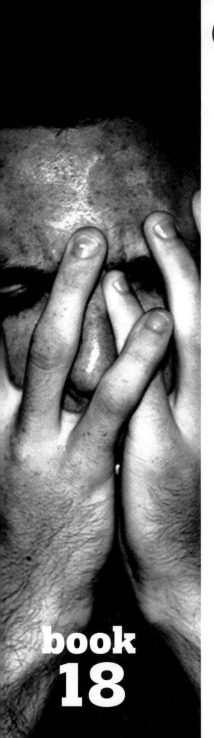

job

staying steadfast

book 18

Job, Proverbs, Psalms, Ecclesiastes, and Song of Songs might collectively be called the Bible's "wisdom literature," though the book of Psalms is actually intended for use in corporate worship. These five books feature a wide variety of writing styles, including prose, poetry, riddles, and even legal jargon. But the common focus among them is the practical, real life wisdom of how to live out a relationship with God in every matter of daily life.

The book of Job is the self-titled story of a righteous man of God whose life included a horrific season of suffering and the loss of his material possessions, his family, and even his health. Job appears to be organized into three sections: an explanation of what triggered Job's suffering, conversations between Job and three of his friends about his plight and why it happened, and God's response and resolution to Job's tragic situation.

Two primary themes emerge in the book of Job. The first is the question of why faithful, good, God-fearing people suffer in this life. The story of Job challenges the common misperception that godly, obedient living somehow automatically protects us from disasters, sickness, and family misfortune in our earthly lives. The struggles of Job's friends in wrestling with this misperception extend for thirty-four chapters. These friends were certain that Job's dilemma was a consequence of sinfulness, for which he had not repented. But even in his misery, Job defended his longstanding upright walk with God and insisted that his suffering was not a punishment from God for wrongdoing.

The second theme is the nature of evil and its impact in the world among God's people. The character called "the Satan" (in Hebrew *ha-satan*, which means "the accuser") is the prince of darkness and all evil. The Accuser gets permission from God, the divine Judge, to test Job's faith to see if his commitment to God will survive tragic, unbearable loss and despair. Though in the story God gives the Accuser a long leash to distract and undermine, God clearly establishes for Job (and for us all) God's position of ultimate lordship and power over heaven and on earth. Even when Job could not answer questions about why he was suffering, he continued to affirm that God is worthy of our affirmation and praise, even apart from the earthly blessings that God often provides.

If you have ever wondered why suffering is part of our human experience, even when we are faithful servants of God, you'll find the questions and answers in the book of Job both challenging and comforting. And if the forces of evil seem to chip away at your faith through daily struggles, stand firm. Greater is God who is in you, than the accuser who is in the world.

THE TWO TESTS OF JOB

_____

_____

_____

_____

_____

_____

_____

_____

_____

_____

A key theme in the book of Job is that forces of evil often test our faith and our relationship with God. In today's reading, God allowed Satan to test Job, God's most faithful human servant. Everything of value to Job (possessions, family, and health) was at stake.

JOB 1:1–2:13

• How did Job react when his possessions and family were destroyed? When his health was destroyed?

• Think of a time when, for reasons beyond your control, you have suffered loss of material possessions, health, or a loved one. How did it affect (or is it affecting) your faith and relationship with God?

MORE SCRIPTURE
Ephesians 6:12-13—Our struggle with the spiritual forces of evil

mon.

ELIPHAZ AND BILDAD'S LOGIC

_____

_____

_____

_____

_____

_____

_____

_____

_____

_____

Job's friends Eliphaz and Bildad believed that suffering is a result of sinfulness and, therefore, Job's plight must have been brought on by unconfessed sins. Job, however, had lived a righteous life and knew his suffering could not be traced to a source of unconfessed sin. Job's misery without logical cause led him to despair even of living.

JOB 5 (ELIPHAZ); JOB 8:1-7 (BILDAD); JOB 10 (JOB)

• Compared with Jesus' explanation of the purpose of innocent suffering in John 9:1-3, what is faulty about the arguments of Bildad and Eliphaz?

• Unlike Job's friends, what friends help you see God's bigger purpose at work when a crisis comes? To whom can you be a friend to support with this perspective?

Job's complete loss of all physical health, family, and material blessings brought him to grief. And God's seeming silence in Job's misery surrounded him with a bewildering, devastating fear of abandonment. But even in the midst of his suffering, Job still named God as his ultimate Redeemer—no matter what.

JOB 19

• Reread Job 19:25-27, and compare it with Hebrews 11:1. What transformed Job's despair into hope?

• Job accused his friends of a judgmental spirit regarding his suffering. How can you ensure a nonjudgmental attitude toward those whom you are called to serve?

wed.

Job's final statement to his friends was a description of practical decisions he had made in daily life in order to keep himself pure and faithful before God. In matters ranging from marital faithfulness, honesty, and justice to providing for the poor and managing money responsibly, Job described his wholehearted efforts to obey God.

JOB 31

• Name the categories of life Job identified in which he had resisted the temptation to sin.

• With which of these do you struggle the most to keep yourself pure, as Job did? What is your biggest incentive to make choices toward godly integrity?

GOD'S FIRST RESPONSE

_____

_____

_____

_____

_____

_____

_____

_____

_____

_____

_____

Despite Job's statements of faith, he also asked God repeatedly why he was suffering. God finally responded to Job from a stormy whirlwind but didn't provide any specific answers to Job's questions. Rather, God put forth many other mighty questions—to which Job had no answers.

JOB 38

• God did not explain any reason for Job's suffering in the divine response to Job. What do you think was God's intended purpose with this series of questions for Job?

• Which descriptions of God's power impress you the most? In knowing that God possesses such power, how does this enable you to face your own problems more confidently as a follower of Jesus?

fri.

GOD'S SECOND RESPONSE

_____

_____

_____

_____

_____

_____

_____

_____

_____

_____

God used the large, frightening crocodile-like animal called the Leviathan as a metaphor to describe God as even more powerful and terrifying. Job's response was full acknowledgement of God's authority over all creation and in the lives of humanity.

JOB 40:1-14; 41:1-34; 42:1-6

• What was God saying about who would ultimately win the contest between God and Satan in regards to how God's plans for creation will play out?

• How would you describe God's demonstration of miraculous power in your life? What metaphor would you use to describe God's strength?

MORE SCRIPTURE
1 John 4:4—God's power is greater

God was unhappy with how Job's friends had misrepresented God's divine character, but God's priority is always about relationship. God's loving-kindness offered a path for restoration of relationship both with Job's friends and with Job himself. Only after Job prayed for his friends did God restore Job's blessings.

JOB 42:7-17

• What factors triggered God's anger at Job's friends, but not with Job himself?

• Think about any circumstance you're currently facing and how the following truths revealed in the book of Job could apply: (1) We are to trust in God as the author of only what is good and right, and (2) God is the one who always has the last word. What perspective or hope do these truths give you?

JOB'S RESTORATION

notes
AND PRAYER NEEDS

Turn the page for this week's Transformations Reflection.

transformations

Inside God's Wallet

Pain. I'm not a big fan of it myself. Job received an unfair share of human pain. As the story goes, God was bragging to Satan about Job one day and got a little carried away, asking Satan if he'd ever checked out Job's faith and trust. Satan took the bait and, with God's permission, set out to prove his favorite evil theory: there's not a man or woman on the earth who won't succumb to rejecting God's power, given the proper dose of pain.

Has God ever bragged on you? As a child, I naively imagined that God did brag on me just a little. In my child-sized brain I could comprehend no other possible explanation for the pain I encountered. Many a time I stood silent as the dad I wanted to love physically struck out at his own children. Day after day I watched as my mom went deeper and deeper into a sea of depression, overcome by the relentless storm of my dad's emotional abuse. My own spirit sagged as I cried out to God night after night, asking why my life should look like this. Why would others my age freely get to live their own child-sized lives, unencumbered by the adult-sized issues that daily threatened my innocent well-being?

And so I imagined that God must be bragging again. God must be pulling out his wallet from the pocket of those big overalls, so faded and worn from creating the world, and opening it up to show the pictures of his kids to Satan. "See here," God points, "this little one won't give up. Her dad is destructive, her mom absent. One by one her siblings are falling away, disillusioned by what they perceive as a lack of love on my part. But this little one, she just won't quit. She's gonna love me no matter what. She trusts that what she sees now isn't all there is, and that tomorrow I'm gonna show up bigger and better than ever. That's my girl."

I wanted to live up to God's overly generous confidence in me. So like Job, I hung in there and chose not to blame God for what Evil had actually invented. It was a valuable lesson that would serve me well in the years to come. Receive pain as part of life, listen to it and learn from it, then trust toward the Promise; but never for a moment think that God caused the pain.

There's another child in God's wallet who didn't give up. Those he wanted to love struck out at him. His mother's heart broke with despair, and for a dark moment in time he felt utterly and intensely alone. One by one his friends walked away, but this One just didn't quit. Three days later he rose again, the Promise bursting with new life for all.

Evil is still inventing ways to provoke us to blame God, but don't succumb to this old trick. God is still pulling out the wallet, bragging to heaven's forces that you aren't going to quit; that now is not all there is; and that tomorrow when the Promise shows up, life will win again.

psalms

songs for the journey

book 19

The book of Psalms contains one hundred and fifty poems reflecting the feelings of authors whose souls were moved by the thoughts of God. The Psalms are attributed to some of the most well-known characters of the Bible (including Moses, David, and Solomon), but many are the product of other writers. The dating of the Psalms is difficult, but the complete book took nearly one thousand years to compile.

Book 1: Psalms 1–41, compiled before King David's death

Book 2: Psalms 42–72, compiled during the reign of King Solomon

Books 3 and 4: Psalms 73–106, compiled during the exile in Babylon

Book 5: Psalm 107–150, compiled during the time of Ezra

Often set to music, psalms were designed to express the dynamics of real life experiences through worship. During times of stability, hymns offered praise to God for acting with goodness and grace. In times of despair, laments provided an opportunity to complain to God, ask for forgiveness, trust God, and ask for God's intervention. Thanksgiving psalms were an immediate response of joy for either a wonderful deed God had done or a reassuring experience of God in a time of instability. Within the New Testament are one hundred direct quotes from Psalms, which shows how they were used in synagogue and early Christian worship.

The Psalms offer two key themes as we read, identify, and worship with them. The first is that we are made in God's image and are therefore worthy of God's love. No matter what our feelings, God desires us to be transparent so we can be transformed more closely into God's image. The second is that God's love is unconditional. God cares about every aspect of our lives! We are not to hide our thoughts or emotions from God. As we become more willing to enter into honest relationship with God, God is able to bless us with spiritual wholeness and health.

This week you will experience the psalms as they were designed: to express dynamic life experiences. The chart below has been provided for you to find your favorite psalms for all moments of life.

Hymn psalms	1–2, 8, 15, 18–19, 20–21, 24, 29, 33, 36, 45–50, 66, 67–68, 72–73, 76, 78, 81–82, 84, 87, 89, 93, 95–101, 103, 104, 110–115, 117, 119, 122, 127–128, 132, 134–135, 144–150
Lament psalms	3–7, 9–10, 12–14, 17, 22, 25–28, 31, 35–36, 38–40, 41–44, 51–61, 64, 69–71, 74, 77, 79, 80, 83, 85–86, 88, 89, 90, 94, 102, 109, 120, 123, 126, 129–130, 137, 139–143
Thanksgiving psalms	1, 8, 11, 16, 18, 19, 21, 23, 27, 30, 32, 34, 40, 49, 63, 65, 67, 75, 91–92, 105–108, 116, 118, 121, 124, 125, 131, 135, 136, 138
Note: Some psalms with mixed style are listed more than once.	

sun.

GOD'S LOVING PRESENCE

_____
_____
_____
_____
_____
_____
_____
_____
_____
_____

These thanksgiving psalms (*todah* means "thanks-giving" in Hebrew) were both attributed to King David, showing the deep faith and hope that he found in being a child of God. King David had a trust in life and hope in death under the watchful care of God.

PSALMS 16; 23

• What specific God-actions did David pray for in his life?

• Psalm 23 is often read at funerals, but it's actually a psalm about living. Which verses of this psalm speak to you?

mon.

WORSHIP AND PRAISE

_____
_____
_____
_____
_____
_____
_____
_____
_____
_____

The sons of Korah, who chanted hymn psalms, were a choir of Levites whom King David had appointed to serve during Temple worship. The Levites, one of the twelve tribes of Israel, were responsible for Temple worship.

PSALMS 46; 48

• What signs of worship and praise to God do you find in these psalms?

• How do Psalm 46:10 and Psalm 48:1-2 speak to you?

CRY FOR HELP

These psalms, both written by King David, are known as psalms of lament. Lamentations are cries for God to act in our lives.

PSALMS 51; 54

• In what ways was David crying out to God to take action?

• Of the ways David cried out to God, which ones are similar to your cries today? How do you hope God will respond?

FAITH IN GOD

This hymn is attributed to Asaph, a Levite whom King David appointed to be the music leader for worship. His name is associated with eleven other psalms and songs. Asaph had become caught up in the chaos of anger, envy, and self-pity, but then he refocused himself upon God.

PSALM 73

• When realizing his jealousy of godless tendencies in people, how did Asaph allow this to affect his own spiritual walk?

• Of the truths Asaph used to refocus himself on God, which ones help you to refocus spiritually?

thurs.

THANKFUL FOR BLESSINGS

_____
_____
_____
_____
_____
_____
_____
_____
_____
_____

Psalm 118 is a thanksgiving psalm written by an anonymous author. This type of thanksgiving is more than a general thankfulness; it is an overwhelmingly passionate, emotional worship response for an experience of God's goodness and grace.

PSALM 118

• For what blessings does this psalm remind you to be thankful?

• Reread Psalm 118:8-9. How have you trusted in others instead of taking refuge in the Lord? What advantages do you gain by trusting in God instead of others?

fri.

THE POWER OF GOD'S WORD

_____
_____
_____
_____
_____
_____
_____
_____
_____
_____

Psalm 119 is the longest psalm in the book of Psalms, and the longest chapter in the Bible. Though considered a hymn, it was likely read aloud rather than sung. Each section contains sentences that begin with the same letter of the Hebrew alphabet (with the sections following in order, from *aleph* to *tav*). This technique is called an acrostic poem, and it functions as a convenient way to memorize and recite poetry.

PSALM 119:1-24

• What is the reassurance found in these verses?

• Reread 119:1-16. How are you hiding God's word in your heart?

MORE SCRIPTURE
Psalm 119:25-176—In praise of God's laws

In these psalms of lament, King David cried out for God's protection and asked God to punish his enemies. In private and personal prayer, David poured out his honest feelings before God and trusted in God's response.

PSALMS 140–142

• What feelings did David pour out in these psalms?

• Write a lament to God about your honest feelings. How is Psalm 142:5-7 a response to your lament?

HONEST TO GOD

_____

_____

_____

_____

_____

_____

_____

_____

_____

_____

notes AND PRAYER NEEDS

_____

_____

_____

_____

_____

_____

_____

_____

_____

Turn the page for this week's Transformations Reflection.

transformations

Image Obsession

When I lived in California, I often crossed paths with a homeless man who had no legs and only one arm. His entire body fit on a skateboard, and he pushed himself up and down the boardwalk with his one good arm. Every day when I saw him struggling past people on bikes, rollerblades, and their own two feet, I would think to myself, "There he goes…made in the image of God." Perhaps not.

I trust and believe that all humans are created in God's image. But I can admit that I've never imagined God as armless, legless, and homeless. I can also admit how awkward it is that I associate God's image with the physical image of humans. Deep down I know it's our spiritual image that "looks" like God. But more often than not, that rationale stays deep down.

We humans probably associate God's image with our own physical image because we live in an image-focused society. Whether it's the media telling us to slather our face with creams and ointments or our parents telling us to iron our shirts, we are obsessed with our physical image, especially when trying to prevent its decay.

We often project this obsession onto our perception of God, sometimes even imagining God to have a perfect physical body. And then when we look in the mirror, we think that our image falls short. I know my body isn't perfect—I lack appropriate muscle tone in my abdominals, my fingernails are ragged, and my head could be mistaken for a bowling ball. I sometimes reason that my lack of physical perfection means that God cannot look like me, which must mean that I'm not like God. This preoccupation with a physical image disrupts my perception of God because deep within my spirit I know that I'm created in God's image. That spiritual connection is the key to my faith in God's grace.

Many of the Psalms call us into prayer and praise by exposing us to God's attributes, such as loving-kindness or omnipresence (e.g. Psalm 139). These attributes help us understand how we are created in God's image. If we stop obsessing over our physical image and start obsessing over our spiritual image, that is by trying to love or be present to others, we can begin to live as we have been called to live—in the true image of God.

proverbs

life rules to live by

book 20

Giving advice is just as important today as it was thousands of years ago. Each of us is on our own journey to understand the complexity of life around us. We are not only searching for practical knowledge, we are also searching for spiritual wisdom.

The book of Proverbs has an educational purpose, for it contains over three thousand statements of practical and spiritual wisdom. These statements take the form of poems, riddles, and metaphors, which the sages called *mashalim* ("proverbs"). These sayings compare and contrast things that the sage observes, to communicate how we are to act.

In the book of 1 Kings, Solomon asks God for wisdom—a discerning heart and the ability to determine right and wrong. This collection of ancient proverbs is traditionally attributed to Solomon, though the sayings were collected over many centuries.

In Proverbs you will find many contrasts and comparisons of two types of wisdom—the wisdom of the world and the wisdom of God. Worldly wisdom tries to ignore God and the boundaries that God has set between right and wrong. When we depend on worldly wisdom, we tend to be self-focused and filled with self-ambition that will eventually destroy relationships, careers, and communities. Wisdom from God always takes into account the interests of others. It is characterized by genuineness and sincerity for both the people we know well and the strangers we may encounter.

At first glance, the book may seem as if it is filled with "one liners," but there are larger themes. In Proverbs 1–9 you will find the importance of a young person learning how to choose his/her friends early in life, discussions about the temptations and pressures young adults will experience as they leave the security of their parent's home, the importance of being obedient to God's wisdom, the risks and consequences of following worldly wisdom, and godly wisdom personified.

Chapters 10–29 contain concise, practical words of advice covering many situations. You may find yourself memorizing and recalling these verses in times of pressure. The concluding chapters (30–31) take a different view of godly wisdom. Chapter 30 presents a choice between piety and skepticism, and chapter 31 contains wisdom about the significant role godly women play in the world.

Proverbs is a guide for making positive choices in life. It covers topics such as marriage, parenting, career advancement, and so on. Proverbs 1:7 reminds us that our first priority must be to "fear the Lord." This phrase means putting God first so that God is able to bless us with godly wisdom. As you grow in respect for God's wisdom, God will provide new opportunities for you to evaluate and understand the truth and beauty of life.

EMBRACING WISDOM

_____
_____
_____
_____
_____
_____
_____
_____
_____
_____

Wisdom is much more than memorizing or quoting Bible verses. Wisdom requires knowledge plus skill. It is not only learning to live but also being able to adapt our life to God's pattern. Wisdom requires complete acceptance and understanding that God's laws are good and right. As Christians we depend upon the Holy Spirit to impart understanding of God's expectations so that we learn the skill of living in a way that honors God.

PROVERBS 1–2

• What benefits of understanding wisdom are listed in Proverbs 1?

• Of the skills for gaining wisdom listed in Proverbs 2, which one do you struggle with the most? How can you improve?

WISDOM VERSUS FOLLY

_____
_____
_____
_____
_____
_____
_____
_____
_____
_____

At the opposite end of wisdom, we find folly (or foolishness). Some of the things listed in this chapter are foolish because they create indebtedness to another person, and others are listed because they are sinful and hated by the Lord. The chapter also gives warnings about laziness and divisiveness.

PROVERBS 6

• What are the seven things listed that God hates most?

• Of the other warnings, which did you need to be reminded the most of today? How will heeding these warnings potentially transform your life?

A SKILLED DESIGNER

Wisdom personified is the one speaking in this chapter. Wisdom is God's tool and the organizing force behind all of creation. Just as a skilled designer creates detailed plans before beginning construction or renovation, God's wisdom ordered the scheme of creation before it appeared and continues to order the scheme of our world.

PROVERBS 8

• What skills does wisdom possess, according to Proverbs 8?

• In 8:10-11, wisdom is compared to wealth. How do you see wisdom to be more beneficial to you than wealth?

THE HEART

Throughout the book of Proverbs, the word "heart" is repeated nearly seventy times. The heart is the driving force, or center, of one's being. How we prepare, nurture, and feed our heart impacts our attitudes, feelings, behaviors, and decisions. Within the following verses we learn that during suffering and difficult times God allows our moral impurities to surface so they can be refined, drawing us closer into God's own heart.

PROVERBS 16:1–17:3

• Of the times "heart" is mentioned in these passages, what blessings or warnings accompany it?

• Which of these blessings or warnings could God use to make your heart more like God's own?

THE LORD

_____

_____

_____

_____

_____

_____

_____

_____

_____

_____

Eighty-four times the words "the Lord" appear in Proverbs. In this passage, we are reminded that God does not see differences between the poor and rich. And the Lord expects each one of us to reach out, protect, and defend those who are poor and needy. No matter our status in society, we will all be held to the same test.

PROVERBS 22

• In Proverbs 22, underline every time "the Lord" is mentioned. What characteristics are identified with "the Lord"?

• Which of these proverbs speak directly to you? What practical applications can you make today?

LESSONS FROM AGUR

_____

_____

_____

_____

_____

_____

_____

_____

_____

_____

We don't know whether Agur represents a real person or if the Hebrew means something else. The sayings in the first nine verses appear to be a conversation between a skeptical person, who is weary of trying to understand God, and a more pious person, who warns that God's words are adequate and that neither poverty nor riches are desirable because they may lead one to deny God. Verses 10-33 offer a separate collection of wise sayings.

PROVERBS 30

• What warnings are given about God's word in 30:5-6?

• Verses 24-28 offer valuable life lessons: ants prepare for the future; badgers know where to find protection; locusts benefit from pooling resources; and lizards seize opportunities. Which animal most represents you?

King Lemuel was likely a non-Israelite king, yet his name means "belonging to God." This wisdom highlights the significant role that mothers play in building character into their children, and thus into society at large. Some have said that this chapter, which was written for a patriarchal society, creates unrealistic expectations (or limitations) for present-day women. Others suggest that it gives women the opportunity to determine the balance that works best for them in terms of family, community, and career.

PROVERBS 31

• For whom are we reminded to speak up and defend in this passage?

• How are you doing in achieving integration between family, community, and career? What changes do you need to make?

notes

AND PRAYER NEEDS

transformations

Check It Out

I'm an information junkie. I don't remember exactly when it all started, but I suppose those long childhood summers spent walking back and forth to the town library put me off to a really addictive start. I joined book clubs and read every biography in the children and young adult sections until books simply weren't enough. I needed magazines and the occasional thrill of a periodical. By the time I reached adulthood, the only high left was the Sunday paper, which to this day I absolutely must read every weekend.

My family knows not to leave reading material in front of me if they want my attention. I can hardly help myself! Info junkies are completely mesmerized by information of any sort and will default to the path of least resistance whether it's the paper, the evening news, or a book on the coffee table. The rooms of my home are strewn with literature and magazines I fully plan to consume, confident that if I fail to read any of them, I will miss some amazing shred of information that on any given day could alter the world as we know it. No doubt about it, I'm addicted to information.

Information and inspiration, however, are two different things. Information has served me well, educating me about people and their crazy lives. Information has entertained me as I have discovered what is going on around the world, new inventions and old deceptions. Information is fascinating and relaxing all at once. It keeps my brain occupied, learning about everything from next week's weather to my vacation spot next summer.

Inspiration goes deeper and alludes to that which is transformational. Wisdom is the fuel of inspiration and the essence of why we have the book of Proverbs. This Old Testament gem comes out of an era when wisdom was a rare commodity. People desired wisdom more than wealth and often asked for it, like the young people today who beg to be mentored by Donald Trump. The ancients knew that wealth without wisdom would soon yield neither but that wisdom without wealth could soon yield both.

God is seeking wisdom junkies. People whose eyes are wide open to life, whose ears are wide open to counsel, and whose hearts are wide open to God. People who humbly ask the hard questions and passionately listen for the answers when they come. People who are absolutely convinced—and even some mature people who are skeptical—that there is a God, that they are not God, and that God alone knows the formula for success in life. God is actively empowering people who are convinced that Jesus is THE WAY in an every-day-I'm-toast-unless-I-follow-him sense.

So I'm thinking of becoming a wisdom junkie. I'm going to check out Proverbs from God's library more often. I'm going to listen harder to those who have traveled the earth just a little longer. I'm going to strew the coffee tables of my mind with God's promises for each new day. I think it will be fascinating and relaxing all at once. Fascinating to hear from the God of heaven, and relaxing to know I'm not that God.

ecclesiastes

thoughts on life

The book of Ecclesiastes is grouped with Job, Proverbs, and Song of Songs as the biblical wisdom books. The title, Ecclesiastes, is a Greek translation of a Hebrew word, *Qoheleth,* that means something like "the Preacher." King Solomon is closely associated by reputation with this wisdom literature, and although there are differing opinions concerning its author, Solomon is attributed as the writer of Ecclesiastes by some Jewish and early Christian traditions. The Hebrew vocabulary suggests that the book reached its present form by the second century BC.

Ecclesiastes does not tell a story; rather, it shares philosophical thoughts on the meaning of life. Several themes are apparent in this book, woven throughout and reappearing in different forms. The central theme of the Preacher is found in the book's first line: "Meaningless! Meaningless!" says the Teacher. "Utterly meaningless! Everything is meaningless!" Using only his own insight and wisdom, the Preacher could find no meaning or pattern in life that made sense. The Preacher's response to this dilemma became the second theme: searching. Rather than wallowing in despair, he actively searched for answers by trying a variety of routes: education, pleasure, and hard work and its resulting affluence. None of these brought the result he craved, but he kept searching. Everyone searches for happiness in life, and in our materialistic society the temptation is to pursue fulfillment through these same means. The Preacher demonstrated the impossibility of finding meaning without God, for money and possessions never bring spiritual fulfillment. Ecclesiastes motivates us to focus our search for meaning on God alone.

Ecclesiastes also addresses purpose in life. By the end of the book and the end of his life, the Preacher reached this conclusion: life is a gift from God and is to be guided solely by God's word and God's Spirit. Even those who love and serve God will find that not everything in life makes sense, and Solomon advised all coming after him: "Remember your Creator in the days of your youth before the days of trouble come and the years approach when you will say, 'I find no pleasure in them'" (12:1). "Fear God and keep his commandments, for this is the whole duty of everyone" (12:13). Solomon wanted others to benefit from his experience, not to repeat his mistakes and miss life as God intended. A life centered in God is satisfying and meaningful and, in the light of eternity, gives insight even to those days that don't make sense.

WIND CHASERS

_____
_____
_____
_____
_____
_____
_____
_____
_____
_____

Having been granted the gift of wisdom, the Preacher's observation of life led him to make conclusions about it. He struggled to find meaning as he chased everything under the sun. Jesus' disciple Peter also agreed that we make conclusions about life based on our observations and experiences. When our priorities do not include God, our efforts are meaningless; but when they include God, great meaning can be found.

ECCLESIASTES 1; 1 PETER 4:1-11

• What conclusions did the Preacher make from his observations? According to Peter, what kind of actions have meaning—and why?

• What are you doing that provides meaning in your life? How can you grow in this area?

mon.

FOR WHOM ARE YOU WORKING?

_____
_____
_____
_____
_____
_____
_____
_____
_____
_____

In life we are often tempted to seek pleasure, especially when we are not content with our circumstances. We try to fulfill our human desires rather than God's. The Preacher tested the human avenues of fulfillment, leaving lessons for us from his experiences.

ECCLESIASTES 2:1-16; 1 CORINTHIANS 15:50-58

• With what activities did the Preacher fill his time, and what did these activities provide? According to 1 Corinthians 15:58, what do we learn about work?

• What does giving yourself fully to the work of Lord mean to you? What practical ways can you do this?

The Preacher's wisdom allowed him to understand the importance of time and how every experience—good or bad—has its time. The Preacher wrote about the greatness of God's gift of life. We need to enjoy our time and respect each season, instead of wishing away the time God has given us.

ECCLESIASTES 3:1-17

• What does it mean that "God has made everything beautiful in its time"?

• Which of the times described in verses 3:2-8 are you in right now? What is God teaching you in this time?

_____

_____

_____

_____

_____

_____

_____

_____

_____

_____

wed.

STRENGTH IN NUMBERS

As the Preacher continued to share his observations of life, he showed compassion for those who were marginalized or oppressed as well as how important it is to have friends. When we build relationships, we gain strength to overcome life's struggles.

ECCLESIASTES 4:1-12

• What benefits come from companionship?

• What difference has close companionship made in your life?

_____

_____

_____

_____

_____

_____

_____

_____

_____

_____

WEALTH AND MATERIAL POSSESSIONS

_____
_____
_____
_____
_____
_____
_____
_____
_____
_____
_____

The Preacher teaches what he had learned from personal experience concerning wealth and material possessions. Finding true fulfillment comes through recognizing and embracing God's provision and fully developing it in a way that honors God.

ECCLESIASTES 5:8–6:7

• What lessons about wealth and money are in this passage? According to 5:18-20, what is God's gift to humanity?

• Describe your relationship with money. How do you feel about the gift of God mentioned in 5:19?

fri.

WORDS OF WISDOM

_____
_____
_____
_____
_____
_____
_____
_____
_____
_____
_____

The Preacher's life was rich with experience as well as financial wealth, and he shared many lessons for life application. As you read today, think about the "life lessons" that apply to you.

ECCLESIASTES 7:1–8:1

• List the benefits of wisdom, as shared by The Preacher.

• Out of the many life lessons the Preacher gave, which spoke to you the most? What will you have to do to live up to this life lesson?

The previous chapters in Ecclesiastes were written to set up this reading. It takes readers on a journey through all the "experiments" of the Preacher to bring them to the "rest of the story." Read and discover the conclusions the Preacher made about his experience.

ECCLESIASTES 11:7–12:14

• What advice does the Preacher give in 12:1? Write the Preacher's conclusion in 12:13-14 in your own words.

• How will you make this conclusion your own?

THE REST OF THE STORY

_____

_____

_____

_____

_____

_____

_____

_____

_____

_____

notes

AND PRAYER NEEDS

_____

_____

_____

_____

_____

_____

_____

_____

_____

*t*ransformations

Computer Control

Bud Sampleton owned, operated, and oversaw everything that happened at his butcher shop. When Bud turned fifty-five years old, business at Sampleton Meats was no better or no worse than when he took over in his twenties.

Bud's son (a salesman for Blue Isle InkJet) recently bought his dad a computer in hopes of making business better. Bud desperately needed the update despite priding himself on being the only business in town that is run on "human brain power." Lately, his error-proof filing system (file cabinet from 1970) had been contradicting its own moniker. Invoices had been lost, shipments were screwed up, and a number of documents needed to appease the IRS had been misplaced.

So with the help of his savvy offspring, Bud learned how operating the computer could save him both time and stress. "They're smart little machines, aren't they?" he said during his lessons. Things picked up around the shop. Bud's four employees were happier because their checks came on time. The IRS was less suspicious. Bud's distributors and suppliers appreciated that they finally had a consistent delivery schedule. Life was good at Sampleton Meats because of one tiny computer.

Well, almost good. After a year and one month of owning and operating his computer, Bud inexplicably went back to his old ways. Bud was skeptical of technology he couldn't control or understand. With the computer turned off, life quickly got bad at Sampleton Meats. Bills were late. Checks were bounced. Hundreds of pounds of beef were thrown away because of overstocking. Critics and family members (whose inheritance dwindled) called Bud Sampleton foolish and stubborn.

Bud is an analogy of the story of the Preacher in the book of Ecclesiastes. God filled the Preacher's brain (his computer) with wisdom. Everything the Preacher did while using godly wisdom turned to gold. People traveled from all over to witness his godly wisdom. Then the Preacher stopped using the "computer" God gave him. He was skeptical of divine technology he couldn't really control.

He started making decisions based on his own desires instead of God's. That got him in trouble, and he realized firsthand that life was meaningless without God.

Bud and the Preacher are proof that humans are control freaks. Bud botched up a perfectly good meat shop because of control issues. Solomon messed up his empire because he started controlling his own life with pleasure-based decisions. Both of them turned off the "computer" that was obviously smarter than them and then tried but failed to manage on their own.

If we use the computer (brain) that God gives us, we have the freedom to let go of control. And learning how to use this computer can become easier if we get a little help and take advantage of the free customer support—or, in techie terms, the Holy Spirit.

song of songs

romantic love

book 22

A graphic description of romantic love in the Bible surprises many, yet the Song of Songs clearly celebrates the love between a man and a woman. Included as part of the poetic wisdom books of the Old Testament, the Song of Songs lyrically expresses the joy and intimacy of marital love and makes a clear statement that this love is the gift of our Creator. While the identity of the author is not stated, many attribute it to Solomon, the third king of Israel. Others believe that this book may be a collection of poems by different authors that were about or intended for Solomon.

Over the centuries, people have embraced different interpretations of this book. The first interpretation accepts this poem at face value: a description of marriage the way God intended marriage to be. Song of Songs is not a factual account; it has no significant plot or story. It simply expresses God's idea of a healthy marital relationship. In contrast to the world's distorted view of sex, this book is a reminder that God's gift is to be enjoyed and used within the boundaries God set. This book gives God's endorsement of marital love as good and pure, as well as powerful, spontaneous, unquenchable, and fulfilling. God created man and woman and established and blessed a lifelong commitment within which mutual fulfillment and oneness could be achieved relationally, spiritually, and physically. In the Song of Songs, God presents an ideal relationship, which is a model to work for within our own marriages.

The second interpretation sees the Song of Songs as an allegory representing God's love for God's people, Israel in the Old Testament. Some early church writers read it as an allegory for Christ's love for the Church in the New Testament. God/Jesus are referred to as the "bridegroom" in many Scripture passages, and God's people/the Church are described as the bride of Christ throughout the New Testament as well. Song of Songs 8:6-7 describes the kind of love our bridegroom demonstrates toward us: a love as strong as death; a flame even many waters cannot quench; a love freely given…no amount of money or effort can buy it. As God's people, this book reminds us of the intimacy and intensity of God's commitment to us, which culminated in God's sacrifice for us through Jesus' death on the cross. We are also reminded of the joy and fulfillment that come when we reciprocate God's love by speaking and demonstrating our love to God without restraint.

The bridal veil separating the bride from her bridegroom (4:1-3) contains a lesson for us: removing the veil came *before* any deep sharing of feelings or intimate physical connection with the bride's partner. On both a human and God-connection level, withholding ourselves will keep our relationships at a shallow level at best. God calls us to joy and intimacy as we release ourselves with abandon to our marriage partner and to God.

sun.

A DECLARATION OF MARRIAGE

_____

_____

_____

_____

_____

_____

_____

_____

_____

_____

_____

God's design for marriage includes deep personal connection and fulfillment within the relationship. God made husband and wife to be equal partners—vocationally, relationally, and within the family. God knew the fullest and most satisfying expression of being "one flesh" came only within the lifetime commitment to the covenant of marriage.

SONG OF SONGS 1:1–2:7; GENESIS 1:26-31; 2:18-25

• How did Adam describe his relationship with Eve in Genesis 2:23? How did the couple in Song of Songs describe theirs?

• The partners in Song of Songs 1 were adept at boosting their spouse's self-esteem and sense of security in their relationship. To whom…your partner, a family member, or a friend…could you give unsolicited affirmation?

mon.

RELATIONSHIP REFLECTIONS

_____

_____

_____

_____

_____

_____

_____

_____

_____

_____

This section of Song of Songs uses many metaphors from nature to describe the couple's relationship. Marriage is a gift that originated in the mind and heart of God, but the "vineyard" of marriage God provides for us must be tended in order to blossom and grow. Any threat to the relationship must be identified and thwarted.

SONG OF SONGS 2:8–3:11; PROVERBS 5

• Song of Songs 2:15 describes "little foxes" as forces capable of destroying a vineyard in bloom. What are some common threats to the success of a marriage relationship?

• Proverbs 5 suggests that untended relationships (including our relationship with God) are vulnerable. What safeguards do you have in place to protect your relationship with your spouse (or with God)?

AN INTIMATE EXCHANGE

In many different ways and situations throughout the Bible we hear, "It's not about you." Grasping and applying this truth is of utmost importance in the contexts of marriage and of spiritual family. As both partners give one hundred percent to their spouse and the relationship, the needs of both partners are met. As all members of God's family give of themselves with no reservation, the needs of the Christian community are met.

SONG OF SONGS 4:1–5:1; EPHESIANS 5:21-33

• How does the relationship between Christ and the church help explain the role of husbands and wives in Ephesians 5?

• How do the marriages around you compare to the description in Ephesians 5? If you are married, how does your marriage compare?

MARITAL GROWTH AND MATURITY

The exclusiveness of the marriage relationship—one person plus one person for life—provides the security and safety for each partner to develop fully into what God uniquely designed for them as individuals and as a team. Knowing "I am my lover's and my lover is mine" frees one to grow in all areas.

SONG OF SONGS 5:2–6:3; 1 CORINTHIANS 6:12–7:5

• Song of Songs 5:6 reveals some sort of separation between the bride and groom. How does the bride ensure their relationship will not be neglected?

• How do you handle situations that threaten to separate you from someone you love? How could Paul's counsel in 1 Corinthians 7 help married couples handle conflict?

THE POWER OF LOVE

_____

_____

_____

_____

_____

_____

_____

_____

_____

_____

_____

Hundreds of songs have been written about the power of love. Because of its power, love must be treated with the greatest caution and respect. The conclusion of Song of Songs resounds with the bride's assertions about the strength of love and her desire to publicly declare their love. The apostle Paul also has much to say about the power of the love we know and share in Christ.

SONG OF SONGS 6:4–8:14; 1 CORINTHIANS 13

• In 1 Corinthians 13:4-8, what are the characteristics that give love its power?

• Rewrite 1 Corinthians 13, substituting the name of Jesus for the word "love" each time it occurs. What new understanding of love does this give you?

fri.

LOVE ONE ANOTHER

_____

_____

_____

_____

_____

_____

_____

_____

_____

_____

_____

We often wonder why our relationships are not what we want or have visualized. God is specific in outlining what it takes to have the kind of intimate relationship God intended. It takes obedience to God's instructions and the desire to treat others as we want to be treated. It's hard work, but the reward is dynamic relationships that grow out of the ordinary, everyday, respectful interactions between family members, friends, and especially marriage partners.

COLOSSIANS 3:1-14; JOHN 15:9-17

• From the Colossians 3 passage, list what are we to take off. What are we to put on?

• How will you follow Jesus' command to "love each other" with the most significant person in your life this week? What will you do?

Song of Songs can be interpreted as an allegory describing the love between Christ and the church. The following New Testament stories describe Jesus as the bridegroom and his followers as the bride.

JOHN 3:22-30; MATTHEW 25:1-13

• How important is the bridegroom in these stories? Why?

• A bride always prepares herself to meet her bridegroom. What step do you need to take to increase the intimacy of your relationship with Jesus? More time in prayer and study? Greater use of your gifts in service? Finding a place of community with other followers? Or what else?

THE BRIDEGROOM AND THE BRIDE

notes

AND PRAYER NEEDS

transformations

Beautiful Sex

Back when minivans and stirrup pants were cool, my family went to a church that was breaking new ground in the land of boring. My brother and I used to take turns "going to the bathroom" two times each during the sermon. I think my mom let us go because she didn't want us taking after our old man, sleeping without shame once the standing portion of the service ended.

I tell you this because I'm slightly peeved right now. I'm twenty-six and reading Song of Songs for the first time. It would've been nice to know fourteen years ago when I was dying of boredom that the Bible had material juicy enough to make the sex education teacher blush. With the Bibles in every pew, I could've been reading about sex and marriage instead of drawing shoddy football helmets on first-time-visitor cards.

If I had known the Bible talked about sex when I was in grade school, I would've made Billy Graham look like an amateur evangelist. I would've been on the playground holding revivals. "Thus saith the good book, 'How delightful is your love . . . Your lips drop sweetness as the honeycomb.'" The kids on swings would've stopped swinging. The girls playing four-square would've stopped. Everyone would've gathered around while I preached the good news that the Bible, infamous for its boredom, talked about sex. I would've been locked away for my suggestiveness. My classmates would've held all night candle vigils protesting my incarceration. Once freed I would've filled the pews of my previously boring church with hundreds of twelve year olds thirsting for God's word.

Perhaps I'm getting carried away . . .

I think my reaction to Song of Songs says a great deal about this day and age. You can agree or disagree, but I think we've ruined sex. I believe we've turned God's beautiful invention into something that is totally misused. With magazines, media, and movies giving the idea that sex is just a casual part of a relationship, sex has lost its meaning. It has lost the intimacy and depth that God intended it to have in marriage. It shouldn't be this way. If God meant for believers to be quiet about the true design for sex, Song of Songs would have been

hidden somewhere other than in the Bible. God created sex for us to use within God's intended plan. It's a gift with endless potential. And yet we've turned that gift into a secular weapon of mass destruction. The number of problems caused by sex is heartbreaking when you read Song of Songs and see how beautiful it should be.

We have the ability to shatter this ridiculous misuse of sex. But it starts at home. Your kids need to know that Song of Songs exists before they turn twenty-six. They need to have you teach and affirm the beauty of sex rather than learn about it from our culture. Sex is wonderful; admit it, because your kids need to hear it. Talking about it is the first step to saving God's beautiful gift. Understanding its true meaning and protection within the long-term commitment of marriage is the second step, and Song of Songs is waiting to help you get there.

isaiah

the messianic prophet

book 23

The definition of a biblical prophet is one whom God has called to draw the attention of the people to righteousness and repentance, and to speak for God. As we've already read so far, God chose a wide variety of individuals to speak on God's behalf: Nathan, Elijah, and Elisha, among others. This week we meet another prophet, Isaiah, whose prophecies are contained in the first of a series of books in the Bible collectively known as the "major prophets" (Isaiah, Jeremiah, Ezekiel). A second series, called the Book of the Twelve (also called the "minor prophets" due to their shorter length), immediately follows the major prophets.

The prophets had specialized roles as spokespersons for God. They were to remind God's people of how to live a righteous life and of the drastic and terrible consequences that would result from disobedience. Many of the biblical prophets were sent especially to confront corruption in the king's government, though Isaiah probably began his announcements from within the royal court.

The prophet Isaiah provided insight into the conditions and events of his lifetime. Although related to the royalty (first cousin of King Uzziah), Isaiah answered God's call to speak to the crumbling southern kingdom of Judah. Isaiah started prophesying in the Jerusalem area in approximately 740 BC at the end of King Uzziah's reign. The utterances in the book of Isaiah span more than forty years and pertain to at least four kings. Other prophets were also active during Isaiah's lifetime, including Amos, Hosea, and Micah.

In addition to calling God's people to turn from sin, restore their relationship with God, and avoid destruction and ruin, the book of Isaiah also provides one of the earliest glimpses of the desire for a messianic redeemer, making Isaiah the most quoted prophet in the New Testament. The first half of the book of Isaiah (chapters 1–39) presents God's message of judgment upon Israel, Judah, and the surrounding nations; the second half (chapters 40–66) offers God's encouragement to the exiles who had been taken into Babylonian captivity and who yearned for a deliverer.

The book of Isaiah gives the reader a deeper understanding of two key attributes of God: justice and mercy. Though angered by sin, God is also moved by compassion to save those who have sinned against God. It is a message to which many of us can relate. Though God requires us to be obedient, God's loving grace is amazing to forgive and restore us no matter how far we have strayed or fallen away. As you read Isaiah, may you fully grasp the compassion of our great God, for the people of Isaiah's time and for us.

LOOK AND LISTEN

_____

_____

_____

_____

_____

_____

_____

_____

_____

_____

_____

Prophets were called in unique ways to become the messengers of God's truth. In this reading, Isaiah describes his unique call. Isaiah's eyes and ears were open to God's directions. Pray that God will open your eyes and ears to God's direction for you.

ISAIAH 6; MATTHEW 13:10-17

• What was Isaiah worried about when he went into the presence of God? What happened to Isaiah in this experience?

• How are you looking and listening for God's call? What is God saying to you today?

NOW AND LATER

_____

_____

_____

_____

_____

_____

_____

_____

_____

_____

Jesse was the father of David—and because of the sin of David's son Solomon, the family dynasty (sometimes called the "House of David") was jeopardized. Isaiah referred to this family's remnant as the stump of Jesse, promising that a shoot would come out of what was thought to be cut off. Though at times we feel stuck, God is working out circumstances for the best, both now and later.

ISAIAH 7; 11

• What problem were the people facing? How did God save them, and what else did God promise?

• What problems is the world facing today? What hope does Isaiah 11:6-9 give you for the future?

MORE SCRIPTURE

Matthew 1:18-23—The fulfillment of Isaiah 7

tue.

WORSHIP IN TRUTH, NOT TRADITION

Isaiah spoke out against the people's empty words. God wants us to truly worship with our lives—not just talk about it. Isaiah prophesied about those who say they love and follow God and then deny God by their practices.

ISAIAH 29; MARK 7:1-13

• How did Jesus (in Mark 7:6-8) appropriate Isaiah's prophecy in verse 29:13?

• How can you keep your worship practices from becoming repetitive and empty?

MORE SCRIPTURE

Isaiah 12–28—Isaiah's prophecies to specific neighboring nations

wed.

CREATOR AND COMFORTER

God provided hope through the prophet Isaiah. This passage shows us God's power to create as well as to provide. We can take comfort that the God of creation is in control, and provides comfort through salvation for those who are weary.

ISAIAH 40; LUKE 3:1-6

• What characteristics of God did Isaiah write about? How do John's words in Luke 3 relate to Isaiah?

• How does it help you to know God is in control of all creation? What promise do we have from these passages?

MORE SCRIPTURE

Isaiah 37–39—Isaiah's connection with King Hezekiah, as described in 2 Kings

THE PROMISED ONE

_____

_____

_____

_____

_____

_____

_____

_____

_____

_____

Christians look to the Servant Songs of Isaiah (chapters 42, 49, 50, 53) to understand the baptism, suffering, and death of Jesus. These passages provided a prophetic message of hope to God's people, even though they did not live to see the promised deliverer who would establish justice throughout the world.

ISAIAH 42:1-4; 52:13–53:12

• What characteristics of Jesus did the early Christians perceive in Isaiah's description of the suffering servant? (See Matthew 26:63-67; Luke 18:31-32; 24:25-27, 44-45.)

• How do you feel about what Christ went through for the sake of humanity? What is your response?

fri.

CONFESSION AND SALVATION

_____

_____

_____

_____

_____

_____

_____

_____

_____

_____

Regardless of our selfish intentions, God desires our actions to be motivated by faith. God's people were engaged in religious practices but not God-practices. God spoke through Isaiah to call them to a new way of life.

ISAIAH 58

• What were the people doing? What did God require of them?

• What differences do you see between what God wanted and what the people were doing? In what ways can you do more of what God asks, rather than just what you want?

GOD ANSWERS PRAYER

In Isaiah 63–64, God's people prayed for deliverance. In Isaiah 65–66, God answered. It is great to know that we serve a living God who responds to us! When we sincerely need something, God provides.

ISAIAH 64:1-12; 66:1-13; MATTHEW 7:7-12

• What did people pray for in chapter 64? What was God's answer?

• What are you praying for? According to Matthew 7:7-12, what can you expect when you go to God in prayer?

notes

AND PRAYER NEEDS

Turn the page for this week's Transformations Reflection.

transformations

Listening for God

Many times throughout my life I've heard individuals say, "God spoke to me and told me" to do this or that, or "God spoke to me and told me" to go here or there. No matter where I am, it seems that people around me talk about their conversations with God. I've also read books of the Bible, like Isaiah, and marveled at how powerfully a prophet like him could hear and then speak God's messages so directly. I wondered what I had done to anger God because God never talked to me in that manner. This bothered me so much that in one instance I looked upward to the skies and said, "Hey, God, just this once how about you talk to me and tell me what you want me to do? I don't care what you say—'Nice haircut' or 'Nice shoes'—anything would make me feel better!"

Over time I slowly came to realize, through talking with other Christians, that for the most part God's communication to us is not verbal. God communicates uniquely to each individual in a variety of ways: sometimes through passions, ideas, or strong feelings; sometimes through Scripture; sometimes through the words of others. The bottom line, I learned, is to be open to God and prepared to answer the call. I was relieved to realize that God had indeed probably been speaking to me all along but I had put my own limitations on the methodology. I made a note to myself not to limit God through shortsighted assumptions in the future.

Then it happened. I was sitting in church one weekend, and the pastor issued an "altar call" following his sermon. It was an invitation to step forward as a physical demonstration of a deeper commitment to my faith. All of a sudden, I felt what seemed like tangible hands pressing my back and heard what seemed like the clear voice of God saying to me, "Go to the altar." Did I jump up and go? Unfortunately, no. Instead, I began to rationalize with God. "Go to the altar, in front of everyone? Why, that sermon didn't really even speak to me this morning. You must have the wrong guy."

A minute passed. The altar call was still in progress, providing an opportunity for me to make a visible statement of God's deepening claim on my life. I kept rationalizing. "God, you can't mean me. I don't need to put myself out there like that." So I sat in my seat until the worship service ended, shocked that God had spoken to and instructed me so audibly at last, yet I was hesitant to acknowledge the instructions and obey.

As I drove home that day, I sheepishly realized a second valuable insight. God can work only through those who, like Isaiah, are willing not only to hear but also to respond to divine communication, whether verbal or through some other means. God's most faithful servants have always been those who put aside their pride and step out to deliver God's message or do God's work, no matter how difficult or menial. Thanks, God, for helping me understand the whole purpose for "hearing" your voice. And yes, I know. I didn't do what you asked this time. Thanks for the forgiveness thing, too.

jeremiah

the weeping prophet

book 24

The book of Jeremiah is named after the prophet by that name. Jeremiah, the son of a priest named Hilkiah, grew up in a small town just north of Jerusalem. He began his call as a prophet as a young man and brought God's message to the Southern Kingdom during the reigns of the last five of Judah's kings before the fall of Jerusalem. Even after some of the Israelites were taken away into exile in Babylon, Jeremiah stayed behind with those who remained, and he prophesied periodically. Other biblical prophets who were active during the same time period include Habakkuk, Obadiah, and Ezekiel.

Jeremiah can be called the "weeping prophet" because he had the distressing responsibility of admonishing the kings and people of the approaching destruction resulting from their disobedience to God. His secretary and friend Baruch faithfully recorded his prophecies, which were given in a wide variety of forms.

We know more about the personal and spiritual life of Jeremiah than any other prophet because of Baruch's careful accounts in this book, revealing Jeremiah's prayer life and ongoing dialogue with God, his interactions with kings and government officials, his commitment to the Israelites, and his agony over the people's unfaithfulness.

Although Jeremiah enjoyed a good relationship with King Josiah (the last faithful king in the history of the Southern Kingdom), the following four sinful kings did not appreciate Jeremiah's gloomy announcements of God's impending judgment. Jeremiah was persecuted for bringing God's prophetic message and call to repentance. This persecution included rejection, false accusations, public ridicule, beatings, and imprisonments—not to mention his own loneliness and isolation. Jeremiah was carried off into Egypt shortly after the fall of Jerusalem.

The book of Jeremiah is not arranged in chronological order but does clearly paint the picture of Jeremiah's central prophetic messages:

- God's people of Israel had backslid into sin and unfaithfulness, and God wanted them to repent—or drastic punishment would result.
- Because of this continuing sinfulness, the Israelites would be scattered and taken into captivity by the Babylonians for seventy years.
- The Israelites would return to Jerusalem, and ultimately God would send a new "branch" who would provide a new covenant.
- God's great desire was (and is) for a personal, faithful relationship, rather than empty rituals.

May the words and message of Jeremiah lead you closer in a new covenant with our God, who longs to live together with you in an intimate, faithful relationship for all eternity.

145

JEREMIAH'S CALL

_____

_____

_____

_____

_____

_____

_____

_____

_____

_____

_____

_____

God called Jeremiah, a young man, to announce judgment concerning the Israelites' sinful behavior. Even though Jeremiah's role as prophet would be dangerous, God promised to provide the right message for Jeremiah and to offer divine protection.

JEREMIAH 1:1-19; 3:6-25

• An almond tree, a boiling pot, and an unfaithful wife were three metaphors God used to speak to Jeremiah. What did each one symbolize?

• What two excuses did Jeremiah attempt to use to avoid accepting God's call? What excuses have you used to avoid doing God's work?

PREDICTION OF CONSEQUENCES

_____

_____

_____

_____

_____

_____

_____

_____

_____

_____

_____

Jeremiah reminded the people of Israel that because they had ignored God and the messages brought by God's prophets, their lives would suffer horrible destruction as a result. Jeremiah's prophecies contained descriptions of the Israelites' sinfulness as well as graphic details of their upcoming devastation and ruin.

JEREMIAH 5:12-31; 6:16-30

• Jeremiah 6:16 indicates that we are to stand at the crossroads of our lives, looking for the "ancient paths" and the "good way." How would you describe this path/way God desires us to follow?

• Jeremiah 6:27 speaks of the "ore" of our lives and the testing of the strength of our spiritual "metal." Read also Paul's words in 1 Corinthians 3:10-15. How does your life "test" right now?

JEREMIAH'S GRIEF FOR HIS PEOPLE

Those who are truly called by God to serve are also given a "heart" for those who are completely lost and far away from a faithful relationship with God. Jeremiah's heart was breaking over the waywardness of the people of Israel, whose distance from God was shown in the dishonesty of their relationships with others.

JEREMIAH 8:18-22; 9:1-10, 23-24; 1 CORINTHIANS 1:26–2:5

• Gilead (Jeremiah 8:22) was located east of the Jordan River and was known for its medicinal herbs and spices. Why couldn't Gilead's balms heal the Israelites?

• Both Jeremiah 9:23-24 and the reading from 1 Corinthians describe the qualities God loves. What are practical ways you can demonstrate that you understand and know the one true God?

AN HONORABLE LIFE SET APART

God required the prophet Jeremiah to refrain from marrying and having children or attending funerals and weddings in order to illustrate that life as the Israelites knew it would soon come to an end. Jeremiah's work as God's faithful servant was lonely. Yet because of Jeremiah's diligence to do God's will no matter how difficult, God was able to use him to influence the course of human history.

JEREMIAH 16:1-18; 17:5-10; PSALM 15

• Compare Jeremiah 17:5-8 and Psalm 15. What characterizes those who are unfaithful to God? What characterizes those who are faithful?

• God will "test the mind and search the heart" (Jeremiah 17:10). What needs to happen so that your heart, mind, and conduct align with God's desires for you?

THE POTTER'S HOUSE

_____

_____

_____

_____

_____

_____

_____

_____

_____

_____

_____

God showed Jeremiah the metaphor of a potter and clay as an example of God's control over the future of God's people. If the clay pot was flawed or imperfect, the potter formed it into another shape. In the same way, God's plans were to allow wayward people to be exiled and then eventually to restore them to their home in Jerusalem and to their relationship with God. Jeremiah faithfully shared this metaphor with the people.

JEREMIAH 18:1-10; 19:1–20:2

• How did Pashhur, chief religious officer in God's Temple, react to Jeremiah's symbol of the potter?

• God's desire is to shape us into effective "tools" for kingdom work. Think of yourself as the clay and God as the potter. How is God shaping you?

BUYING A FIELD

_____

_____

_____

_____

_____

_____

_____

_____

_____

_____

While Jeremiah was imprisoned as the Babylonians attacked Jerusalem, God instructed him to make a strange purchase. Jeremiah bought his cousin's field in Judah and had the deed sealed away for safekeeping. Since the fall of Jerusalem was near and God's people would be taken to Babylon, the purchase of property in Judah seemed useless. But God had a message to communicate through Jeremiah's purchase.

JEREMIAH 32:1–33:9

• What was God's intent in directing Jeremiah to buy land in Judah as God's people were being deported into Babylon?

• Jeremiah reassured the people that God would miraculously restore them. Have you ever experienced God's restoration after destruction? What restoration are you praying for right now?

Jeremiah's helper, Baruch (a scribe by profession), wrote down all of the prophecies about God's judgment and the impending exile to Babylon. He then read these scrolls to the people and to the king's leaders. The king treated these scrolls with disdain and destroyed them, but God demonstrated sovereign power by ordering Jeremiah and Baruch to write the scrolls again.

JEREMIAH 36

• The people of Judah fasted to prepare for the reading of God's word. The king had a different response. What was it?

• What central truth about God and God's desire for our lives have you learned this week from Jeremiah?

MORE SCRIPTURE

Jeremiah 46–51—Jeremiah's prophecies to various nations

Jeremiah 52—A summary of the fall of Jerusalem, as Jeremiah had warned

BURNING OF THE SCROLL

_____
_____
_____
_____
_____
_____
_____
_____
_____
_____

notes
AND PRAYER NEEDS

_____
_____
_____
_____
_____
_____
_____
_____
_____
_____

transformations

If Jeremiah Had a Cell Phone

God said to Jeremiah: no family, no funerals, and no weddings. I imagine his phone conversations went something like this:

11 a.m.   Jeremiah's friend Barak calls.

"So listen, Jer, last night I met this girl who is totally in love with you. Trust me, I about fell off my barstool when she told me. But she's serious, she wants to marry you, dude!

Jeremiah rubs the sleep out of his eyes and says, "Sorry Barak, not interested."

"Jer, did you hear me? She's a special woman—with all the great qualities you would want in a wife. Now, put on some clothes and get over here. We're meeting her for lunch."

"I'm sorry, Barak. She's gonna get stabbed and starve to death. And then birds are going to eat her. I really can't let her be a part of that."

2:35 p.m.   Jeremiah's Uncle Boris calls.

"Jeremiah, hey, it's your Uncle Boris."

"Hey, Uncle."

"Jeremiah, I have horrible news. My wife died last night."

"I'm so sorry, Uncle. She was a great woman."

"Yes. Yes she was. Anyway, I was hoping you could say a few words at her funeral. You were her favorite nephew, you know."

"Sorry, Uncle. I'm busy that day."

"I haven't said the day yet, Jeremiah."

"I have stuff."

"Jeremiah, have you lost your mind? My wife—your aunt—has died and the funeral is in two days. Now I expect you there!"

"No can do, Uncle. God said he's done mourning for us and told me that I am, too. So I won't be able to speak at Aunty's funeral. I understand that means I probably won't be invited to the Family Fish Fry next year."

9:46 p.m.   Jeremiah's neighbor Shleb calls.

"What do you need, Shleb? I'm in the middle of something."

"I'm getting married, Jeremiah! The arrangements were made today. Can you believe it?"

"No."

"So listen, I want you to be my best man. You've been a great neighbor—a quiet neighbor—but really great. I'd be honored if you said yes."

"No."

"Ha. You and your jokes, Jeremiah. Come on over for a little bit and we'll celebrate."

"Sorry, Shleb. The Lord is going to end all this joy and gladness you're currently experiencing, and I really can't be a part of that."

I can't imagine what it must've been like for Jeremiah. His obedience to God caused him a life of isolation and rejection by God's people. I'm thankful in obeying God that I have the benefit of relationships. Jeremiah shows me how blessed I am to experience the "joy and gladness" of God's presence, as well as my family and community every day.

lamentations

songs of mourning

book 25

Pain and suffering are often pathways that lead to transformation and development of godly character. Hebrews 12:7-12 reminds us that a sign of God's love is God allowing struggle and discipline as tools for our healing and growth. Although some forms of suffering should not be considered redemptive or intended by God, Scripture assures us of God's willingness to work in any situation to bring healing and restoration (Romans 8:28).

God allowed tragedy and destruction to overwhelm God's people in Judah as a horrifying result of their sinful behavior. Yet God's hand of judgment also brought with it a promise of hope for restoration. But first, the people who had refused the care of their loving God had to learn deep lessons revealed only through sorrow.

The book of Lamentations is an expression of that deep sorrow. It's a set of dark, emotional funeral songs for the city of Jerusalem. The author, sometimes assumed to be the prophet Jeremiah, was an eyewitness in 586 BC to the fall of the once proud city of God. Lamentations expresses grief over the fall of Jerusalem, reminding Judah that great penalty and pain come as a result of sin and that out of the most significant seasons of brokenness can come powerful restoration of relationship with God.

Lamentations was carefully crafted with three of its five chapters arranged in an acrostic format containing twenty-two verses, the first word of each verse corresponding to the twenty-two letters of the Hebrew alphabet. One chapter has sixty-six verses, with each third similarly laid out. (Scholars speculate that this format was useful in assisting memorization, or as part of public liturgy.) The final chapter of Lamentations also has twenty-two verses but is in the simpler form of a prayer.

Each section expresses a different aspect of the grieving process.

Section 1: Tears over the fallen city of Jerusalem

Section 2: God's anger at God's people, with grave consequences

Section 3: A cry of despair and a prayer for mercy

Section 4: Vivid accounts of the final siege on Jerusalem by the Babylon-ians

Section 5: A description of the need for restoration and a request to God for that restoration

As you'll understand through your readings this week, Lamentations is a universal expression of pain and suffering to which all of us can relate. Like the people of Judah did so long ago, embrace and respect sorrow as a path, however undesirable, to the spiritual healing and restoration that God intends.

sun.

PAINFUL JUDGMENT

_____

_____

_____

_____

_____

_____

_____

_____

_____

_____

Jeremiah expressed his grief over the fall of Jerusalem. Jeremiah used personification to depict Jerusalem as a grieving woman in pain and distress. As we grow in our relationship with God, we learn that our sins warrant consequences because our God is just. Paul teaches in Romans that though God's judgment is painful, we can be transformed in God's presence and trust in God's mercy.

LAMENTATIONS 1; ROMANS 8:18-28

• Why was Jeremiah grieving?

• How have you felt in times when you have let God down? What assurance does Paul give us in Romans 8:26-27?

mon.

A PARENT'S DISCIPLINE

_____

_____

_____

_____

_____

_____

_____

_____

_____

In Lamentations 2, we see the final, terrible consequence for God's people that came as a result of ignoring God's warnings for generations. Though God's discipline sometimes seems harsh, God has a reason for using discipline. Much like a parent disciplines a child to protect him or her from future mistakes, God teaches God's children to listen and honor God's ways.

LAMENTATIONS 2; HEBREWS 12:4-13

• What does Paul say about God's discipline in Hebrews 12:5-6? What does God's discipline produce?

• When have you ever knowingly ignored God's warnings or deliberately chosen a path of disobedience? What were the consequences?

For many years people have sung the wonderful hymn "Great Is Thy Faithfulness" (Lamentations 3:23) to affirm that God is never absent, even during times of struggle and difficult challenges. In today's reading, Jeremiah's words of sorrow shifted into a prayer of hope and redemption. When God's judgment is upon us, restoration is around the corner if we turn to God.

LAMENTATIONS 3

• What about the nature of God caused Jeremiah to have hope, according to Lamentations 3:21-26?

• How have you experienced God's great faithfulness? How have you responded?

GOD'S FAITHFULNESS

wed.

FALSE SECURITY

Israel's false sense of security had kept the people from responding to God's repeated warnings of judgment (Lamentations 4:12). Though they had turned away from God, they still expected God's protection and provision. God wants to protect us and to provide for us, but also wants us to protect ourselves by following God's commands.

LAMENTATIONS 4;
HEBREWS 10:26-39

• What serious message does Hebrews 10:26-31 teach us? What message does Hebrews 10:35-39 have for those who are faithful?

• How would you describe your attitude toward God's approval or disapproval of your life choices? What truths from today's readings speak most urgently to you?

thurs.

A NEED FOR RESTORATION

_____

_____

_____

_____

_____

_____

_____

_____

_____

_____

Throughout Lamentations, Jeremiah expressed grief over the devastating physical destruction of Jerusalem and also expressed a desire for its restoration. God's concern, however, was first and foremost for the spiritual restoration of people. Just as God wanted God's people to return to spiritual faithfulness rather than to selfishness and sin, so God also wants this for us.

LAMENTATIONS 5; ACTS 3:18-20

• What is the cry of Jeremiah's heart in Lamentations 5:21? According to Acts, what does God require for restoration?

• Put Lamentations 5:21 into your own words as you write a prayer to God asking for restoration.

fri.

PAST AND PROVISION

_____

_____

_____

_____

_____

_____

_____

_____

_____

_____

Jeremiah grieved in Lamentations that, before Jerusalem's fall, he had reminded God's people repeatedly of how God had allowed drastic consequences in the past when they had been unfaithful—but they didn't listen. In 1 Corinthians 10, Paul used this same approach and reminded one of the New Testament churches of some past history (found in Numbers 14) in order to teach them a lesson about staying faithful and resisting temptation.

NUMBERS 14:1-35; 1 CORINTHIANS 10:1-13

• In Numbers 14, what did God's people do that displeased God? What consequence did they receive?

• According to 1 Corinthians 10:13, what does God provide to help us stay faithful? In what current situation do you need this help?

SPIRIT OF HOPE

The book of Lamentations is a universal expression of pain and suffering to which we all can relate. A central message throughout all Scripture is that pain and suffering in our lives are often the pathways leading to true spiritual growth and transformation. In Romans, Paul wrote specifically about the godly character development that can happen in us when we persevere (hang tough) in suffering.

ROMANS 5:1-11

• According to Romans 5:3-5, what are the benefits of persevering in times of suffering?

• God does not ask that we be thankful for difficult times, but that we have a spirit of thankfulness for God's provision during those times. What has God provided to help sustain you during life's challenges?

notes

AND PRAYER NEEDS

transformations

The Faces of Loss

Loss comes with many faces. In the book of Lamentations, Jeremiah wept over the loss of relationship with God that the Israelites experienced as they rejected God. He grieved their corporate loss of God's presence and loving guidance. The ongoing sinfulness and selfishness of God's people broke God's heart and, Jeremiah, knowing the long-term consequences of the people's actions, wept the tears of God.

Loss also comes on a personal level, sometimes through no fault of our own. The reality of failed relationships. The frustration of blocked life dreams. The fear of overwhelming circumstances and loss of control. The pain of losing a job. The anguish over the loss of health. The actuality of death. Each life experience brings change, heartache, and hopefully the motivation to seek Jesus' presence and understanding.

Sometimes loss comes as a result of a positive personal choice to fully commit to the call of God. Loss gives us a chance to encounter and then choose how we react to change. When I struggle with difficulties of my own, I remember two friends who model God's directive to "give thanks in all situations"—when it's easy and when it's not. They inspire me to be positive and trust God even in the painful things of life. They are my heroes. Tom and Elaine Sampley heard the call of God and chose to leave a thriving business, beautifully appointed home, friends, and family to serve on the mission field in the Czech Republic. Elaine attests to how right this decision has been for them, regardless of the personal cost. Pressing on in the hard and often lonely work of presenting Christ to a former Communist and atheistic nation, they have gone through the loss of their oldest son in a car accident. The last two years have been filled with the recovery and residual physical effects of a disastrous, freak accident with their second son. They are the embodiment of Jeremiah's declaration, "Because of the LORD's great love we are not consumed, for his compassions never fail. They are new every morning; great is your faithfulness" (Lamentations 3:22-23).

Blessed are those who mourn loss. And blessed are those who choose to believe that in God loss always has the potential to create good. The authenticity and reality of our relationship with God is not in the ease of life but in how we live in obedience to God within life's challenges. Our spiritual connection with our Creator grows quickly in the crucible of crisis as we trust and, by faith, give God thanks and praise for God's involvement. I am grateful for people who graciously model commitment to faith in the pain and loss of real life. They encourage me and urge me onward to live as God planned.

ezekiel

God's visionary

book 26

The book of Ezekiel shares powerful insights about God. Ezekiel used passionate and bizarre methods to act out God's messages, and these methods became a hallmark of his prophetic career. Following God's instructions, he ate scrolls; shaved his head; and spent 430 days (the same number of years the Israelites were enslaved in Egypt) lying on his side, looking at a model of Jerusalem to describe the coming siege. Although people often misunderstood and resisted God's messages, Ezekiel did whatever was necessary to draw their attention to God.

The book of Ezekiel contains oracles, a particular type of speech based in either judgment or salvation. Israel had tempted fate for generations, ignoring God's messengers who warned of coming destruction if they refused to listen to God. God's judgment began with three deportations of Israelites from Jerusalem to Babylon. The second deportation in 597 BC sent many of Judah's spiritual and political leaders to live in exile, including Ezekiel and Judah's King Jehoiachin. A few years after his arrival as a refugee in Babylon, Ezekiel began his prophetic career. Despite Ezekiel's passionate warnings, the remaining Israelites could not comprehend that their beloved city and Temple would be destroyed. In 586 BC Babylon's King Nebuchadnezzar reduced Jerusalem and its Temple to rubble and sent the third group into exile.

Ezekiel contains strong warnings of judgment followed with prophecies of hope for those who repent. In the last eight chapters, God promised the exiles their return to the Promised Land and the reestablishment of Temple worship. Ezekiel's final prophecies promise a new heaven and earth. Ezekiel's pronouncements for Judah suggest some lessons for us:

- We must never underestimate the seriousness of disobedience against God or the depth of God's anger over sin. God will allow us to experience the consequences, calling us to repent.
- There is always hope. God, through Jesus, offers pardon and restoration no matter how far from our spiritual home we have wandered.
- God is not confined to one location but is Lord over all the earth. The Holy Spirit brings God's glory (presence) into the new temple that God is building, the hearts and lives of individuals submitted to God.

Ezekiel modeled the purpose to which all God-followers are called: "They will know that I am the Lord." We who know the Lord, like Ezekiel, are accountable to urgently call those around us to a relationship with God. Are you willing to purposefully risk and do whatever is necessary to make that happen?

sun.

CALLED TO BE A PROPHET

_____

_____

_____

_____

_____

_____

_____

_____

_____

A prophet of God was like the watchman for a city, positioned on the city wall and entrusted to cry out the news of enemy attack. Ezekiel's responsibility was to sound the alarm of God's coming judgment to the Israelites living in Babylon. Allowed to speak only when God spoke through him, Ezekiel was silent the rest of the time.

EZEKIEL 1:26–3:27

• Three times God told Ezekiel, "Do not be afraid." What in this account would have been intimidating or frightening for Ezekiel?

• What is your role in sharing the message of God with the people in your family, workplace, and community? What from this Scripture could help in overcoming any fear or intimidation for you as you share God's message?

mon.

OBJECT LESSONS

_____

_____

_____

_____

_____

_____

_____

_____

_____

Rather than just verbal messages, God had Ezekiel use symbolic actions (physical object lessons) to create an indelible visual image for the Israelites. Ezekiel acted out the siege of Jerusalem before it actually happened and described what would ultimately happen to God's people. His drama failed to convince his audience, but the message held true and has meaning for us today. We are not to underestimate our sin or God's demand for our obedience.

EZEKIEL 4–5

• What did God say would happen to Jerusalem (5:8-17)?

• Sometimes it takes radical methods to get our attention and alert us to the need to change. How do you sense God trying to get your attention in order to bring about transformation in you?

PROMISE TO THE EXILES

When King Solomon dedicated the Temple, the glory of the Lord (God's presence) filled the Temple. At that time God warned the people that their disobedience would cause Israel to be uprooted and the Temple to be rejected. Ezekiel 8–11 describes Ezekiel's vision of the corruption of the Temple and the resulting departure of God's presence. True to God's compassionate nature, God promised that not all would be destroyed. Those in captivity would be protected and would one day return to the Promised Land.

EZEKIEL 11

• What role did God play for those in exile (11:16)? What hope did God give the people in Babylon?

• Look again at 11:19-20. How do your heart and spirit compare to what God describes here?

PERSONAL RESPONSIBILITY

The Israelites had become fatalistic, believing that their situation was determined by the choices of their predecessors. Ezekiel held out the truth that God was at work in them, allowing them to change direction through confession and repentance. Circumstances of life influence us but do not necessarily determine our future. Each person is free to make responsible choices, and we are held accountable for those choices.

EZEKIEL 18

• What characterizes the unrighteous person? What characterizes the righteous?

• What choices have you made that mirror choices made by your parents? What choices have you made that are different? How have these choices made a difference for you?

thurs.

SHEPHERDS AND SHEEP

_____

_____

_____

_____

_____

_____

_____

_____

_____

_____

Thirteen years after the destruction of Jerusalem, during which Ezekiel spoke warnings to many nations, Ezekiel began a new ministry as a prophet of hope. His new message was about the restoration of God's people. God, through Ezekiel, condemned the leaders (shepherds) of Judah that mistreated and misguided the people (the sheep) and promised a new Shepherd who would care for the sheep eternally.

EZEKIEL 33:30–34:31; JOHN 10:7-15

• What happened to God's people because of poor leadership? What did God promise to do? How do these promises connect with the mission of Jesus?

• What types of leadership have you experienced in your family, school, work, or church? In what ways could you more closely reflect the approach of the Good Shepherd with those whose lives you influence?

fri.

DRY BONES

_____

_____

_____

_____

_____

_____

_____

_____

_____

_____

The dry bones are a metaphor through which Ezekiel brought God's word of hope to spiritually dead and dying people. Only God can breathe new life. Even at the point of absolute hopelessness, as demonstrated by these conquered and oppressed people, God supplies power to restore individuals and nations.

EZEKIEL 37

• The Northern Kingdom, Israel, and the Southern Kingdom, Judah, were divided following the reign of King Solomon. What was the point of the stick metaphor for these two nations? Who would be their king?

• In what dry area do you need God to breathe new life into you?

GOD'S GLORY RETURNS

The final eight chapters of Ezekiel contain apocalyptic visions concerning events that would happen in the future. Nineteen years had passed since Ezekiel saw the glory of God leave the Temple. Ezekiel's vision of the new Temple was the assurance that God's relationship with people would be restored and God would again live with them. In the New Testament we are assured of God's presence literally within us as we live in relationship with God through God's Son, Jesus.

EZEKIEL 43:1-12; REVELATION 21:1-7

• What was God's expectation of people in order for God to live among them?

• Describe a time when God felt distant to you as well as a time when you felt deep connection with God. What made the difference?

notes
AND PRAYER NEEDS

transformations

Poster Boards in the End Zone

If you have ever watched any sporting event, especially football, you have seen him. The guy who stands in the end zone, holding up the white poster board with the black block lettering: JOHN 3:16. Admit it: at least once you thought that guy looked a bit wacky.

Many centuries ago God's prophet Ezekiel did things that make our guy in the end zone look pretty tame. He ate scrolls; shaved his head; and spent days lying on his side, looking at a model of Jerusalem. I'm sure the ancient Israelites thought he looked a little wacky, too.

Now consider the people who saw the sign—someone cheering in the stands, another watching TV from home, or perhaps the woman sitting beside our end zone guy on the bus. Imagine that she returns home and digs out the Bible she got in third grade Sunday school. Since the binding has only been cracked open a couple of times, the book is stiff. "What is John 3:16?" she wonders. She has never really looked through the Bible, but she knows there should be a table of contents. Her finger follows down the line. She finally finds John and skips to chapter 3. What she finds next changes her life forever. "For God so loved the world…God did not send his Son into the world to condemn the world, but to save the world."

"Surely not me," thinks the reader. That nut job at the game couldn't be as bad as me. What has he done? Why did he have the guts to hold up a sign like that?

Grace is what brings us to God. Grace is what makes God go out of the way to be in relationship with people. Grace is what motivates people like Ezekiel and our end zone guy to stand out from the crowd and make a statement for God. They have experienced God themselves and yearn for others not to miss it. Consider what incredible things can happen through someone who takes a risk and does whatever it takes to draw attention to God.

Back to our reader. She begins to search for more understanding of this passage in John. In her quest, she learns that no matter how far she has disobediently wandered from God, if she is willing to connect with God, God will be there. Graciously, lovingly, joyfully.

Now imagine our reader with the courage to stand in the end zone of the next game with a sign of her own. And imagine that one more person reads it and wonders. How full of poster boards could our end zones become if we heard God's message of restoration, responded, and stepped out a little with it? How might the world change around us? Perhaps Ezekiel and that guy in the end zone are not so wacky after all. Perhaps they just understand grace and want the whole world to know about it.

daniel

courage and conviction

book 27

Daniel, the final book of the major prophets, provides a narrative history of the life of Daniel and his friends as well as Daniel's apocalyptic visions foreseeing the course of world history until the end of time.

Daniel was among the first group exiled to Babylon in 605 BC. King Nebuchadnezzar recognized the potential of this teenager, positioning him for leadership within the royal palace. Daniel was found to be trustworthy as a leader and government official. Although given the Babylonian name Belteshazzar, his birth name Daniel (meaning "God is my judge") became the measure for how he lived his life. Daniel's integrity, character, and single-minded commitment to please God were legendary even in his own day. The prophet Ezekiel pointed to Daniel as a role model for wisdom and determination to do what was right. Daniel's conviction and courage guided him through a career spanning the entire seventy years of Jewish captivity in Babylon.

The book of Daniel is easily divided into two parts. The first six chapters recount personal stories of Daniel while the last six contain apocalyptic visions describing events yet to come. Through the visions of Daniel and other prophets, God demonstrates control of historical events and provides hope for those who stay faithful in times of persecution. In the cosmic battle of good and evil, God wins! Like Daniel, we are called to be faithful and dependent on God for victory in the daily battle within our own lives.

Perhaps the greatest message from Daniel is the reminder that God's people are called to humbly follow God and demonstrate full obedience, even while living in a hostile world. Daniel was an excellent example of how to live and work with people who do not share or respect our beliefs. He offered an excellent, honorable sacrifice to God every day through his effective service, showing high regard and diligence even to kings who did not worship God. Since the days of Abraham, God had intended to use God's people to reach the world. Though he was taken far from his homeland, Daniel's actions in Babylon convinced others to honor God; in response to Daniel's respectful demonstrations of faith, the decrees issued by the Mesopotamian kings Nebuchadnezzar and Darius recognized the supremacy of God and influenced an entire empire.

Daniel was unwavering in his determination to obey God, and his resolve allowed him to impact significantly the godless rulers who surrounded him. We are reminded this week that when God calls us to a role within a power structure (family, business, or community), we too can be true to God and have influence in the course of history.

sun.

A YOUNG MAN'S CONVICTION

_____
_____
_____
_____
_____
_____
_____
_____
_____
_____

Daniel was taken from Judah to Babylon as a prisoner while he was still a young man. This Scripture reveals the strength of his character, identifying him at a young age as a man of principle. Determined to keep God's law, Daniel wisely showed sensitivity and a positive attitude while doing so.

DANIEL 1

• How was Daniel faithful to God in this passage? What was the outcome?

• In what situation do you feel the most pressure to fit in? What actions could you take in that situation to remain faithful?

mon.

INTERPRETING NEBUCHADNEZZAR'S DREAM

_____
_____
_____
_____
_____
_____
_____
_____
_____
_____

King Nebuchadnezzar asked the astrologers and wise men to do what was humanly impossible. Through his reliance on God, Daniel received an unexplainable outcome. Because of his deep connection with God, Daniel knew how to serve King Nebuchadnezzar, save the wise men of the kingdom (including himself) from a certain death sentence, and give God opportunity to be revealed to the world.

DANIEL 2

• Daniel was proactive in addressing the king's demand. What else did he do that affected the outcome of his dream interpretation (verses 17-23)?

• What are you facing that seems impossible? From this story of Daniel, what could you put into practice in order to move forward in God's power?

Just as they did in choosing to follow God's dietary laws, Shadrach, Meshach, and Abednego resolved ahead of time to worship the one true God and establish that daily practice in their lives. Settling in our minds that our relationship with God is ultimately more important than life itself and committing to a course of action that honors that truth prepares us to make the right decisions in times of crisis.

DANIEL 3

• In the three men's response to Nebuchadnezzar, of what were they unsure? Of what were they absolutely sure (3:16-18)?

• How prepared are you to take a stand for God in the midst of a crisis? What could you do to prepare yourself more fully?

Daniel had been in service as an advisor to the Babylonian kings for over sixty years. King Belshazzar discounted God by using items set apart exclusively for Temple worship as common dinner utensils. The king needed Daniel to unravel the prophetic significance of a mysterious message written on his dining room wall.

DANIEL 5

• In verses 18-24, in what ways was the king "weighed on the scales and found wanting"? What did Daniel say would happen as a result?

• If God weighed your life on the scales (took inventory of your life) right now, where would you be found wanting? What will you do to fill in this spiritual deficit?

DANIEL IN THE LION'S DEN

_____
_____
_____
_____
_____
_____
_____
_____
_____
_____

At the time of this incident, Daniel was over eighty years old and still one of the top administrators in the Persian government. He had faithfully and consistently modeled his devotion to God to the leaders of several empires, convincing them of the reality of God and God's power to save. Because of his character and integrity, the only place his enemies could attack him was his faith.

DANIEL 6

• Satraps were governors of areas within the Persian Empire and reported to the king's top administrators. What was the underlying motivation for their attack on Daniel? What was Daniel's response to the king's decree?

• Daniel's faith journey spanned decades. As you progress in your faith journey, what trials have increased your faith?

THE SON OF MAN

_____
_____
_____
_____
_____
_____
_____
_____
_____
_____

The last six chapters of Daniel contain visions about the heavenly council and the end of time. The title "Son of Man" was used ninety-three times in the book of Ezekiel to refer to someone who was merely human. In Daniel, this apocalyptic title referred to a specific ruler over the whole earth, whose kingdom would overshadow all earthly kingdoms and would never end. In the New Testament, Jesus applied this title to himself (Matthew 26:62-64).

DANIEL 7

• What will the kingdom ruled over by the Most High be like (verse 27)?

• Daniel's vision instills confidence in God's control and authority over all things. How do you need your confidence in God's control strengthened?

Daniel's final vision strained him physically, emotionally, and spiritually, and God sent a messenger to walk him through it. Daniel saw the battle between good and evil up close, and heard God's promise of hope for all true believers in the midst of trials and suffering.

DANIEL 10:1–11:1; 12:1-13

• In Daniel 12:1-4, what good news does God have for God-followers? What is the bad news for those who close their minds and hearts to God?

• We find wise counsel in Daniel 12:13. Rather than focusing on the end times, followers of Christ are to focus on developing our relationship with Jesus and serving him. What will you do to draw closer to Jesus?

MORE SCRIPTURE
Mark 13:26-37—Jesus' advice concerning the end times

notes

AND PRAYER NEEDS

transformations

The Boss of Me

One of my favorite characters in the history of *Saturday Night Live,* is Arianna, the ditzy cheerleader who together with her partner, Craig, managed to cheer their way through many a painful ordeal. When faced with a particularly critical (albeit imaginary) taunt from her friend Alexis, Arianna would pull up into her one-hundred-pound Spartan-clad frame, place her hands on her hips, and boldly state, "You're not the boss of me!" Call it great boundaries or a confident spirit; it never hurts to establish to whom in life we are truly responsible. Sooner or later we must all decide who exactly is the Boss of us.

Daniel of Babylon (formerly known as Daniel of the royal family of Jerusalem) could've been challenged to know whom his loyalty and responsibility should follow. Was it the government he'd grown up under back in Israel? Was it Nebuchadnezzar, king of Babylon? The circle of friends Daniel hung out with? How could this handsome, well-educated young man possibly sort his way through the maze of authority challenges presented through the unique transitions of Daniel's short life?

Daniel possessed an Arianna attitude. "You're not the boss of me," informed Daniel's steadfast response at every turn. Each time Daniel was told to do something that violated his internal spiritual and moral code, Daniel respectfully demonstrated this deep conviction. He knew in no uncertain terms who was the Boss of him.

"Daniel, it's time for dinner. The king's best food and wine are here, ready for you at the table." But Daniel resolved not to defile himself with the king's food and wine. *"I've committed to eating only healthy food, and…in all due respect, you're not the boss of me."*

"Daniel, you and your friends will either fall down to worship when the music plays, or you're going into that furnace set on 'extra crispy.' Now what's it going to be?" *"Oh King, the God we serve is able to rescue us, and we wouldn't worship your gods anyway. With all due respect, you're not the boss of us."*

"Daniel! If you can read the writing on the wall for me, you'll get the purple robe, the gold chain, and the royal treatment! Daniel of Babylon, come on down!" *"King Bel, I'll read the writing, but you can keep the clothing and the clout—I don't need them. My God is the revealer of all mysteries and, no offense intended, you're not the boss of me."*

"Daniel, you've really done it this time. We told you not to pray to your God, and what did you do? Now we have to throw you to the lions. We don't like this any better than you, but you leave us no choice!!"

And from the bottom of that den early in the morning, Daniel's voice rang out clear, *"Oh king, I've never been more alive, for I was found innocent in God's sight and God shut the mouths of the lions! This God—Provider, Protector, Wisdom, and Defender—has always been the Boss of me!"*

HOSEA: ISRAEL'S FINAL PROPHET

Hosea was a prophet of the northern kingdom of Israel who addressed his own people. Hosea was the final prophet that God sent to Israel to warn of impending doom if the people did not repent of their faithless ways and become obedient. Unfortunately, they did not listen. They were not only defeated by their enemies from Assyria but were also exiled throughout that brutal empire.

The theme of Hosea is God's grace-filled love and compassion. The prophet Hosea is best remembered for the unusual instructions that God gave him to symbolize God's own experience with the wayward people of Israel. God directed Hosea to marry a wife who would be unfaithful, leave him for others, and prostitute herself to ungodly partners. Then God instructed Hosea to take her back, restore his relationship with her, and provide her with all possible blessings. This was to symbolize God's distress when the people of Israel turned their backs to the one true God and worshiped false idols. Just as Hosea took back his unfaithful wife, so God longed to take back God's people, forgive them, and restore a blessing-filled relationship with them.

JOEL: THE LORD IS GOD

The name of this prophet means, "The Lord is God" (literally, Yahweh is God). We know nothing about Joel except what is written in this short book. The date of his ministry is uncertain. Most believe Joel was a resident of Jerusalem. His words of prophecy and warning are directed to the southern kingdom of Judah.

The theme of Joel's message is "the day of the Lord," defined as a time of punishment for God's faithless people, followed by a restoration of relationship with God. Joel described an impending plague of locusts and a drought, horrifying efforts to call the people back into obedience to God. Joel saw the waves of locusts as a representation of the thoroughness of God's judgment on the people but also urged his listeners to remember that God would withhold this judgment if they repented and returned to God.

Joel announced an ultimate "day of the Lord," when an outpouring of God's Spirit would come upon God's people, miracles would take place, and a final cosmic day of reckoning before God would occur. In the book of Acts, Peter referred to the words of the prophet Joel when the Holy Spirit fell upon the people on the day of Pentecost. Similar descriptions of the final or "end times" are also found in the book of Revelation.

sun.

HOSEA'S REAL LIFE ILLUSTRATION

_____

_____

_____

_____

_____

_____

_____

_____

_____

God called Hosea to demonstrate literally the dynamic between God and God's unfaithful people Israel by marrying Gomer, an unfaithful wife. God even instructed Hosea to name his children according to the dark, prophetic warnings that God sent in an effort to call the people back into obedience. As a symbolic of God's willingness to restore relationship with the Israelites, God directed Hosea to take back Gomer and restore his marriage with her.

HOSEA 1–3

• What loving and forgiving characteristics of God do you see in this reading?

• Hosea demonstrated complete obedience to God, no matter how difficult or challenging God's requests. What is the most challenging request that God is now making of you? How are you doing?

mon.

GOD'S DISFAVOR

_____

_____

_____

_____

_____

_____

_____

_____

_____

The people of Israel assumed that God's anger would last only a short time and that God's loving care would quickly resume. But God's response through Hosea let them know God's true desire was for their acknowledgement of faithfulness at the heart level, not only through religious sacrifice.

HOSEA 6:1-7; LEVITICUS 26:3-17

• According to Hosea, what did God request of the people in order for them to receive God's blessings? What blessings of God are named in Leviticus?

• What is God trying to teach you right now through the consequences of your actions—or what have you learned in the past?

SOWING AND REAPING

Hosea reminded his people of the importance of preparing the ground and sowing the right "seeds"—those of righteousness—in order to reap the harvest of God's love and care. Hosea also used the image of the love of a father for his son to describe God's commitment to the Israelite people.

HOSEA 10:12–11:11

• What was the spiritual meaning when Hosea urged the people to "break up" their "unplowed ground" (10:12)?

• As you look over the whole of your life (relationships, character, spiritual integrity, handling of your possessions), is there any "unplowed ground" you need to break up in order to plant seeds of godly obedience? In which of these areas? Name your next step to get started.

GOD'S FRUITFULNESS

Hosea's urging to the Israelites included strong advice about denouncing the human strength of their eventual conqueror, the neighboring country of Assyria, and acknowledging God as the only source of provision. In the final chapter of this book, Hosea likened God to a tree providing people with fruitfulness.

HOSEA 14

• Reread verse 9. Why do some walk easily and others stumble on God's "way," or path?

• According to Hosea, living in obedience to God brings fruitfulness. In what ways have you "blossomed" (been transformed) since you committed yourself to following Jesus?

thurs.

THE DAY OF THE LORD

_____

_____

_____

_____

_____

_____

_____

_____

_____

The short book of Joel opens with a trumpeting, authoritative call to all people of all times to take note: God was (and is) preparing for dramatic action. "The Day of the Lord" not only referred to the approaching judgment of God's people for their sinfulness but also to the final, ultimate day of judgment for all humankind.

JOEL 1:1-12; 2:1-11

• The swarm or "nation" of locusts Joel described was to bring judgment to all parts of the lives of God's sinful people. What did Joel prophesy would be the results of the locusts?

• Have you ever had a wake up call like the locusts, a time in which a major event made you immediately realize you needed to get your relationship with God in order? What happened?

fri.

GOD'S LOVE AND CARE

_____

_____

_____

_____

_____

_____

_____

_____

_____

Joel brought a powerful message of restoration for those who asked God for forgiveness and returned to a life of faithfulness. According to Joel's prophecy, God longs to lavish blessings upon obedient people.

JOEL 2:12-32; PSALM 103

• What similar descriptions of God are found in the readings from Joel and Psalm 103? Which do you find the most powerful, and why?

• What might it mean that God longs to restore our "years the locusts have eaten" (Joel 2:25-26)? Has God ever restored blessings from years when you were lost from God?

MORE SCRIPTURE

Acts 2:14-21—Peter quoting Joel on the day of Pentecost

VALLEY OF DECISION

Joel described a "valley of decision." The Hebrew word for "decision" in this passage means a strict, biting judgment—in this case, with God as the ultimate judge. Joel brought a picture of divine judgment, then eventual restoration between God and God's people. The city of Jerusalem, sometimes called Zion, was named as the location where God and God's people would be fully reunited.

JOEL 3:14-21; PSALM 24

• God's "holy hill" is a metaphor for the Temple in Jerusalem. What requirements were named as necessary in order to ascend the holy hill and meet God?

• We make most important decisions of spiritual obedience in the valleys (low times) of our lives. What has been your most recent "valley of decision"? What has been the result?

notes

AND PRAYER NEEDS

Turn the page for this week's Transformations Reflection.

transformations

Our Heart's Devotion

Does grace mean that I can do whatever I want and God will forgive me in the morning?

Our local newspaper recently ran a letter from a man who is pleading for forgiveness from his wife of twenty years and bemoaning the fact that she refuses to forgive him. It seems he had an affair fifteen years ago that almost ended their marriage. She forgave him back then, and all has been well since. However, the old flame got in touch recently via e-mail, and he innocently responded. What followed was a six-week correspondence back and forth, "just catching up." Oh, and some cell phone calls, which "meant nothing." When his wife received an anonymous letter revealing this recent friendship renewal, she came undone and demanded a divorce. The man said that even his teenage daughters are upset with him, and he questioned how in the world everyone, especially his wife, could be so lacking in understanding and forgiveness. The following week, a full page of opinion letters from local newspaper readers was published.

This story is what I think of now as I ponder God's grace. The book of Hosea records a similar dilemma concerning an unfaithful partner and a longsuffering spouse. The story in Hosea is a metaphor for God's relationship with God's wandering people, and it makes a strong statement for the love, acceptance, and grace God offers those who choose to return to God. We can ask the same questions of both situations: Should the unfaithful spouse (God's people) expect forgiveness? Why did the unfaithful spouse cheat again? Does the unfaithful partner truly love the spouse? Does the faithful partner (God) have reason to question the partner's love and commitment? Is this marriage one of the heart, or simply a paper registered at the courthouse?

Here's the deal as I see it. We serve a God who has all these answers. God doesn't need to guess with us. God knows exactly when we love God and when it is a sham. God knows when we made a mistake and when we have a plan to use God while trying to cover up sin in our lives. What we expect has little to do with what we are going to get from God. God does not argue with us, or read all the opinions we may have on this subject. God desires our heart's devotion and our seeking God's love in our lives. God desires that we grow in our relationship with God, not attempt to find loopholes in it. God does not divorce us, but we are playing a pointless game with ourselves if we have simply filed a paper at church instead of developing a relationship.

AMOS: LOSING FOCUS

Amos announced God's message using metaphors from his life experience as a shepherd in Judah. Amos' ministry took place around 760 to 750 BC, a time when the northern kingdom of Israel had become prosperous. As the people adjusted to this prosperity, they became materialistic and self-centered, denying their relationship with God.

The book of Amos can be divided into three sections. The first section (Amos 1:1–2:16) announced God's judgment on Israel and its neighbors. Amos warned of God's impending judgment and the resulting consequences if the people did not return to God. Amos used repetitive language to call each nation into account, addressing their sins and justifying God's judgment. The second section (Amos 3:1–6:14) defined why God was judging the Israelites. Instead of traveling to Jerusalem to worship, they began to worship in Bethel, Gilgal, and Beersheba, sites that ultimately proved to be a distraction from what God had commanded. God's people even constructed their own idols, representing the sinful lifestyles they had chosen. The third section (Amos 7:1–9:15) recorded Amos' visions of God's future judgment of Israel, and the personal rejection Amos received as a result of his messages. With one brief exception (5:14-15), Amos offered no hope for the future of the northern kingdom of Israel, which indeed ended in exile, never to return.

OBADIAH: WORSHIPER OF THE LORD

The book of Obadiah is the shortest book in the Old Testament. Little is known about Obadiah, but his name means "worshiper of the Lord." It is believed that Obadiah's ministry took place after the Babylonians invaded Jerusalem in 587 BC. Unlike several other prophetic books that spoke to many nations, Obadiah proclaimed God's judgment on the nation of Edom, a people who harassed the Israelites and took pleasure in Israel's misfortune. Obadiah's message to Edom was that "the day of the Lord is near for all nations. As you have done, it will be done to you; your deeds will return upon your own head" (1:15). He announced God's coming judgment and the restoration of Israel and its rule over Edom.

Believing in God is not enough. Amos and Obadiah remind all God's followers that we cannot ignore injustice. Israel was guilty of ignoring and abusing the poor. We, too, are accountable to worship God through our treatment of others. God wants us to identify our complacency, repent, and return to God. God will bless our lives as we seek to bless others.

GOD KNOWS

_____
_____
_____
_____
_____
_____
_____
_____
_____

God chose Amos, a farmer and shepherd, to address the sins of many nations. "For three sins...even for four" was an expression that meant "many," as Amos described the specific sins of each nation. Regardless of the extent to which we try to ignore our sinfulness, God knows and will bring us all into account.

AMOS 1–2

• Whom was God judging? According to Amos 2:4-16, what were the sins of Judah and Israel, and what led them astray?

• What false gods do you struggle with? What can you do to prevent them from distracting you from God?

CAUSE AND EFFECT

_____
_____
_____
_____
_____
_____
_____
_____
_____
_____

Amos asked rhetorical questions to expose God's impending judgment of the sins of the people of Israel. God's judgment is not arbitrary. God uses judgment to transform people from their sinful state into a holy spiritual relationship with God.

AMOS 3

• According to 3:7-11, how did God use Amos? What message did God send to the rich in verse 15?

• Even as followers of Jesus, our consciences can become desensitized—and the difference between right and wrong can become blurred. When has God jolted you back to reality?

MORE SCRIPTURE
Romans 3:21-31—Righteousness through faith

MISPLACED FOCUS

Despite God's command to worship only in Jerusalem, in the Southern Kingdom, the Israelites in the Northern Kingdom worshiped at Bethel, Gilgal, and Beersheba. These locations were more convenient for them, but these places were also sites for worship of Baal. God does not want us worshiping at our convenience. God desires our true, heartfelt worship.

AMOS 4–5

• What message of hope did God give in Amos 5:14-15?

• What distractions have taken you away from true worship? List ways that you can maintain your God-focus.

MORE SCRIPTURE

Philippians 4:4-9—Rejoice in everything

POISONOUS PRIDE

According to Amos, the prosperity of Israel had led the wealthy to prideful living. Their comforts led them to a focus on self and a mistreatment of the poor. God had stern judgment for this behavior. For followers of Jesus today, the book of Romans provides a specific picture of the attitudes God desires from us. When we rely on our own abilities and receive success as our own, we are living in a dangerous place.

AMOS 6; ROMANS 9:9-21

• According to Amos 6:7-10, what consequences from God did Israel's pride bring?

• What prideful thoughts or attitudes do you battle? How can you ensure that God receives the credit for your successes?

STANDING FIRM

_____
_____
_____
_____
_____
_____
_____
_____
_____
_____

Amos' prophecy against the Northern Kingdom was not well received by the religious leaders of his day. Amaziah, the priest of Bethel (one of the sites used for worship of Baal), appealed to King Jeroboam to deport Amos back to Judah. Like Amos, sometimes God calls us to take a stand—even when it won't be popular.

AMOS 7; 1 CORINTHIANS 10:1-13

• Why did Amos resist leaving the Northern Kingdom? What was God's response to Amaziah through Amos?

• At different times, all of us are called to take a stand for God. How can you make certain you're prepared, even for unexpected opportunities?

FROM DESTRUCTION TO RESTORATION

_____
_____
_____
_____
_____
_____
_____
_____
_____
_____

Amos described God's relentless pursuit of God's people in order to bring judgment upon them and then, for the southern kingdom of Judah, to bring restoration. The psalmist provides reassurance that God lovingly pursues us just as relentlessly today. No place is too obscure to be out of reach of God's love.

AMOS 9; PSALM 139

• According to Amos 9:11-15, what were the actions God would take to restore God's people?

• Just as Amos indicated no one could escape God's judgment, Psalm 139 says no one is exempt from the pursuit of God's love. To which message do you most relate, and why?

Although Esau forgave his brother Jacob for stealing his birthright (Genesis 27–28 and 32–33), Esau's descendants, the Edomites, feuded against Jacob's descendants, the Israelites. The Edomites were bigger, stronger, and lived in fortified cities in the mountains above Jerusalem. God sent Obadiah to warn them of the consequences for their mistreatment of the Israelites.

OBADIAH 1-21

• According to verses 3-4, what was the attitude of the Edomites? For what did God judge the Edomites in verses 10-15?

• When have you ever been like the Edomites, either standing aloof or actively undermining those who need your help? What change of behavior does God expect of you?

transformations

On Target

When I was in the Navy, I had the opportunity to qualify for dive school. I was serving on a submarine that was required to have qualified divers for special operations. In order to qualify for dive school, each applicant had to pass several physical tests designed to weed out those who wanted to go but did not have the drive to make it. The tests challenged our physical strength as well as our ability to remain calm while accomplishing a task under water.

Each test was performed under the supervision of full time Navy divers. These guys are a special breed. They are paid to work out, swim, and operate in some dangerous situations. One job requirement is to be a bit of an adrenaline-junkie. Dive instructors are the watchdogs of their community, a brotherhood of hard-core individuals who are anything but faint of heart. They take seriously the requirements that protect the integrity and image of those who will someday be called divers.

One of the tests was to swim 500 meters in under 12 minutes and 30 seconds. This would be a reasonable time requirement for the test if it weren't for a little twist. You could only use the sidestroke or breaststroke, and you could not allow your head to go under water. This style of swimming is good for a leisurely Sunday afternoon swim. It's not good for a speed test. Even veteran swimmers had a hard time adjusting to the head-above-water stroke. On the surface (pardon the pun), it might seem like a vindictive ploy of the hard-core dive instructors to make their selection process that much harder. But after a little digging, I realized there is more thought behind this particular stroke.

When swimming at sea, especially in rescue diving, it is important to keep your eye on the target. Rolling seas, crashing waves, and powerful currents can wreak havoc on your sense of direction. Without a fixed target, a diver can waste valuable energy swimming in the wrong direction. The dive instructors know that it's not important just to complete the task with the easiest stroke. And they know better than anyone that the hard way is sometimes the best way.

As with the requirements for dive school, God's requirements aren't easy. But many times we want to take the easy road. It is faster, less demanding, and seems to take us to the right place. It is only after we have invested way too much energy that we realize we have gone in the wrong direction. I guess that is why God sent Amos and Obadiah as divine "dive instructors" to remind the people of the right way and to turn their focus on God. Though we may not fully understand why God requires us to live a certain way, it is only when we are focused on God, and not trying it our way, that we can truly stay on target.

JONAH: THE RELUCTANT PROPHET

Jonah was known as the reluctant prophet because of his rebellious attitude and disobedience to God's call. Jonah lived during the reign of Jeroboam II (2 Kings 14:23-29) and prophesied during the same time period as Amos and Hosea. Jonah prophesied to Nineveh, the capital city of Assyria, as well as to the people of the northern kingdom of Israel.

Through Jonah's story we grasp the depth of God's grace:

- Like Jonah, we cannot hide from God. God judges disobedience but always offers a second chance through forgiveness and restoration.
- God's grace extends beyond Israel to all people. Even the Assyrians (Israel's sworn enemies) were equally worthy of love in God's eyes. God shook Jonah's paradigm and continues to shake ours today by sending the gospel of grace to unlikely places and people.
- God cares more about our values and inner character than rote obedience. Jonah took hold of his second chance to obey God but was not fully aligned with God's purpose. God's progressive work within us will transform our heart attitude to reflect God's grace to others.

MICAH: SECOND CHANCES

Micah, who served as prophet at some point during 750-686 BC, was concerned with the growing evil in the Southern Kingdom. As a result of Micah's prophecies, King Hezekiah put in place reforms that reestablished an official faith through the observances of God's law. But idol worship was still widespread, and the poor were being cheated and robbed.

In Micah, we read the following:

- Micah warned of judgment for sin yet promised hope for the future when God's people turn to God.
- Judah was proud to believe "right" and observe "right" practices, but God is interested in those who choose to be right with God and reflect God's love, justice, and compassion.
- God will not tolerate unrepentant sin forever and will act with swift judgment, yet God's forgiveness is total and complete for those who confess and turn to God. God balances justice with mercy.
- Micah declared God's peace and justice for all people and forecast their establishment through the coming earthly reign of the Messiah. What Micah envisioned is possible today because of Jesus' presence through the Holy Spirit and the empowerment of Jesus' followers to be instruments of peace and justice in the world.

This week, may Jonah and Micah help you grasp the importance of a heart right with God—and the power of demonstrating God's love, justice, and mercy to the unlikely people in unlikely places within your circle of influence.

RUNNING FROM GOD

_____
_____
_____
_____
_____
_____
_____
_____
_____
_____

Jonah was called to head east to the Assyrian capital of Nineveh to do a specific job for God, and he promptly booked passage on a ship heading west. A variety of reasons could explain Jonah's resistance to God's call: fear of facing Israel's cruel Assyrian enemies, nationalistic prejudice against the Assyrians, or anger over God's offer of mercy to Israel's enemies. God showed Jonah that disobedience is never justified, regardless of our feelings or attempts to rationalize our actions.

JONAH 1; LUKE 8:22-25

• What effect did the storm have on Jonah? On the sailors? On Jesus' disciples when they encountered a storm in Luke 8?

• What is most likely to cause you to run and resist God?

JONAH'S PRAYER

_____
_____
_____
_____
_____
_____
_____
_____
_____
_____

During this time of Israel's history, it was commonly believed that God was found only in the Temple in Jerusalem. Jonah, far from Jerusalem, experienced God in the belly of a great fish—and his view of God expanded. God is available to us, like Jonah, anywhere and at any time, no matter how far we may have run. Through God's grace and forgiveness, God hears and responds to the prayers of all who seek God.

JONAH 2; PSALM 118:1-18

• Circumstances were obviously out of Jonah's control. In the midst of his situation, how did Jonah respond to God?

• Write a prayer to God concerning a situation in your life in which you feel out of control. Where in this situation can you, like Jonah, express gratitude and hope?

The central message of the book of Jonah is that God is the God of all people and all places. Our connection with God comes through God's grace and forgiveness, not our association with a certain people group or belief system. Jonah was thankful for God's grace and mercy for himself and his nation but did not have the mind of God concerning others, a sin Jesus described in Matthew 16. God will not tolerate a self-centered attitude.

JONAH 3–4; MATTHEW 16:21-26

• Mercy is forgiving and serving others, even when they don't deserve it. Where in these verses from Jonah can you identify God's mercy?

• From whom are you most tempted to withhold mercy? What could you do to show them the mercy of God this week?

The people of Israel often worshiped false gods. Micah described this false worship as an ever-expanding, incurable infection that spread from Israel's capital of Samaria to Judah's capital of Jerusalem, infecting all surrounding cities. According to Micah, God's only recourse was judgment, resulting in the deportation of the people of both Israel and Judah away from their homelands.

MICAH 1:1–2:5

• In 1:3-7, Micah described Israel's spiritual disease. How does the prognosis for Israel impact Micah personally (1:8)?

• When correcting someone we love, we often experience pain. With whom and in what circumstance is this most often true for you?

thurs.

JUDGMENT AGAINST OPPRESSIVE LEADERS

_____

_____

_____

_____

_____

_____

_____

_____

_____

In Micah's day, the people of Judah were prosperous and materialistic. Although they observed the outward practices of religion through offering sacrifices, true devotion to God was lacking. False prophets spoke what the people wanted to hear, the people practiced idolatry along with the worship of God, government officials were corrupt, and the poor were oppressed. Micah spoke out against these evils.

MICAH 2:6–3:12

• Micah addressed at least three groups of leaders. Who were they? Why was he especially hard on them?

• How can you follow God more closely in order to positively influence those around you?

fri.

GOD'S PLAN OF RESTORATION

_____

_____

_____

_____

_____

_____

_____

_____

_____

_____

The people of Judah would suffer the consequences of their sin through exile in Babylon. Micah announced the safe return of God's people to Jerusalem after the exile. He anticipated a ruler who would be born in Bethlehem, free his people, and lead them in a time of peace. Today we know that promised ruler as Jesus.

MICAH 4:1–5:4

• In 4:6-8, what does God promise those who have suffered and been treated unjustly?

• According to Micah, the Messiah would be the source of peace—an inner peace for individuals and a lack of conflict among nations. Where are you experiencing the peace of Christ now? Where do you need more of his peace?

MORE SCRIPTURE
Matthew 2:1-12—Compare Micah 5:2, which foretold a ruler who would be born in Bethlehem.

GOD'S REQUIREMENTS

In the midst of Micah's writing is the clear statement of what God wants people to do: act justly, love mercy, and walk humbly with God. Micah saw God demonstrating those very things: a willingness to act justly and show mercy to those who repent of their disobedience, and to walk long-term with those who are faithful.

MICAH 6:6–7:20

• Throughout his book Micah contrasts justice with compassion, judgment with mercy. In what ways do you see those contrasts within the nature of God as described in 7:14-20?

• Assess the development of the qualities God wants to see in your life. Are you just and fair in your dealings with other people? Do you show mercy to those who sin against you? How is God teaching you humility?

AND PRAYER NEEDS

transformations

$4 Coffee

Cameron needs coffee. He's falling asleep to the harmonizing hum of florescent lights and computer screens. It's 3:30 p.m. There's coffee downstairs. It's free. It's convenient. It's not what Cameron wants. He wants a four-dollar coffee from Starbucks. He wants an afternoon break even though his lunch lasted a little longer than it "technically" should have and every ten minutes he stops for a quick game of online poker. One could argue that Cameron's entire day is a break. He would disagree, of course. He'd tell you he's a hard worker who gets his job done on time. He may pause from time to time to rejuvenate himself but that's just part of his process, he'd say. Healthy break-taking is a crucial component of the office DNA.

At 3:32 p.m. Cameron grabs his keys. He pops his head into his manager's office and tells him he's running to the post office. "You need anything while I'm out?" Cameron asks. His manager replies, "Actually, Cameron, before you leave I want to talk to you for a few minutes."

As Cameron sits, his manager shuts the door behind him. They talk of office-wide changes. Productivity is down. Corporate is unhappy. Cameron suddenly feels like a shoehorn has been stabbed into his stomach. He's getting fired. He should've seen this coming. He needs this job. What will he do without this job? How will he buy food? Underwear? Starbucks lattes?

"Corporate has given me two weeks to trim the fat, Cameron. I need you to be my eyes and ears out there. Help me decide who stays and who goes." Cameron can't believe it. He wants to tackle his manager he's so excited. He mumbles out repeated thank-you's and skips downstairs for a free coffee.

For two weeks Cameron is corporate's watchdog. Via e-mail and the occasional, condescending personal interaction, Cameron informs his coworkers of the fat-trimming. He makes notes of his office mates abusing everything from personal calls to lunch breaks. Cameron has a list. He shows his list to everyone.

Finally, Cameron presents the list to his manager with zest and attention to detail. His manager decides to give everyone a second chance. "Look what happened to you after you got one," his manager chuckles. Cameron is furious. He told people they were getting fired, and now he'll look like a fool. Cameron pleads for his manager to reconsider. "Fire them, they deserve it," he practically yells. His manager is surprised. "Cameron, I'm not sure it's right for you to be angry here."

Cameron was a fool. And his foolish soul mate was Jonah. Both of them were given a second chance even though they didn't deserve one. Jonah was saved by a giant fish. To me, that seems like reason enough to be saturated with grace. He should've been oozing grace all over everybody. Same with Cameron. In a better world with happier endings, neither Jonah nor Cameron would have turned self-righteous and judgmental. Cameron, for example, would go to Starbucks and buy every person who didn't get "fired" a four-dollar coffee.

NAHUM: PROPHET OF THE IMPOSSIBLE

It is believed that Nahum was a citizen of the southern kingdom of Judah whose ministry took place during the same time frame as that of Zephaniah, Jeremiah, and Habakkuk. Nahum's name means "comfort," and the message God sent him to share was designed to comfort the beleaguered people of Judah.

Approximately a hundred years before Nahum was born, Jonah brought a prophecy of destruction against Nineveh, the flagship city of the neighboring country of Assyria. After Jonah's prophecy, the Ninevites repented, and God withheld punishment. But years later, Judah was again suffering from Nineveh's cruel attacks.

So Nahum announced a horrific and final fall of this sinful city. At the time, his message seemed ridiculous. The city of Nineveh boasted that it was capable of withstanding a twenty-year attack, so well fortified were its one-hundred-foot-high walls. But God's power of punishment was greater. Nearly fifty years after Nahum's announcement of judgment, the Tigris River flooded and destroyed part of the city's walls, which allowed the army of Babylon to enter quickly and destroy Nineveh by fire. Nahum's central message was confirmed: God is ultimately Lord over all governments, human affairs, and history.

HABAKKUK: LIVING BY FAITH

Rather than a prophecy from God that was announced to the people, Habakkuk is the record of a conversation with God on behalf of the people of Judah.

Habakkuk questioned why God appeared to be ignoring the increase of the sinful behavior of God's own people. The reply shocked Habakkuk. God's intent was to allow the Babylonians (the chief world power after destroying Nineveh in 612 BC and defeating the entire country of Assyria) to punish Judah with repeated military attacks and ultimate defeat. Habakkuk, disbelieving at first, ultimately accepted God's greater wisdom. The final chapter of this book is Habakkuk's psalm of praise to God's power and authority.

Scholars believe that Habakkuk most likely addressed God with his concerns about the future of Judah shortly before its first invasion by the Babylonians in 597 BC (resulting in the first exile of Jewish leaders from their homeland). Habakkuk, often quoted in other books of the Bible, was the originator of the call for God's people to "live by faith" rather than by works or sight. Habakkuk also gives us a paradigm by which to understand our relationship with God as a safe space to ask the hard questions of life, and to expect answers—even when God surprises or challenges our perspective.

GOD IS IN CONTROL

_____

_____

_____

_____

_____

_____

_____

_____

_____

Nahum's message of prophecy against Assyria's capital city, Nineveh, was filled with descriptions of God's ultimate power over all heaven and earth. The one true God of justice and judgment, according to Nahum, always ultimately deals with those who are sinful and disobedient—and cares for those whose faith is fully in God.

NAHUM 1; PSALM 18:1-19

• What specific illustrations of God's power are given in today's readings? Of God's protection?

• Nahum 1:15 was understood by early Christians as the mission of Jesus. The image is used in Romans 10:16 to describe Christians who spread the gospel. What good news and peace has Christ brought you? Are you sharing it?

mon.

THE POWER OF GOD'S JUDGMENT

_____

_____

_____

_____

_____

_____

_____

_____

_____

Nineveh, flagship city of Assyria, was well fortified against invaders. Its long, high city wall was also surrounded by a one-hundred-and-fifty-foot-wide, sixty-foot-deep moat, making an attack against it a formidable challenge. But according to Nahum, the fall of sinful Nineveh would not be the result of human effort alone. The act of God's judgment would provide the conquering power.

NAHUM 2; PSALM 44:1-8

• According to Nahum 2:13, what aspects of defeat did God plan to bring to Nineveh?

• Psalm 44 reminds us that our victories come from God, not from our own efforts. Right now, what victories are you relying on God to accomplish through you?

Nahum's prophecy against Nineveh concluded with a graphic description of the results of Nineveh's fall. God's word through Nahum to the Ninevites was that their evil deeds and behavior would be exposed for the rest of the world to see.

NAHUM 3; JOHN 3:19-21

• Nahum's announcement that Nineveh's fall would be "fatal" (3:19) came true—Nineveh was never restored. What reasons did Nahum give for this?

• The book of Nahum is a reminder that God will always have the final word, no matter how cruel and sinful the situation. For what specific concern or issue does this truth bring you encouragement and hope?

The first chapter of Habakkuk reveals a conversation between the prophet and God. Habakkuk expressed concern about the sinfulness of the southern kingdom of Judah, and he wondered aloud why God seemed to ignore the situation. God assured Habakkuk of Judah's eventual judgment at the hands of the enemy army of Babylon.

HABAKKUK 1:1–2:1

• What was Habakkuk's reaction to God's proposed strategy of punishing the sinful people of Judah by using the even more sinful Babylonians?

• Just as God welcomed Habakkuk's questions, God also welcomes our difficult questions. What would you like to know from God or have greater understanding about? Write your question in the form of a prayer, and then spend some time listening.

CONSEQUENCES OF SIN

_____
_____
_____
_____
_____
_____
_____
_____
_____

Habakkuk's conversation with God is believed to have taken place as Judah experienced the imminent first invasion by the Babylonians. Habakkuk announced that "the righteous will live by faith" (2:4), a phrase quoted in the New Testament books of Romans, Galatians, and Hebrews.

HABAKKUK 2:2-20; ROMANS 1:16-20

• God identified five sinful behaviors that bring a person to ruin, each introduced by the phrase "Woe to the one." What are these, and what consequences result from each?

• In Habakkuk 2:20, we read about God's desire for "all the earth to be silent before him." When during this day can you plan to be in silence before God? What spiritual benefits might you gain through this practice?

fri.

GOD AS VICTOR

_____
_____
_____
_____
_____
_____
_____
_____
_____
_____

The final chapter of this book contains Habakkuk's acknowledgment of God's coming judgment against the people of Judah, plus statements of affirmation of God's power and authority. Some scholars believe this third chapter of Habakkuk was used as a psalm and sung as part of worship in the Temple.

HABAKKUK 3

• What statement of confidence is expressed in verses 17-19? Rewrite it in your own words.

• Habakkuk found spiritual encouragement for the present by remembering great and mighty victories of God in the past. What memories of God's past victories in your own life encourage your faith today?

Psalm 68, like Habbakuk's final chapter, is a dramatic description of confidence in the power and authority of God over all creation, and also in God's specific care for people in need. From playing the expansive role of Lord over the entire universe to caring for even the tiniest details of those who are in need, our God is indeed a God who saves.

PSALM 68:1-20

• From Psalm 68, what specific categories of people in need does God care for, and what does God provide for each?

• Look at your response to the first question. Which category applies to you? Which provision do you need to trust in faith that God will provide for you right now?

A GOD WHO SAVES

notes

AND PRAYER NEEDS

Turn the page for this week's Transformations Reflection.

transformations

Enemies Within

I've never been one to read something just to get it done. Asking hard questions along the way is good practice that leads to growth, and I need all the growth I can get. To the same degree that I am willing to wrestle, God is able to show up and teach me more. No pain, no gain.

Reading the book of Nahum has caused me to ask this hard question: Who are the people who "plot evil against the Lord" (Nahum 1:9)? Where do these evil plotters live, and what's their day job? What do they do that seems an affront to the God I attempt to serve? These and other questions tend to work away at me. I can't confront the meaning of this brief prophetic book until I know who the present-day plotters are. In any struggle, my first line of defense has always been to identify the enemy.

Enemies. The ancient Scriptures refer to them often. On the surface, my life reveals no such creatures. I live in a lovely home on a quiet, tree-lined street in a small American town of twenty churches. No one is marching for peace. No one is refused food or shelter. No one is ostracized openly for their beliefs, skin color, or family size. Oppression and violence occur on other continents in different time zones. I can't seem to identify the enemy, the ones who plot evil against the Lord.

Perhaps my enemies don't have names like Saddam or Adolph or Fidel or Osama.

Perhaps the enemies I will most likely encounter have code names and fake IDs. Alias identities like Fear (he's huge), Doubt (Fear's partner in crime), and Anger (this guy's a double agent—working for me and against me all at the same time), not to mention Selfishness—the one who whispers in my ear that *it's all about me*.

Yes, these would represent the Mafia of My Mind, the Enemies of Present Day that threaten to "plot evil against the Lord." Rather than outwardly attack the kingdom efforts we attempt as the organized community of faith, these agents of evil subversively attack the spirits we house as humans. God's best purposes, whether to feed hungry bodies or forgive hostile hearts, are completely foiled when I seek to control my circumstances. When I unleash my anger onto undeserved targets, all in the name of "ME," "MYSELF," and "I," I deem my enemies as powerful as the Ninevites who exercised violence over Judah. Evil plots against the Lord.

So today, my prayer is that God would flood my heart with living water to destroy the walls of today's enemies. Fuel the same fires that destroyed Nineveh's sinful heart, dear God, to conquer the true enemies within. Allow that each day I would confront the evil that plots against you, Lord. Evil that might even show up inside a lovely home on a quiet, tree-lined street in a small American town of twenty churches.

ZEPHANIAH: FROM RUIN TO RESTORATION

Through many of the Old Testament books, God's people experienced ups and downs in their faithfulness, often through the influence of their kings. Some kings led the people away from God, but King Josiah called the Southern Kingdom to spiritual obedience after the book of the Law was found in the Temple (2 Kings 22:1–23:25). During this time, God called Zephaniah to warn the people of impending judgment for their lack of obedience. Zephaniah announced God's word from 640–621 BC and had three main messages:

• Judgment is coming.

• Do not be indifferent to God.

• Find joy in restoration.

Zephaniah proclaimed, "Seek the LORD, all you humble of the land, you who do what he commands. Seek righteousness, seek humility; perhaps you will be sheltered on the day of the LORD's anger" (Zephaniah 2:3). But despite God's admonition, the people of Judah did not commit themselves to God, and judgment came. The prophecy in chapter 3 announced God's judgment and also God's intended restoration.

HAGGAI: SPEAKING OUT

In 586 BC God's Temple was destroyed, and the Babylonians overthrew Jerusalem. Though the people of Judah had been taken into exile in Babylon, the Persians overthrew Babylon. The Persian king Cyrus allowed the exiles to return to Jerusalem in 538 BC. Upon their return, the exiles began to rebuild the Temple but were stopped by their enemies early on.

In approximately 520 BC, God sent Haggai (along with Zechariah) with a message for those who had returned from exile and were living in Jerusalem. Haggai was the first of three prophets to address God's people after their return. During the eighteen-year suspension of the work of rebuilding the Temple, God's people had shifted their focus to restoring their own homes and businesses. Haggai and Zechariah successfully challenged them to return to rebuilding God's house rather than their own (Haggai 1:4).

Both Zephaniah and Haggai obeyed God's command to speak out, and God worked through their messages. God needs people who will overcome their fear and speak out on God's behalf. Just as God used Zephaniah and Haggai, God wants to use us to speak boldly the message of hope. Sharing our spiritual story may not be about the rise and fall of a nation or temple, but it is about the rise and fall of an individual. It is a story of God's love for us and of the restoration that comes from walking with God.

sun.

RIGHTEOUS JUDGMENT

_____
_____
_____
_____
_____
_____
_____
_____
_____
_____

Years of influence from other cultures had led God's people to combine idol worship with the worship of God. God had restrained judgment long enough, and it was time to bring God's people back to true worship. In this passage, Zephaniah proclaimed God's distaste for the people's unfaithful practices and spiritual complacency.

ZEPHANIAH 1:1-13; MATTHEW 22:34-40

• Zephaniah's message was one of judgment. What would the people experience as a result of God's punishment?

• What cultural influences have crept into your relationship with God that keep you from worshiping God alone?

mon.

WOEFUL WARNING

_____
_____
_____
_____
_____
_____
_____
_____
_____
_____

Many times God's prophets used the phrase "the day of the LORD is near," referring to God's impending punishment for sin. Zephaniah proclaimed, "The *great* day of the LORD is near," signifying that great suffering would come as a result of the people's sin unless they humbled themselves before God. Just as God's people needed to heed God's warning through Zephaniah, we need to hear and respond to God's call to faithfulness every day.

ZEPHANIAH 1:14–2:3; PSALM 81

• What warnings did God give the people? What did God command them to do in Zephaniah 2:1-3?

• What does Psalm 81:13-16 say to you about what God desires to provide you as a faithful follower?

In the book of Genesis, God judged Sodom and Gomorrah for their sinfulness and the harm they brought on Abraham and his family (Genesis 18–19). In today's passage, God judged other nations for their treatment of God's people. Though God required God's followers to be obedient, God also brought others into account for their behavior.

ZEPHANIAH 2:4-15

• In this reading, whom did God judge, and what did they do to provoke God?

• Take a few moments to reflect and identify times when you knew God was protecting you from harm. How does it feel to know that God is concerned about your well-being?

_____

Zephaniah's message was one of both judgment and hope. Though God despises the proud, this passage shows the love and compassion God has for the humble. It is through this love that God longed to restore people. Read about God's reaction to those who are proud and live for "outward show" and compare it to God's reaction to those who are humble and truly transformed on the inside.

ZEPHANIAH 3

• According to verses 1 and 4, how did the people demonstrate their pridefulness? What was God's response to this in verses 5-8?

• In verses 9-20, Zephaniah shared God's plan for restoration. Which of these promises do you need to embrace to bring about God's restoration for you? Why?

PRIORITIES

_____

_____

_____

_____

_____

_____

_____

_____

_____

_____

The first of the Jewish exiles had returned to Jerusalem after years of captivity in Babylon. Though they had initially begun rebuilding God's Temple, enemy threats deterred their efforts for a number of years. God used the prophet Haggai to bring a wake-up call to the people (who had gradually shifted focus to their own selfish ambitions). God wants to bless us, but God also requires us to make God our first priority. Until we give God the rightful place, we will never be fulfilled.

HAGGAI 1

• How were the people unfulfilled in verses 5-9? What consequences of their selfishness are described in verses 10-11?

• In what ways have you put other people or things before God? What results are you experiencing? How can you demonstrate God is "number one"?

fri.

ENCOURAGING WORDS

_____

_____

_____

_____

_____

_____

_____

_____

_____

_____

After years of living in exile, God's people were finally being restored to what God had intended for them. Through Haggai, God addressed the spiritual condition of the people and their need to seek holiness. God promised to bless the people and assured their leader Zerubbabel of his call. Though the people of God suffered the consequences of their sinful decisions, God brought them back when their priorities were straight.

HAGGAI 2

• How does the physical restoration of the Temple relate to the spiritual restoration of the people in verses 3-9? What does God promise for both?

• In terms of your personal spiritual rebuilding, what stage are you in: laying the foundation, strengthening the structure, or doing the finish work?

PERSONAL RESTORATION

Because we all have sin in our lives, we all are in need of restoration. As David wrote in Psalm 51, true recognition of sin against God brings great sorrow and the desire to make it right. God is always available to restore us to a right relationship when we turn to God.

PSALM 51

• From Psalm 51, what is God's part in our restoration? What is our part?

• Write a psalm (prayer) of your own, expressing your need and desire for restoration with God.

notes

AND PRAYER NEEDS

*t*ransformations

Frontal Lobe Theory

I have a theory that I haven't yet tested or proved. My theory deals with the human brain. I would like to suggest that a small portion of our brain (frontal lobe perhaps) is devoted to the task of getting our priorities straight. I also suppose this part of the brain works at its peak performance in or around kids. Ready for some evidence?

When I was a little kid, my priorities were straight because they were simple. Love God. Love mom and dad. Love brother. Don't cross the street without looking both ways. So when I did things like cannonball my brother's head, I was sent to my room to reflect/understand that pouncing on brother's head does not line up with priority #3: love brother.

In grade school, priorities were added because there were more things to love. The environment became the biggest. I found out our ozone is dying. So it became a priority to avoid aerosol like it was radioactive plague. I found out baby seals are choking on plastic bags, so I demanded paper when my mom was given the choice at Kroger. In just a couple years my priority list became: Love God. Love family. Save earth.

Perhaps the portion of the brain in charge of priorities gets tainted as kids get closer to becoming teenagers. It did for me. Selfishness crept into the list. Instead of "Love God and family" topping the list, "Make sure friends think I'm cool" became the top priority. Once I reached my teens, I no longer sang road trip songs with my family on the way to Nashville. Keeping up with fashion trends, like knowing when I should and shouldn't tight-roll my pants, became more important than saving baby seals.

High school was the same way. Coolness trumped everything. I had a fine-tuned walk that I did in study hall to show the throngs of staring girls that I was their long-awaited dream boat. As I went through college, I remained pretty faithful to this priority of self. (Please note: there were times when my priorities were straight. My mom would be sad if I didn't include this disclaimer.)

My point is, as I got older, God moved farther down on my list of priorities. This is significant because everything we do is affected by whatever tops our list. Priorities determine actions. When I was little I recycled like I was single-handedly saving Mother Earth. And you can see how that changed as I got older. Priorities turned inward.

As an adult, I still struggle to place God at the top of my list, even though I know that is how it should be. Everything falls into place when God is the priority. That's what Haggai was trying to get across. If my priority becomes something that adults worry about, such as blissful retirement, then everything I do will focus on retirement.

I need to look to kids for inspiration here. That was Jesus' advice, "Come as a child." And I think part of that call correlates with my frontal lobe theory. Kids have their priorities straight because those priorities are simple. Love God. Love family. Don't pounce on brother's head. You can't really go wrong with those.

ZECHARIAH: YAHWEH REMEMBERS

Zechariah, whose name means "Yahweh remembers," was among the Jews who returned to the Promised Land after the Babylonian exile; he began prophesying in approximately 520 BC. After the initial project of rebuilding the Temple began, progress ground to a halt. Zechariah, along with Haggai, was instrumental in encouraging the people to resume the work. Known as the prophet of hope, Zechariah projected the future of Israel through the years of oppression and domination by ruthless empires to the eventual triumphant coming of a messiah. Chapters 9–14 are an apocalypse, or description of the "end times."

The main emphasis of Zechariah's book is timeless: no matter what happens, God is always in control and at work in the world. As described in Zechariah's final prophecy, God intends for all people from all nations to respond to God's grace and invitation to be in relationship with God. We, as God's representatives in the world, are responsible for presenting this invitation to all. The book of Zechariah helped the Gospel writers understand the meaning of Jesus' suffering, death, and resurrection. It was quoted in Jesus' final days. The book of Revelation also drew from Zechariah, as it told of the end of history as we know it and of Jesus' return to set up his physical and spiritual kingdom on earth.

MALACHI: HOPE IN MESSIAH

Malachi's book was written as a dialog between God and God's people, through which God is compared to a father, pleading with God's children to acknowledge their sin, repent, and return to God. Ministering between 460–430 BC, Malachi presented a tragic picture of the restored community that had endured the years following the return from Babylonian exile. While Zechariah and Haggai ended their ministries with ringing words of hope, Malachi ended his ministry in despair. There was no lasting impact from the warnings of earlier prophets; the people continued in a downward slide of sin that resulted in spiritual lethargy and distance from God. The list of issues Malachi addressed is similar to the ones we face today: materialism, hypocrisy, and complacency. By doing the bare minimum spiritually and halfheartedly practicing their "religion," the people missed out on a relationship with God.

Though circumstances change, and though God's response to those events can be influenced, God's character does not change. The prophets remind us that God, who is loving and just, wants to be in relationship with us like a worthy parent. Now, as then, God holds us accountable for our sin, takes away our guilt, and revives us from our lethargy as we return to God.

sun.

PROPHETIC VISIONS

_____

_____

_____

_____

_____

_____

_____

_____

_____

_____

_____

Zechariah's sayings were often framed in prophetic visions. God gave Zechariah eight visions in chapters 1–6. Today we look at two of these visions, which deal with Judah's restoration and the rebuilding of the Temple under the leadership of Zerubbabel and Joshua, the high priest.

ZECHARIAH 1; 4

• What was the source of God's anger (1:14-15)? What was God's promise?

• In Zechariah 4:6, God charged Zerubbabel to rebuild the Temple in the power of the Spirit, not in his own human power or might. In what life situation do you need to take this verse to heart?

mon.

PROPHETIC SYMBOLS

_____

_____

_____

_____

_____

_____

_____

_____

_____

_____

_____

Zechariah used symbols to describe Judah's immediate circumstances, as well as the events connected to the messiah who would come in the distant future. Joshua, the high priest, represents the coming messiah (also referred to as the Branch).

ZECHARIAH 6

• From the description of a Davidic messiah in verses 12-15, list what Jesus the Messiah would do.

• 1 Corinthians 6:19-20 describes each follower of Jesus as God's temple. In what ways are you cooperating with the Spirit in caring for your body, which is God's temple?

MORE SCRIPTURE
Revelation 6:1-8—The vision of the future, comparable to Zechariah's

Zechariah rebuked the people for ritualistically going through the motions of their religion without heart involvement. He reminded the people of God's requirements of obedience and holiness, along with God's promise of restoration through repentance.

ZECHARIAH 7–8

• What were the people to do differently (7:8-10; 8:16-17)? What would be the different result (8:20-23)?

• What must you do to prevent going through the motions of religion and instead grow in your relationship with God? What different result could you expect?

MORE SCRIPTURE
Zechariah 9–14—The future of Jerusalem and its people, including specific prophecies of the coming messiah

An oracle is the authoritative word of God given through one of God's prophets. Zechariah's oracles revealed the culmination of God's plan and made it clear that there was a great day coming when all of God's creation would be restored to God. An all-powerful ruler, who would be pierced and struck down on behalf of people, would later return to earth to reign over a new, sin-free community. According to Zechariah, God is in control of all of history.

ZECHARIAH 12–13

• According to 12:10–13:1, what will come about as the result of God's chosen one being pierced?

• According to 13:9, God will test the character of the faithful in order to refine them. How do you sense God refining you now?

thurs.

NEGLECTING GOD

_____

_____

_____

_____

_____

_____

_____

_____

_____

_____

_____

Malachi addressed the sins of Israel, particularly complacency and hypocrisy. His strongest words were for the priests, those who were commissioned to lead Israel in true worship but who encouraged spiritual compromise through corrupt practices. As followers of Christ, we have become part of God's priesthood and are to serve God by leading others with excellence and integrity.

MALACHI 1:1–2:9; 1 PETER 2:4-12

• What worship practices brought about God's anger?

• According to 1 Peter 2:4-12, we are God's holy priests. What about your life is less than excellent and pure? How will you improve?

MORE SCRIPTURE

Numbers 25:1-13—The covenant God made with the tribe of Levi

fri.

BROKEN COMMITMENTS

_____

_____

_____

_____

_____

_____

_____

_____

_____

_____

A parallel of how we learn faithfulness to one God is through a lifetime of faithfulness to one marriage partner. We often create our own problems with God and others through our self-centeredness and hard hearts. Although God allowed divorce because of the hardness of humans' hearts toward each other, it is contrary to God's intent for us, which is to live in a dynamic lifelong union.

MALACHI 2:10-16; MATTHEW 19:3-11

• According to Malachi, what faith commitment does God want between husband and wife? What does this have in common with a relationship with God?

• What steps do you take daily to "guard yourself in your spirit and not break faith" with those with whom you are in a covenant relationship (God, spouse, family, church)?

THE LORD DENIED

God continually calls people to repentance and restoration, but the complacent Israelites denied any wrongdoing or separation from God. Everyone will experience the anticipated Day of the Lord: those who deny the Lord will experience God's raging fire of judgment, but the faithful will feel the healing warmth of the Son.

MALACHI 2:17–4:6

• In what ways had Israel made God weary? What attitudes and actions led to lukewarm faith and compromised lifestyles?

• When we withhold what is rightly God's, we become complacent. How are you cooperating with what God expects from you financially? How are you experiencing God's protection and provision?

notes

AND PRAYER NEEDS

transformations

Crazy for You

I've never thought of myself as crazy. Crazy people are the ones who do things that just don't make sense. They act outside of the rational norm. Crazy behavior is scary behavior—no telling what will happen next. Predictability goes out the window. Come to think of it, I don't even like crazy people.

But on that hot August day in the summer of '86, I became a crazy person.

It started out with great promise. Vacations always found our family of five at the same beloved campground, a wooded human nest adjacent to an enormous white beach on the western shore of Michigan. It was getting close to lunchtime, and our three-year-old had informed us he was hungry, yet we put him off. We weren't quite ready to leave our paradise of castle-building, kite flying, and dune running on the beach to go get lunch.

In amongst other fun-loving families on the beach, I remember losing sight of the kids but feeling confident that the older two were with the hungry three-year-old. Moments later, however, our little guy was MIA. Nowhere. And something inside of this mother snapped. I became Crazy Woman.

I deployed the family to the dunes and beach, ordering them to ask every single person if they'd seen the cutest little blond three-year-old alive. Then I tore into the campground on foot, a mother panther with muscle and energy seething. My mind raced ahead to what might have happened to my baby. I ran to the camp office and ordered them to stop all incoming and outgoing traffic. We had to close ranks and fortify the borders! Next, my legs took me the full circumference of the campground, inspecting, asking, interrogating. WHERE'S MY CHILD? Lost in the dunes? Kidnapped by a violent criminal? Or even more frightening, fighting for breath out in the lake? All I could see was his picture on the side of a milk carton and my obituary in the paper, for I could not bear the thought of going on without him.

Rounding up over the hill to our own campsite, I took in an absolutely incredible scene. There, under the dining canopy, perched atop the picnic table was Mr. Adorable chowing down on a box of Cheez-Its® (he was hungry, remember?). Running to him, I snatched him up and hugged him with the type of uncontrolled emotion that sends kids into therapy for years to come. Lost kid becomes found kid. Crazy Woman cries.

The books of Zechariah and Malachi depict a God who, frankly, comes off as Crazy. Through these prophets, I see a Divine Parent who says crazy things, threatens crazy consequences. I see a desperate God, almost out-of-control desperate, closing ranks, fortifying the borders, whatever it takes to rescue the beloved children. I honestly don't understand it until I remember that day on the beach, until I relive the feelings of Crazy Woman, and then it comes to me. God is out-of-control Crazy—for us.

orientation to the New Testament

The sixty-six books of the Bible tell the most important story of all: the overwhelming love of God for people and the length to which God is willing to go to be in relationship with them.

The first thirty-nine books (the Old Testament) reveal God's promises to the people of Israel during times of stability and periods of suffering. Out of their exile was born the yearning for and promise of a deliverer who would save the people of God from cruel oppression. The last twenty-seven books (the New Testament) record the fulfillment of God's promise to provide a deliverer, a messiah, who is Jesus.

During the time frame between the testaments, God was still at work, gradually shaping world events to prepare people to receive the Gospel (the good news of God's provision through Jesus). Conquests by Alexander the Great in 330 BC led to a common, universal language (Greek) through which news could quickly spread. The New Testament writers probably had access to a Greek translation of the books of the Old Testament, which was completed in Egypt by 150 BC.

With the rise of the Roman Empire came good roads, protected sea routes, open borders, and an army-enforced peace that facilitated the speedy transmission of the gospel across thousands of miles. The Jews over time had been gradually scattered across the area surrounding the Mediterranean Sea. Many Jews remained in Babylonia. Some of their religious practices were diluted by merger with other cultures. With God's people—dispersed and under submission to the Roman Empire—longing for the promised messiah to appear, the rest of the world was being prepared for Jesus' arrival as well. The intersection of the dramatic promises of the Old Testament and these cultural factors is well described in Galatians 4:4-5: "When the fullness of time had come, God sent his Son, born of woman, born under the law, to redeem those who were under the law, so that we might receive adoption as children" (NRSV).

The New Testament books were written within a period of about one hundred years following the time of Jesus. Almost one half of the New Testament consists of the Gospels (the first four books, which are called Matthew, Mark, Luke, and John). These books contain accounts of the life and ministry of Jesus, told from the four distinct perspectives of four different authors. Written between AD 60–100, together they give a composite view of Jesus, whom they identify as the Christ (Messiah). The daily readings from each of the Gospels in this edition of the *Transformation Journal* were chosen to reflect the unique content of each Gospel.

The book of Acts recounts the early history of the church (the communities made up of the first followers of Christ who were scattered across the ancient Near East and southern Europe). The apostles (the early church leaders, including Jesus' original disciples) fed these young churches spiritually through a series of letters positioned in the back of the New Testament that gave encouragement and instruction and are known as the Epistles. The apostle Paul wrote many of the first thirteen letters, the first of which was written in approximately AD 50, making these letters the earliest New Testament writings. Some letters (such as Ephesians and Colossians) circulated among clusters of early churches, and the author is uncertain. The other authors of the Epistles included Jesus' closest disciples Peter and John as well as Jesus' half-brother James. The New Testament ends with the Revelation of John, which describes the end of time and Jesus' second coming to earth.

The theme of covenant (an unbreakable but conditional promise) is integral to the New Testament, just as it is to many stories and books of the Old Testament. The Old Testament describes the covenant made between God and Abraham that was extended through Isaac and Jacob to the people of Israel. This covenant was established through the Law given by God to

Moses and written on tablets of stone on Mount Sinai; it was to guide the people in obeying God and living according to God's word. Many Old Testament prophets describe the disobedience of God's people, caused by their inability to keep this covenant. Six hundred years before Jesus was born, the prophet Jeremiah spoke of a "new covenant" that would be internal (written on hearts of flesh) and lived out through a personal relationship with God. Through Jesus' sacrificial death and resurrection, this new covenant is offered to all people. Through the power of the Holy Spirit, given to everyone who is in a personal relationship with Jesus, we are empowered and equipped to live in obedience to God.

Several terms you will repeatedly encounter when studying the New Testament offer a rich understanding of the new covenant and our faith. They include:

- **Salvation**: Spiritual rescue from sin and death. Redemption. The reconnection with God accomplished through Jesus' death on the cross. The result of placing trust in Jesus and entering a personal relationship with God through him.

- **Grace**: The love God offers to every human being, even when it is undeserved. An approach to humanity that provides reconnection with God, with no strings attached and no need to earn God's love.

- **Holiness, or Sanctification**: The process by which a follower of Jesus conforms more and more to the image of Christ. This process is made possible by the presence and power of the Holy Spirit in the believer's life.

- **Faith**: Placing complete trust and confidence in God. The ability to rely fully on God, not on self.

- **Justification**: To be set free from guilt or blame. To become righteous. The state of forgiveness we live in when we confess our disobedience to God and God wipes our spiritual history clean.

An understanding of the dynamics between several key people groups in the New Testament also gives greater insight into our study of the Scriptures. These groups include:

- **Pharisees**: A strict Jewish sect, whose name means "separatist." Pharisees carefully observed the Law (Torah) in every detail. The Pharisees' obedience, focus on holiness, and rigorous effort to keep the Law and preserve Jewish tradition distanced them from the general Jewish and Greco-Roman populations.

- **Sadducees**: These descendants of the ancient priesthood were more casual about the Law than the Pharisees. They doubted the likelihood of supernatural miracles, and they disagreed with the Pharisees by denying the possibility of resurrection. The Sadducees controlled the priesthood and the operation of the Temple, and some were people of wealth and position who worked to accommodate the foreign occupational government in order to preserve their own status and power.

- **Scribes**: Copiers of the Law, the members of this group were part of a profession rather than a religious group. They were regarded as authorities on the Scripture and frequently were teachers. They were often linked with the Pharisees in Scripture and were more closely related to their outlook on faith.

- **Samaritans**: When the Assyrians conquered the Northern Kingdom in 721 BC, the upper region of Israel was taken into exile. Those who were left intermarried with the people of the region, producing the Samaritan people. Viewed as a "mixed breed" both religiously and racially, the Samaritans were considered "unclean" by the Jews and experienced severe discrimination.

Like the world of Jesus' day, the time is ripe for us to share the life-changing message of God's grace, offer of salvation, and power for life-change with the people within our spheres of influence. May the words of the New Testament (both challenging and healing) inspire you to touch the people around you for Jesus.

matthew

Jesus as Messiah

book 40

The book of Matthew is the first of the four Gospels (accounts of the good news of God's provision through Jesus). It connects the Old Testament Law and prophets to the New Testament proclamation that Jesus is the Messiah. Matthew, also known as Levi, wrote his account in approximately AD 60. Until he answered the call to be one of Jesus' twelve disciples, Matthew was a Jewish tax collector working for the Roman government. This was one of the least respected professions of the day. But Matthew's response to Jesus and resulting radical transformation took him from being one considered a traitor to the Jewish people and his spiritual heritage, to one of the most influential voices in the development of the Christian faith. Through his records of Jesus' life and ministry, and for a culture that was thoroughly under the thumb of the Roman Empire, Matthew wrote a persuasive argument to Jewish leaders, revealing Jesus as the Messiah, the Promised One, who was anticipated by Old Testament prophets and visionaries.

Matthew's account contains many occasions in which Jesus defended his identity from the attacks of the Pharisees and Sadducees, the Jewish religious leaders of that time. They had placed their faith in God's promise, described throughout the Old Testament, that a ruler would come to set them free from bondage. They assumed this would be freedom from political bondage and foreign enemy occupation. Instead, Jesus came as the king who would bring freedom from spiritual bondage to sin and provide the power to live in obedience to God. Jesus proclaimed his mission to them in Matthew 5:17, "Do not think that I have come to abolish the Law or the Prophets; I have not come to abolish them but to fulfill them." Jesus' purpose was different than what they had imagined, but even more powerful.

The book of Matthew records more of Jesus' teachings than any of the other Gospels. Matthew also recounts many of Jesus' parables, stories and metaphors based on common, everyday experiences that reveal spiritual lessons. The parables in Matthew teach what the kingdom of heaven is like, as well as the characteristics of citizens of the kingdom of heaven. Jesus used these parables to invite his listeners to enter into a spiritual relationship with him and become citizens of God's eternal kingdom.

Matthew tells the story of Jesus' life from his humble birth to his triumphant resurrection. This Gospel represents the radical teachings of Jesus that not only contradicted the religious thinking of his time but also challenge us today. Through Matthew's persuasive writing we receive an invitation to experience radical life transformation as Matthew himself did and become faithful followers of Jesus ourselves. This week's readings have been specifically chosen to honor Matthew's distinctive emphasis upon Jesus as king and how we can live as citizens of the kingdom of God.

sun.

DIVINE DELIVERANCE

_____

_____

_____

_____

_____

_____

_____

_____

_____

_____

Though he was not born in a royal setting, Jesus' miraculous birth has impacted upon the world more than any other event. Read Matthew's account of the birth of Jesus, God's Son and Savior of the world, and how God provided a way out of tough circumstances.

MATTHEW 1:18–2:23

• What difficulties surrounded the birth of Jesus? How were they miraculously overcome?

• In what difficult situation do you need God to work a miracle today?

MORE SCRIPTURE

Luke 1:5–2:20—A detailed account of Jesus' birth

mon.

WORLD TURNED UPSIDE DOWN

_____

_____

_____

_____

_____

_____

_____

_____

_____

_____

Today's reading is the first of three focusing on the Sermon on the Mount (given by Jesus on a mountainside by the Sea of Galilee). Jesus' teachings turned the religious thinking of his day upside down and provided guidelines for those who want to live as true citizens of God's kingdom.

MATTHEW 5:1-48

• What "upside down" lessons did Jesus teach about how we are to treat other people?

• In what relationship could you apply a lesson from the Sermon on the Mount? What steps will you take?

MORE SCRIPTURE

Luke 6:20-36—Luke's consolidated version of the Sermon on the Mount

SECRET SERVICE

We are in our second day of Jesus' teachings from the Sermon on the Mount, which encourage us to work out of pure motives in order to go deeper with God. According to Jesus, we must make a choice of whom we are going to serve. When we seek God, rather than the approval of those around us, we enter into God's provision and can live a life of peace rather than worry.

MATTHEW 6

• What activities are we to do "in secret"?

• What rewards come from living a life free from worry? What do you worry about the most? How would your life change if you trusted God's provision?

wed.

IT'S NOT EASY

Finish reading Matthew's account of Jesus' Sermon on the Mount. This chapter provides great teachings, each of which has challenging application for our lives. As he did in the first century, Jesus confronts our selfish mindset and calls us to respond according to his priorities.

MATTHEW 7

• List the main lessons presented by Jesus in this chapter.

• Which lesson is most challenging for you? Write a prayer asking Jesus to transform your mindset on this issue into his viewpoint.

thurs.

KINGDOM TEACHINGS

_____

_____

_____

_____

_____

_____

_____

_____

_____

_____

Throughout his book, Matthew presents Jesus as a king or ruler who stands for something different than the rulers of the Roman Empire. Jesus used parables (stories based on common everyday experiences that reveal spiritual lessons) to describe the spiritual Kingdom over which he reigns.

MATTHEW 13

• According to Matthew 13:10-15, why did Jesus speak in parables?

• Which of the "soils" best represents your current spiritual condition? What changes, if any, need to be made?

MORE SCRIPTURE
Matthew 25—Jesus' parables on preparing for his second coming to earth

fri.

FAITHFUL FRIEND AND FOUNDER

_____

_____

_____

_____

_____

_____

_____

_____

_____

_____

Of Jesus' twelve disciples (or followers), Peter was among those who had a special relationship with Jesus. Although he was quick to act, sometimes before thinking, Jesus appreciated his bold responses. God doesn't expect us to be faultless, but he does expect us to be faithful. When we are faithful like Peter, we gain a new identity in Jesus.

MATTHEW 14:22-32; 16:13-20

• What happened when Peter, in the boat, was focused on Jesus? What happened when he became distracted?

• In what area of your life do you sense Jesus calling you to step out of the boat and walk by faith? What could be distracting you from following that call?

Jesus pointed out how far the religious leaders of his time were from living out the two greatest commandments. His harshest treatment of people was toward those who taught one thing and did another, thereby influencing others to do the same. Jesus requires integrity of heart, soul, and mind.

MATTHEW 22:34-40; 23:1-39

• What was Jesus' main complaint against the religious leaders of his day?

• In what ways do you need to grow in how you demonstrate God's love? What can you do to increase your integrity of heart, soul, and mind?

transformations

Red Letters

I received my first Bible for Christmas when I was in the fourth grade. It was a white, leather-bound Bible, a King James red-letter edition that I've kept to this day. Starting out in the book of Matthew, I remember being strongly attracted to Jesus while reading the red-letter words of the Gospel, but now as an adult looking over these Jesus quotes, I'm not quite sure why.

Reading through Matthew, I'm struck by the upside down kingdom that Jesus describes, the bold and brash behavior to which Jesus ascribes. Most days it must have been altogether awesome and infuriating to hang out with the guy. Just when you thought you had him all figured out, he'd throw a curve ball and bash your navel-gazing theology all to pieces.

Blessed are you when people insult you, persecute you and falsely say all kinds of evil against you because of me . . . if anyone strikes you on the right cheek, turn to them the other also. Love your enemies and pray for those who persecute you.

None of this feels natural to me. It's the opposite of how I want to think, feel, and act. I'd like to love my enemies, but when they grow real faces and accuse me with real voices, I lose my like-to. What was Jesus thinking? Where was he coming from?

For I have not come to call the righteous, but sinners.

Not fair.

The girl is not dead but asleep.

Not rational.

I did not come to bring peace, but a sword.

That's not what they promised me in Sunday School.

Whoever finds their life will lose it, and whoever loses their life for my sake will find it.

How's that?

I want to be smart and right. I hate being slow of mind or flat-out wrong. Then those red letters pop out again:

The Father has hidden these things from the wise and learned, and revealed them to little children. Ugh!

Forgiveness seems overrated. How about if I start with forgiving once, maybe twice?

I tell you, not seven times, but seventy-seven times.

I'm getting on top of things now, God. Please bless me, my family, and the things and people I love.

The last will be first, and the first will be last. I tell you the truth, the tax collectors and the prostitutes are entering the kingdom of God ahead of you.

So why, in my early days, did my affection for Jesus grow while my feelings of self-importance shrank? How could this straight-walking, truth-talking man so attract my affection?

I think it was the red letters. As my reading went further into Matthew's Gospel, the color red became more intense. I saw Jesus modeling the core truths of the words he'd spoken, and the high cost of sacrifice bled out all over the page.

They spit on him, and took the staff and struck him on the head again and again. After they had mocked him, they took off the robe and put his own clothes on him. Then they led him away to crucify him.

In the end, I realize I don't want a nice God, a savior who tells me I'm right. I want the Truth, for it sets me free. I want The Way in, not a way out. And above all, I want Life. The Life that was described and written on a cross for you and for me in bold red letters, the Jesus I've grown to love.

mark

Jesus as servant

The power, fast pace, and simplicity of the Gospel of Mark has held enduring appeal for Bible readers throughout the world. Containing concise and compelling accounts of Jesus' life, death, and resurrection, the Gospel of Mark is written in a straightforward style, consistent with the conversational Greek language of Jesus' day.

It is suggested that the author of this book was a young believer named John Mark, whose mother offered her home as a meeting place for the early church (Acts 12:12). John Mark was not one of the original twelve disciples, but he joined his cousin Barnabas on the apostle Paul's first missionary journey to share the message of Jesus. John Mark soon returned home, and Paul refused to take him along on his next missionary journey; yet in some of Paul's letters to the early churches we read that John Mark was with Paul again during Paul's imprisonments in Rome. John Mark also spent time doing ministry with the disciple Peter (1 Peter 5:13). Through the eyewitness accounts of Peter and the powerful influence of Paul, God equipped John Mark, the servant who initially abandoned the mission, to document for all time the faithful servant life of Jesus Christ.

The Gospel of Mark does not appear to have been intended as a chronological account of everything Jesus said and did. Mark carefully chose events that would relate to those living in the Roman culture who knew what it was to be a servant. He filled the final few chapters with a careful recount of the crucifixion and resurrection, Jesus' ultimate act of service. The remainder of the book reveals Jesus as the radical servant leader representing the new kingdom truths of God. Mark has been called the "Gospel of Action" because it contains only four of Jesus' parables (stories) but reports eighteen miracles. Mark paints a striking picture of Jesus as a controversial challenger to the religious thinking of his culture, a spiritual leader with authority over evil, and a healer who brought miraculous health to the sick.

A key theme of Mark's gospel centers on the identity of Jesus. Early on, Jesus told those who clearly understood that he is the Son of God to remain silent. Later he acknowledged his supernatural identity to his disciples but warned them also to keep it a secret. Not until Jesus' final hour, when the centurion guarding Jesus on the cross exclaimed, "Surely this man was the Son of God!" (Mark 15:39), was his identity publicly acknowledged. Jesus' powerful earthly ministry, filled with miraculous works of the Spirit, was shrouded in mystery until the end.

Written two thousand years ago, the Gospel of Mark still brings fresh energy and excitement about Jesus to its readers. May Jesus, who moves swiftly, courageously, and confidently through the pages of this Gospel, empower you through the Holy Spirit for service on his behalf.

book 41

JOHN THE BAPTIST

_____

_____

_____

_____

_____

_____

_____

_____

_____

_____

Jesus' cousin John grew up as a fiercely independent prophetic figure who followed God's call into the desert wilderness. His unorthodox style provoked the attention of the religious leaders of the day, as well as attracted people who desired to be forgiven and baptized. John was surprised when Jesus asked for baptism. This event launched Jesus' Spirit-led teaching and healing ministry.

MARK 1:1-11; MATTHEW 3

• What did John mean when he said, "Produce fruit in keeping with repentance" (Matthew 3:8)?

• What words came from heaven when Jesus was baptized? Describe a time you felt God's love and blessing upon you.

MORE SCRIPTURE
Luke 1:5-38—The early life of John the Baptist

JESUS AS SERVANT LEADER

_____

_____

_____

_____

_____

_____

_____

_____

_____

_____

In today's reading we see Jesus as servant, not only with crowds of people but also with individuals. Jesus refused to let the traditions of Jewish synagogue leaders prevent him from healing a handicapped man on the Sabbath, a sacred day. As his ministry grew, Jesus selected twelve followers to train and mentor as spiritual servant leaders.

MARK 3; LUKE 6:12-16

• Jesus spent all night praying before choosing his disciples. What principle was Jesus modeling for all believers?

• Jesus considered his spiritual relationship with his followers as valuable to him as his blood relatives. Because of your relationship with Jesus, who has become your spiritual "family"? What roles do they play?

AUTHORITY OVER EVIL

Mark's report of the life of Jesus gives many examples of his authority over evil and his role as healer. No matter what the circumstances, Jesus, compassionate servant of the people, always knew how to deal with each individual's needs.

MARK 5

• What instructions did Jesus give the man who was healed at the tombs? Why was this important?

• With whom in Mark 5 can you identify the most: the man living at the tombs, the father pleading for Jesus to heal his daughter, or the woman who approached Jesus in the crowd and touched him? Write a prayer asking Jesus for healing, or a thank-you prayer for the healing he has already brought.

GOD'S PROVISION

After Jesus trained his disciples, he sent them out in pairs to teach and to heal those in need. When they returned with many "success" stories of God's power at work, Jesus showed them yet another miraculous demonstration by feeding a crowd of five thousand. Slow to learn, the disciples needed one more lesson about God's provision. A few days later they watched as Jesus fed a group of four thousand.

MARK 6:30-44; 8:1-21

• In Mark 8:14-21, Jesus was disappointed in his disciples. In spite of the major miracles they had seen, what did they still not understand?

• In Jesus' day, bread was viewed as a precious symbol of God's provision. What "bread" do you need to ask God to multiply to meet your needs?

THE MOUNTAIN AND THE VALLEY

_____
_____
_____
_____
_____
_____
_____
_____
_____
_____

The experience Peter, James, and John shared with Jesus on the mountaintop is known as the "Transfiguration." In Jewish tradition, God often appeared in a cloud. For that reason, the disciples immediately recognized Jesus as the awaited Messiah when the Transfiguration happened. After they returned to the city, Jesus had another opportunity to demonstrate God's miraculous power in a practical way.

MARK 9:2-29; MATTHEW 17:1-20

• The Transfiguration was so inspiring that the disciples wanted to build shelters and stay there. Why do you think Jesus led them back to life in the city instead?

• Prayer keeps us vital and empowered by God. How connected through prayer do you stay with God? How can you improve?

JESUS AND PRIORITIES

_____
_____
_____
_____
_____
_____
_____
_____
_____
_____

Most people in Jesus' day believed that the signs of success and favor with God were financial wealth and material possessions. But Jesus challenged popular thinking in his teachings about God's real priorities. Even his disciples struggled to understand the new definition of "greatness" Jesus described.

MARK 10:17-45

• Jesus redefined the purpose of having material blessings as the ability to help others, and said that a relationship with him was more important than family. Why do you think the rich young ruler went away sad?

• According to Jesus, the path to spiritual "greatness" is serving the needs of others. What percent of your life reflects this priority? What percent is still focused on your own set of priorities?

This teaching of Jesus is one of the most difficult to understand. His disciples were eager to know when and how God would accomplish ultimate earthly victory and reign eternally over all creation. Jesus left the exact time to God, but he described what his followers can expect.

MARK 13

• According to this passage, what challenges can followers of Jesus expect as a result of their faith? What does Mark 13:11 promise that God will provide?

• The most important instructions for believers are given in Mark 13:32-37. What do you need to do to stay spiritually prepared?

MORE SCRIPTURE
1 Thessalonians 5:1-11—More instructions about being prepared

WAIT AND WATCH

_____

_____

_____

_____

_____

_____

_____

_____

_____

notes

AND PRAYER NEEDS

_____

_____

_____

_____

_____

_____

_____

_____

_____

_____

_____

_____

transformations

Divine Restraint

As a Christian I've been asked why I buy the Jesus story. "How can you be sure he's the Son of God?" In the past I've struggled to come up with good answers. "Um…I…it's what I grew up believing?" F minus. Not having a good answer to this Jesus question is like a doctor not having an explanation for why he or she wants to "go ahead and amputate." Typically, the people who ask this question are not currently buying Jesus, but they may be shopping. So it's not okay for a Christian to have a dumb answer for such a smart question. I've been working on my answer because I have some friends who need to be convinced to go ahead and amputate. I mean, they need to understand why I believe Jesus is the Son of God.

I have different reasons for believing almost every day. It's much like my marriage. Some days I know and believe my wife loves me because she does fifty-seven loads of laundry and doesn't say a word. Other days I know because she sings Celine Dion love ballads to me. That may be a lie, but you understand my point. I believe in Jesus for different reasons all the time. Earlier in the week it was because he answered a prayer in a way only he could've thought up. Tomorrow it may be because of his patience with me. Today it's all about his restraint. I'll give you a few examples.

If I were Jesus, I would have skipped on water instead of just walking. And not just that one time but all the time. I never would've seen the inside of the boat. While the disciples were fishing, I would've been skipping around telling them to try fishing on the other side. Not Jesus. He had divine restraint.

If I were Jesus, I would've had a hard time keeping the future secret. When my best friends asked when I was coming back to earth to save them, I would've spilled the kidney beans. When I wasn't preaching or healing, I would've taught the disciples how to play baseball. "This game is going to be huge someday, guys!" I'd say. And after I got them to understand that "stealing" was okay in baseball, I'd talk serious trash. I'd smash a home run and tell Peter (the pitcher), "Oh Petey! Babe Ruth is EN FUEGO today!" Not Jesus. He had divine restraint.

If I were Jesus, I would've ridden into Jerusalem on something much cooler than a donkey. Like a unicorn. Or a dump truck full of sandwiches. I would've given everyone a ride after we ate sandwiches. Not Jesus. He had divine restraint.

When Jesus was being tortured on the cross, he could've called down a fleet of the baddest army angels in heaven to come and torch everyone. The very people whom Jesus came to save were whipping, stabbing, scourging, and ridiculing him. With the smallest head nod, Jesus could've shown his killers Old Testament-style wrath. But not Jesus. He had divine, non-human restraint. That's my proof and the reason I believe—today.

Luke

everyone is invited

The Gospel of Luke was written by a Gentile (someone who is not a Jew) to other Gentiles. In Colossians 4:14, the apostle Paul acknowledged Luke as a doctor as well as his dear friend. Luke authored an intricate, detailed record of Jesus' life. Luke addressed his gospel to Theophilus, most likely a high Roman official who was seeking to know more about the rumor of a spiritual leader named Jesus. It was Luke's desire to give a thorough and orderly account so Theophilus would understand precisely Jesus' miraculous nature and life witness. It is believed that Luke also wrote the book of Acts to Theophilus, recording the empowerment of Jesus' disciples after his resurrection and the stories of the early Christian church.

Luke offers a distinct perspective. Where Matthew's account recorded the family line of Jesus linking him to Abraham, father of the Jewish faith, Luke traced Jesus' lineage to Adam, the father of all humanity. This emphasized the importance of Jesus as Savior for all people, both Jew and Gentile. Luke was not a personal eyewitness to Jesus' ministry. However, his companionship with the apostle Paul during missionary journeys most likely provided the environment in which Luke learned the stories of Jesus' life. Luke's excellent command of the Greek language and his carefully ordered report provide us today with a beautiful and thorough description of Christ's time on earth. Given humanity's history of relationship with God, Luke's goal was to verify the liberating good news of Jesus as the spiritual fulfillment of all that had gone before.

Jesus is specifically presented as teacher and healer, empowered by the Holy Spirit for his miraculous work. Luke also highlighted other important themes in his account of Jesus' ministry. For example, Luke gives great detail about important women in Jesus' life: Elizabeth's pregnancy with John the Baptist, Mary's pregnancy with Jesus, his friends Mary and Martha, and other notable women of faith. Luke also provides vivid pictures of Jesus in prayer, records words of praise, emphasizes Jesus' concern for the poor, and underscores Jesus' compassion for those who are spiritually lost. Most significantly, Luke included Jesus' requirement of complete obedience in order to become his follower: prioritizing Jesus over the competing importance of family, friends, finances, and possessions.

Jesus saw all of humanity as valuable in God's eyes. The Gospel of Luke reveals our Savior as the One who came so everyone who believes in him may be saved, regardless of race, gender, or social status. From the sinful woman who anointed Jesus' feet to the Pharisee who scolded her for doing so, Jesus brought love and compassion for all. And just as he did with Theophilus so long ago, Luke invites us today to personally encounter the Son of God through his teachings, his miracles, and his gift of eternal life.

book 42

sun.

TEMPTATION

_____

_____

_____

_____

_____

_____

_____

_____

_____

_____

Having been baptized by John, Jesus was filled with the Holy Spirit. After overcoming the temptations to disobey God's call to serve, Jesus proceeded with his powerful earthly ministry that fulfilled Old Testament prophecy and ultimately changed the lives of countless people.

LUKE 4:1-30

• In what ways did Satan tempt Jesus? How did Jesus respond each time?

• What tricks does Satan try on you, to distract you from being obedient to God? What helps you keep from falling for his tricks?

MORE SCRIPTURES
1 Corinthians 10:12-13—Advice on facing temptation

mon.

LOVING SAVIOR

_____

_____

_____

_____

_____

_____

_____

_____

_____

_____

Living a "religious" life is not the same as being sold out for God. As Christians, we are called to honor God and love others—regardless of their position. No matter what our history has been, God is capable of forgiving us and transforming us into new eternal life with God, from the inside out. When we see those around us through the miracle of this truth, we are empowered to offer others love and compassion. God desires us to be ready every day for opportunities to follow this example.

LUKE 7:36-50

• How did the sinful woman honor Jesus? What was Simon's reaction? What lesson did Jesus teach his friend?

• To whom do you have trouble demonstrating love? Why? What can you choose to do to treat them as Jesus would?

We often think of and celebrate the free gift of new life in Jesus, but the whole truth is that following Christ also has a cost. Jesus pointed out the change of priorities and level of trust necessary to be a true follower. Even our relational obligations to friends and family come second to our obedience to God.

LUKE 9:57–10:24

• According to the conversations Jesus had in Luke 9:57-62, what kept these individuals from fully following God? In Luke 10, what instructions did Jesus give to the "harvest workers" who were willing to be fully faithful to follow him?

• What "cost" have you experienced in following Jesus? What's the next hard step for you in following Jesus even more fully?

God's people had developed a prejudice against the citizens of Samaria. The Samaritan people were the result of intermarriage, in violation of God's law, and were therefore despised by the Jewish people as "unclean." This well-known story is a reminder that God is pleased when we show prejudice-free compassion and comfort to those in need. God calls all of us to reach out to those who are hurting and broken.

LUKE 10:25-37

• Describe each passerby who did not help the man. What reasons do you think each had for ignoring him?

• What excuses do you use to avoid serving someone in need? In what way is Jesus telling you to "go and do likewise"?

MORE SCRIPTURE

John 4:1-26—Jesus and a Samaritan woman

thurs.

PASSION FOR THE LOST

_____
_____
_____
_____
_____
_____
_____
_____
_____
_____
_____

Jesus worked hard to show how relentless God's love is for every one of us, using parables (stories) to provide real-life examples. No matter what our spiritual distance from God or how far we are "lost," God never quits seeking to bring us back into a loving relationship. Jesus was sent as the ultimate effort to embody God's love for the lost. Notice specifically how Jesus explained God's passion to "find" those who have left God's protection.

LUKE 15

• Who represents God in these parables? What diligence did each one show to find what was lost? What did each one do when the lost object was found?

• Of the two sons in Jesus' third parable, with which do you most identify? How does it feel to receive God's unconditional love?

fri.

OVERCOMING OBSTACLES

_____
_____
_____
_____
_____
_____
_____
_____
_____
_____
_____

Jewish men who worked as tax collectors for the Roman government were despised in their day. A tax collector's salary was earned through collecting over and above what the government called for. Taking financial advantage of citizens had tainted all tax collectors' reputations. Jesus used an unlikely character, a tax collector named Zacchaeus, to teach about God's redeeming power.

LUKE 19:1-10

• What characteristics are seen in Zacchaeus? What choices did Zacchaeus make that allowed "salvation" to come to him?

• With which of Zacchaeus' characteristics can you identify? Which parts of your daily living need to shift to Jesus' priorities?

MORE SCRIPTURE
Matthew 9:9-13—Jesus' other encounters with tax collectors

QUIET TIMES

Near the end of his life, Jesus chose to spend his final "free" hours with the followers who had been at his side for the three years of his ministry. Together they celebrated the Jewish Passover meal, a religious occasion commemorating the day God delivered Israel from Egyptian bondage. Jesus proclaimed a whole new covenant that his death and resurrection would fulfill. He then went to the Mount of Olives to pray.

LUKE 22:1-46

• What was Jesus experiencing in his final hours of freedom? What did he pray (Luke 22:42)? What happened (Luke 22:43)?

• What from the example of Jesus encourages you to trust God's ability to provide the right solution, even if you can't see it yourself? For what do you pray when you are faced with tough situations?

notes
AND PRAYER NEEDS

Turn the page for this week's Transformations Reflection.

transformations

Searching for the Originals

My bachelor days are numbered. I'm soon to be married. Wedding planning—I am finding out—is not an incredibly enjoyable experience. I've always thought the process could and would be simple and comfortable. And it really has been except for a few minor bumps (pebbles) in the road.

The other morning I ran into a small pebble. As I was getting ready for work I received a call from my fiancée. Morning calls from her are unusual. Something was wrong; I heard it in her voice. It was very slight, but it was there. "Are the engagement pictures sitting on the counter?" she asked. "Uh…no," I replied. I heard her heart sink.

Several weeks ago, we had had our engagement pictures taken. They were to be used for our engagement announcement in the paper. I don't like to brag, but the photos turned out great. So we showed them off to family, friends, and the occasional stranger on the street, if we could interest them.

After a long pause, my fiancée said the pictures were lost. She had looked in her car, in both of her purses, and everywhere else she could think to look. I immediately searched my apartment, looking for any sign of our pictures. I called my mom and had her check her house. My fiancée's mom was doing the same, but no pictures. We retraced every step we'd taken in the last week. We called the grocery store and Wal-Mart because she remembered having them with her in a "building." I called the bank because most of our free time is spent there preparing for the wedding. If there were a hotline, we would've called it. If there were suspected thieves, we would've rounded them up and played good cop, bad cop. Those pictures were alone and probably starving out in the dark, cruel world, and we were desperate to find them.

When something of true value is lost, desperation becomes a powerful motivator. Jesus told similar stories in Luke 15 when he taught that there is value in the one. He said that lost sheep, coins, and ultimately people matter greatly to God. The pictures we lost were originals. They captured a specific moment of our history that could never be reproduced. The sun will never catch the sparkle in my fiancée's eyes the way it did in those photos. The smiles we had from being months from marriage will never be the same because we'll never be months away from marriage again. We wanted to find those photos so desperately because we knew they could never be duplicated, replaced, or even substituted.

God sees us the same way. In God's eyes we are originals that can never be duplicated. God loves us so much that God sent God's son to die for us so no one would be lost. Incredibly, the photos were eventually found. Even more incredible is the length to which God went to find me.

john

Jesus, the Son of God

The fourth Gospel was written by another faithful witness to the life of Christ. This writer is traditionally believed to be the disciple John, although no author is named within this account. John was a partner with his father and brother (James) in their prominent fishing business along the Sea of Galilee. From there Jesus called them to leave their nets and become "fishers of people." John and James, along with Peter, made up the inner circle of the twelve disciples. In John 20–21, John is called "the disciple Jesus loved," an indication of his position as Jesus' closest friend. John offers the insight, understanding, and interpretation of what Jesus said as only a close friend and eyewitness could provide.

The Gospel of John was one of the last New Testament books written. John lived to an old age and completed his gospel in the city of Ephesus around AD 90. He had had sixty years, much of it living in exile, to sort through which of Jesus' "many signs" (20:30-31) he would include in his gospel. By the end of the first century, aberrations to the Christian message (such as the Gnostics) were developing and teaching that Jesus was not God. The early church needed a clear theology (the understanding of who God is and what God is about) to uphold the truth and integrity of Jesus' teachings. More clearly than any other gospel writer, John presented Jesus as fully God and fully human. Rather than launching the story of Jesus with his physical birth, as Matthew and Luke did, John traced the origin of Jesus back into eternity itself. From the outset, the purpose of John's writing was his stated mission: "that you may believe that Jesus is the Messiah, the Son of God, and that by believing you may have life in his name" (John 20:31).

Beyond reporting the historical events of Jesus' life and ministry, John reflected on the meaning behind the events. He wrote in long explanatory discourses rather than in the simple parables of the other Gospels. Using the biblical number for perfection, John used seven miracles Jesus performed, seven names to identify who Jesus was, and seven "I am" statements that Jesus made about himself to emphasize the deity of Christ. John concentrated on Jesus' activities in Jerusalem rather than his ministry in Galilee; almost half of John's book is dedicated to the last week of Jesus' life and his sacrificial death and resurrection. The last nine chapters give us a glimpse of Jesus' intimate time alone with his disciples. These teachings about his mission, the Holy Spirit, and how to love one another are found only in the Gospel of John.

John wrote a "universal" gospel, emphasizing to all people everywhere the need for a relationship with Jesus in order to know God. Now as then, John's book speaks in a life-transforming way as he calls all people to faith in Jesus, the Son of God.

book 43

sun.

THE LAMB OF GOD

_____

_____

_____

_____

_____

_____

_____

_____

_____

_____

The main purpose of the Gospel of John is to present Jesus as God. Jesus was the "Word" who existed before time and came to earth as the sinless Lamb of God, an offering on our behalf. John was clear in teaching us how to respond to Jesus on a heart level.

JOHN 1:1-34; 3:1-21

• To both Jews and Greeks, the "Word" meant the Supreme Being ruling the universe: God. What do you learn about the "Word" in John 1:1-15?

• After reading John 3:1-21, where are you in the spiritual birthing process: still considering, newly born, growing and developing, or _____?

MORE SCRIPTURE

John 2:1-11—Jesus' first miracle, recorded only in John's Gospel

mon.

THE BREAD OF LIFE

_____

_____

_____

_____

_____

_____

_____

_____

_____

_____

Through spiritual rebirth, we enter into a new life with God. Centuries before, God provided manna (bread) for God's people in the wilderness (Exodus 16), requiring them to depend on God every day for their needs. Now Jesus, the Bread of Life, promises to sustain our relationship with him by providing everything we need to support this new spiritual life.

JOHN 6:25-69

• What hard teaching shook the faith of many of the disciples? What did they want from Jesus?

• When you hit hard spots in your faith, how are you likely to respond? Why?

MORE SCRIPTURE

John 10:1-21—Jesus describes himself as the Gate and the Good Shepherd

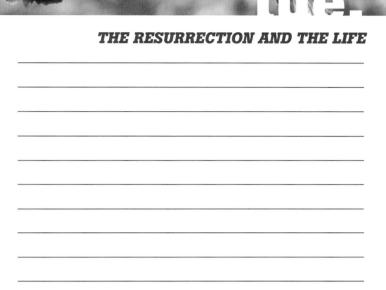

THE RESURRECTION AND THE LIFE

Beyond the circle of twelve disciples, Jesus was close to a family that lived in Bethany, a small town close to Jerusalem. Mary, her sister Martha, and her brother Lazarus provided a safe haven through their home and friendship for Jesus during his public ministry. Jesus used his relationship with them to demonstrate a powerful truth: Jesus makes his resurrection power available to his followers every day.

JOHN 11:1-53

• Why did the religious rulers plot to kill Jesus as a result of this incident?

• In what area of your life do you need Jesus' resurrection power to bring new life for you?

MORE SCRIPTURE

John 13:1-20—Jesus washed the disciples' feet

THE WAY, THE TRUTH AND THE LIFE

John 13–17 is known as the Upper Room Discourse. John includes us in an intimate time with Jesus and his disciples on the night before his death. Jesus gave specific teachings on community, prayer, and nurturing a vital relationship with him. He also introduced the Holy Spirit as the one who empowers us to live the new life found in him.

JOHN 14

• According to verses 21-31, how did Jesus demonstrate his love for the Father? How are Jesus' followers to demonstrate love for him?

• After reading verse 6, how would you respond to someone who asserts, "There are many ways to God"?

thurs.

THE VINE

_____

_____

_____

_____

_____

_____

_____

_____

_____

_____

Jesus calls his followers to a lifestyle far beyond what is possible through our human efforts. Rather than an outward conformity to a set of rules, God cares about our inner attitudes and an obedience that comes out of love. We are empowered by the Holy Spirit living within us and flowing through us to keep God's command to love one another.

JOHN 15:1–16:15

• According to John 16:7-15, what are the roles the Holy Spirit plays in the life of Jesus' followers?

• Fruit is produced only on living branches that are connected to (remain in) their life source, the vine. When is it most difficult for you to "remain in the vine"? Why?

MORE SCRIPTURE

John 17—Jesus' prayer for his disciples, including us

fri.

JESUS' CRUCIFIXION AND RESURRECTION

_____

_____

_____

_____

_____

_____

_____

_____

_____

_____

After Jesus' betrayal, desertion, and illegal trial, he was executed by the excruciatingly painful method of crucifixion. Jesus fulfilled all of his teachings about love through his willingness to sacrifice himself for everyone—those who hated him as well as those who loved him. Through his resurrection, the power of death has been broken forever, and those who follow him will live with him for eternity.

JOHN 19:1–20:18

• Why did Pilate not follow his conscience (19:4) and release Jesus?

• What part of this account holds the most meaning for you at this point in your life?

MORE SCRIPTURE

John 18–20—The full story of Jesus completing his mission

JESUS' POST-RESURRECTION APPEARANCES

Following his resurrection, Jesus made several appearances to his disciples, confirming their call to continue his mission. Because of Peter's betrayal, Jesus addressed him specifically. This chapter is the final piece of John's carefully constructed presentation of evidence supporting Jesus' claims to be the Son of God.

JOHN 20:19–21:25

• Consider Thomas' journey from doubt to faith. In what ways are you most likely to doubt God? What steps can you take to move to trusting God?

• In what ways did Jesus reassure Peter of his restoration and offer him his trust?

MORE SCRIPTURE
Luke 24:1-53—More of Jesus' post-resurrection appearances

notes
AND PRAYER NEEDS

transformations

Mud 'n Spit Miracles

Having said this, he spit on the ground, made some mud with the saliva, and put it on the man's eyes. "Go," [Jesus] told him, "Wash in the Pool of Siloam" (this word means "Sent"). So the man went and washed, and came home seeing. (John 9:6-7)

Have you ever wondered what it really takes to make a miracle happen? From our own limited perspectives, we imagine God with sparkling magic potions carefully arranged in a glittering heavenly toolbox. Maybe with a few wands thrown in for the really tough jobs.

God's best work, however, has always been done with amazingly ordinary stuff—water, mud, spit, a piece of stale bread, a barn, a teenage girl, twelve dysfunctional disciples. God uses ordinary objects in regular places with everyday people. The good news for every single Jesus-follower on the planet is that miracles happen when the Divine intersects with the ordinary.

Mud 'n spit. I'm fascinated with the Gospel of John, with the earthiness of everything Jesus did while he lived among us. If Jesus were walking on earth today, I don't know how he would heal the blind man in John 9. Perhaps instead of using mud and spit, he'd use some thick espresso or aromatic candle wax. On that particular day, however, Jesus spat in the dust, made a clay paste with his saliva, rubbed the paste onto the blind guy's eyes, then told the man to go wash in a pool. That's creativity. That's using what you have, where you have it, and with whom you have it—and that's the part I love! Stories like this give me hope that I can do it, too. I'm an everyday person. I've been touched by heaven, empowered by God. I can use the ordinary stuff that God has already put in me and around me to begin to change the world.

You and I are called to the business of mud 'n spit. Modern-day mud surfaces in the form of possessions and pieces we offer for kingdom use: homes to open for community and connection, cars to transport friends to places of provision, gardens to plant for beauty and restoration, and food to prepare for hungry souls.

Spit originates inside the human body, and our individual DNA is mapped out into every single drop of the stuff. To add spit to the dry earth is to infuse our unique personalities into the possessions we hold, to breathe life into everyday acts of kindness and grace. While Jesus could have used water from the well close by, he chose instead to use the saliva God had put inside of him.

God is all about empowering each one of us with the Holy Spirit, uniquely gifting us to be part of making miracles happen. We are everyday people using ordinary objects in regular places, creating powerful moments of transcendence. There are plenty of blind persons walking aimlessly on the earth who need God-encounters. Never underestimate the power of what can happen when the Divine Spark of heaven intersects with your ordinary earthly offerings. Someone is waiting to be touched by God, and no wands are needed. Miracles will occur right where you are, all because of a little mud 'n spit.

acts

the early church

book 4

Acts, a book packed with accounts of Jesus' apostles (disciples) acting out their call from Jesus following his resurrection, creates a bridge in the New Testament between the Gospels and the Epistles (the letters to the early churches). Acts provides the early church's historical background, making the letters of the apostles richer with meaning. Written by Luke, a Gentile physician and Paul's traveling companion, the book of Acts is considered the continuation of Luke's Gospel. While Luke was not an eyewitness to the events contained in his Gospel, he was definitely part of the happenings in Acts. It is believed that Luke wrote Acts sometime between AD 55-66.

The real story in Acts is about the presence and work of the Holy Spirit. In fact, some have suggested that this book should be called "The Acts of the Holy Spirit," rather than "The Acts of the Apostles." Acts faithfully reports the Spirit directing and empowering the apostles as they lived out their radical commitment to Jesus. While Acts also describes other early church leaders, the focus is chiefly on Peter and Paul. As the church grew, an important development took place: the new believers who were Gentiles (non-Jews) were included equally with those of Jewish background, and Peter and Paul were the primary leaders of the two parts of the church. Peter was the chief apostle to the Jews, and Paul was the chief apostle to the Gentiles.

Through a series of stories, sermons, and speeches, the book of Acts traces the development of the church from 120 praying people in a room in Jerusalem to a network of communities stretched along the Mediterranean Sea. During the thirty years it took for Christianity to spread from Jerusalem to Rome, the early church experienced many things:

- Jesus continued his activity on earth in and through his followers through the ministry of the Holy Spirit.
- Signs and wonders authenticated the ministry of the Holy Spirit.
- Persecution strengthened the church and spread the gospel to new lands through followers willing to lay their lives on the line for the truth.
- Discipleship communities developed, with unreserved commitment to each other and service to those outside the community.

Today the same Holy Spirit will fill and empower all who surrender themselves not to an intellectual belief system but to a life sold out to Jesus. Like the New Testament church, we must seek community with other followers of Jesus while we purposefully serve and reach others for Christ. There is no limit to the influence we as the church can have while Jesus, through the power of the Holy Spirit, continues his activity through us.

sun.

SPIRIT POWER

_____

_____

_____

_____

_____

_____

_____

_____

_____

_____

Jesus ascended into heaven and promised the power to carry on his mission to the followers he left behind. The power of the Holy Spirit transformed their lives and those of countless others. Peter turned from a fearful coward to a bold spokesperson for Jesus, and Jesus' followers became a vital, caring community that attracted people to him. The same Holy Spirit is available to those who follow Jesus today!

ACTS 1:1-8; 2:1-47

• What qualities characterize the first century community of Jesus followers? How did they go beyond doing religious activity to being the church?

• What part did God and the disciples each play in the witnessing of the disciples in Acts 2? How does this encourage you as you apply Jesus' commission in 1:8 to your own life situation?

mon.

IN JERUSALEM

_____

_____

_____

_____

_____

_____

_____

_____

_____

_____

Empowered by the Holy Spirit, the disciples were able to fulfill Jesus' promise in John 14:12: "All who have faith in me will do the works I have been doing, and they will do even greater things." No longer on the defensive before the Jewish leaders, they boldly proclaimed the only "name given under heaven by which we must be saved." Even when threatened, Peter and John could not stay quiet about Jesus.

ACTS 3–4

• From Peter's speech in 2:11-21, what is the purpose of signs and wonders like the healing in today's reading?

• Turning to God in repentance brings forgiveness and "times of refreshing" (3:19). How do you desire God to refresh your spirit?

IN JUDEA AND SAMARIA

Many times we question the unexplainable trials we face. But God uses these challenges to bring about God's plan for individuals and the world. Today's reading describes how God worked through persecution experienced by the early church to spread the word about Jesus. We are assured that God is in charge of the church (God's people) and will prevail over any force trying to destroy it (Matthew 16:18).

ACTS 7:59–8:3; 9:1-31

• Considering Paul's history, what was Ananias risking in being obedient to God's direction?

• Barnabas means "son of encouragement" (Acts 4:36), and he demonstrated this character quality with Paul in 9:26-28. To whom could (do) you serve as an encourager?

_____
_____
_____
_____
_____
_____
_____
_____
_____
_____

wed.

TO THE ENDS OF THE EARTH

The early church was birthed out of Judaism, which taught that God's people were to be a blessing to all people on earth but were to stay separate from foreign nations and the false gods those nations worshiped. No wonder the inclusion of Gentiles (non-Jews) in the New Covenant through Jesus caused difficult questions. Ministry to the Gentiles opened up the way to spread the good news of Jesus to the ends of the earth.

ACTS 10

• What difference did the connection between Peter and Cornelius make for them and for the church?

• What prejudices could you be holding onto?

MORE SCRIPTURE

Acts 15:1-35—The Council at Jerusalem approves and embraces ministry to the Gentiles (non-Jews)

_____
_____
_____
_____
_____
_____
_____
_____
_____
_____
_____

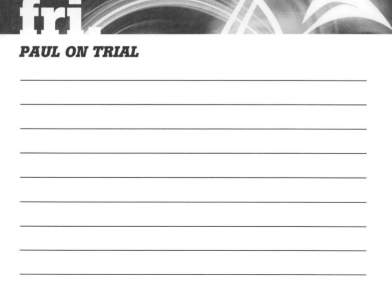

thurs.

PAUL ON MISSION

_____

_____

_____

_____

_____

_____

_____

_____

_____

_____

_____

_____

Paul, with a variety of traveling companions, went on three missionary journeys to spread the news of Jesus to the people living in the areas surrounding the Mediterranean Sea. The stories in Acts give examples of Paul's experiences among the Gentiles. Today's reading finds Paul in Philippi, a city in Macedonia, and emphasizes the influence family members have on each other.

ACTS 16:6-40

• Years later, Paul wrote to the Philippians from a jail in Rome. How does his message in Philippians 4:4-13 explain his behavior in today's story?

• Paul's negative experience ended up benefiting the jailer and his family. Describe a time when someone has benefited from your time of testing.

fri.

PAUL ON TRIAL

_____

_____

_____

_____

_____

_____

_____

_____

_____

_____

_____

Paul returned to Jerusalem after his third missionary journey, where the prophet Agabus predicted his arrest (21:10-11). Paul was soon defending himself before religious and government officials. As a Roman citizen, Paul had the right to have his case heard by the emperor or the emperor's representative in Rome. Paul addressed Festus, the Roman governor of Judea, and King Agrippa, the Roman-appointed Jewish ruler of northern Palestine, before he was sent to Rome.

ACTS 25:13–26:32

• Why was Paul was on trial (26:19-23)?

• An ox goad (26:14) was a sharp instrument used to move cattle. Jesus was telling Paul he was only hurting himself by resisting him. What are you resisting?

Paul's goal was to preach about Jesus in Rome. His arrival came at the expense of imprisonment, shipwreck, and many other challenges, but Paul never lost sight of his God-given purpose. Along the way he continued to teach, heal, and encourage others. He lived under house arrest in Rome while awaiting his trial, with freedom to teach, write, and influence others to follow Jesus.

ACTS 27–28

• List events from Acts that support the fact that God wanted Paul to get to Rome. How did God protect Paul?

• According to Romans 8:28, God can use challenges to bring about God's plan for our lives. How is God working to accomplish God's will in and through you?

notes

AND PRAYER NEEDS

Turn the page for this week's Transformations Reflection.

transformations

Texas Instrument

Let's say (just for fun) that right before Jesus left for heaven he gave the disciples a box of Texas Instrument calculators. Let's also say that all the disciples were speechless except Peter. So picking up a calculator, Peter looked over to Jesus and said, "Are you going to tell us what these are or just watch us poke at them?"

"They're calculators," Jesus said with a wry look.

"Is that a made-up word? Or are you being serious?" Peter lacked patience.

"They help you with math. So, for example, remember when we fed all those people on the mountain?"

"Yeah, there were like 5,000 families."

"Right. So how many people did we feed?" Jesus waited for a minute as Peter stared blankly. "That's where these calculators come into play. If each family had 3.2 members we multiply 5,000 by 3.2 for a grand total of 16,000." Jesus loved multiplication.

"That calculator just told you that?" Peter was dumbfounded. He asked Jesus to show him how the calculator worked. He pointed to the "divide" button and asked Jesus, "What's this one do?"

"We don't use that button. Actually, disciples, listen up. I need you all to take this button and remove it from your calculators. In our line of work, division is the devil."

Jesus hates division. Unfortunately, humans love it. We use everything from race, age, hobbies, and religion to divide ourselves into separate groups. We even divide our groups into cliques and our cliques into cronies. If Jesus could break the division button off or out of our brain, he would. That would solve a lot of problems, but it would also interfere with the whole "free will" thing.

Division is the devil. It's the opposite of what Jesus taught. Can you imagine what the early church would say about today's church? The early church was made up of thousands of people with "one heart and one soul." They were able to take on evil and spread the gospel with ONE united front. Today's church is divided into hundreds of denominations. We may share the same soul, but we're a divided front.

Can you picture what would happen if we stopped hitting the divide button? Can you imagine the power we'd have over evil if millions of Christians started marching together as ONE united front? It would look like the early church. Thousands came to know Christ on a daily basis.

It would take a monster calculator to figure out how many would come to know Christ if today's church undivided itself and became one united front. That kind of math would require one of those scientific calculators with lots of buttons. I call those calculators "something I never learned how to use." Because I agree with Jesus, division is the devil.

romans

the gospel explained

Having introduced the apostle Paul and some of his missionary journeys in the book of Acts, the New Testament now begins its journey into the letters of Paul with the letter to the believers in Rome. Paul's letter to the church at Rome is prestigiously placed first, and its placement is not because it was the earliest letter written but because it has no match in depth or scope in describing the gospel, or good news of Jesus Christ. In fact, Romans is probably one of the most profound letters ever written about God and humanity.

Paul wrote this letter around AD 58 from the city of Corinth. He was on his third missionary journey and had stopped in Corinth to correct and build up the church he had started in that city. Most of Paul's letters were written to churches that he had planted and were for correction, encouragement, or both. This letter to the church at Rome was written for very different reasons. Paul had never been to Rome and had not started that Christian community, but Paul had heard about them and their great faith.

Paul's initial reason for writing was to inform them of his plans to visit Rome and to request assistance from them for his missionary journey to Spain, in order to take the gospel of Christ there. He also took this opportunity, however, to give them in the same letter a complete and thorough understanding of the gospel message. Not knowing fully of their origin as a church, Paul wanted to make sure they were firm in their understanding of the Christian message.

In the first eight chapters Paul methodically yet profoundly lays out:

- the problem of humanity caused by sin and rebellion from God
- our need for salvation
- the solution through the death and sacrifice of Jesus Christ
- the cleansing and power that the Holy Spirit brings to our lives
- the truth that this salvation is freely given to those who have faith in God through Jesus Christ, enabling them to be called God's children and to become heirs to eternal life

It is from this great grace and mercy that the last few chapters of the letter to the Romans then turn sharply from spiritual issues to daily action. This turn takes place at Romans 12:1-2, which explains that, because of this great salvation and new life, we should live our lives for God. This is truly our loving response and our daily worship. The final chapters give specific instructions on how to live in the church, in the community, and in the world as people of witness, service, and love, sharing this same Jesus Christ to those around us.

book 45

OUR CONDITION OF NEED

_____

_____

_____

_____

_____

_____

_____

_____

_____

Paul spends the first part of his letter explaining the condition in which humanity finds itself because of sin and spiritual rebellion against God. Even though God can be easily seen in the wonderful creation of the world, we have all rejected God and live for our own selfish desires.

ROMANS 1:18-32; 3:9-20

• What are some of the ways God's "invisible qualities" (1:20) are clearly seen in creation and in the world around us?

• What are some of the areas of your life you continue to struggle to control? How can you better seek God's control on a daily basis?

mon.

THE REMEDY FOR OUR SIN

_____

_____

_____

_____

_____

_____

_____

_____

_____

_____

Because our need for forgiveness and reconciliation with God is so great, it takes a supernatural act to bring us back into a right relationship with God. Because we can never pay for this debt of sin we owe, Jesus came to pay the debt for us with his own blood and freely offers us a new life with God.

ROMANS 3:21-31; 5:1-11

• What was God's role in rescuing us from sin and death? According to Romans 10:9-13, what must we do to receive this great gift?

• Since God has demonstrated such a great love by dying for you, what can you do today to show God love in return?

tue.

THE OUTCOME OF CHRIST'S SACRIFICE

Because we have received such amazing grace to forgive our sins, we are free to live a life that is pleasing to God. But God doesn't leave it for us to do on our own. The Holy Spirit comes into our lives and gives us the power to live according to God's will and plan, and not to our own sinful nature. Because we have the Spirit, we also have new life and are now considered God's children and heirs to all God's promises.

ROMANS 6:8-23; 8:1-17

• Since we are now free from slavery to sin and have become God's own children, how are we to live on a daily basis? As heirs of God, what will we receive as our inheritance?

• How can knowing you are a child of God help you through your life's struggles this week?

wed.

THE BLESSINGS OF GOD'S GRACE

Our restored relationship with God brings fantastic blessing and promise. There is no situation that can separate us from God's working power and love. And even as we wait for God to restore us and this world back to glorious perfection, we continue living under God's magnificent protection and provision.

ROMANS 8:18-39

• List all the promises you find in this passage of Scripture. What is the most powerful one for your life right now?

• How will God's powerful protection and provision inspire you to be a witness? In what way can you be "more than a conqueror" for Christ?

239

RESPONSE: LOVING IN OUR COMMUNITY

_____
_____
_____
_____
_____
_____
_____
_____
_____

The way we show God our appreciation for God's grace is by daily offering our lives to God. By allowing God to transform our hearts and minds, we can then serve and truly love our sisters and brothers with whom we live. The transforming power of God in our lives will lead us to commit our lives to serving others.

ROMANS 12

• How are we to know and understand God's will? What practical ways are we to show God our great appreciation for God's mercy and grace?

• What is the gift you use to serve the body of Christ? How will you use it this week?

fri.

RESPONSE: LOVING IN OUR WORLD

_____
_____
_____
_____
_____
_____
_____
_____
_____

Another response to God's great mercy is to live with love and respect for the whole world. Paul compels us not only to be model citizens, obeying legitimate law and government, but also to shine like light in this dark world and become agents of love to all our neighbors.

ROMANS 13

• What are the reasons for submitting to governing authorities?

• How can your godly life be a light of hope shining in this dark world? How will you show love for the people you encounter today?

Our final obligation is to look out for those whose faith is not strong. Paul addresses certain cultural practices of his day as well as timeless truths and advice for all followers of Jesus. Our actions should never be centered only on the freedom our faith in Christ gives us but also on how we can build up our brothers and sisters in their faith.

ROMANS 14:1–15:6

• How does Paul want us to treat those whose faith is weaker than ours? How are we to build up their faith?

• What actions can you take to make sure that Christian sisters and brothers around you are encouraged and built up? What steps of peace and mutual support do you need to take to ensure this?

RESPONSE: LOVING THE WEAK

notes
AND PRAYER NEEDS

transformations

Fly High

The morning was incredibly hot, and perspiration was already dotting my face. Driving down the highway in my SUV with four friends, I could think only of the impending ordeal that soon would split my life into two parts: before and after. At 3 p.m. my date with destiny would be manifest from the altitude of 10,000 feet over the Greene County skies. This height-challenged mother of three would jump from a plane.

I'm not crazy about risk-taking adventure stunts, and I'd never seriously considered jumping from a plane. Most days I'd discouraged my kids from climbing to the top of the jungle gym. Nothing great can happen if one constantly chooses the easy road, however, so on this hot July day my mind gave my body a larger-than-life "to-do" list that included a skydive. It was my divine appointment.

This resurrection life you received from God is not a timid, grave-tending life. It's adventurously expectant, greeting God with a childlike, "What's next, Papa?" God's Spirit touches our spirits and confirms who we really are.

Arriving at the airstrip, I signed a lot of papers, waiving my right to sue should anything go wrong. (Like I'd be around to sue them, should the inevitable occur.) I watched a training video and then got a ten-minute discourse from my assigned tandem-master. I remember praying that he'd not been out drinking the night before.

We climbed into the plane and crammed ourselves in like sardines in a hot metal can. Ascending slowly up the 10,000 feet, my heart raced ahead. This could be it. *I wish I'd told my kids where I was going. Why hadn't I said one more "I love you" to my husband? When was the last time I'd thanked my mom for hanging in there all those years?*

Intentionally willing myself out of the plane was the hardest thing I've ever done, but, once out, there was certainly no turning back. Nothing to do but try to catch my breath and wait for the chute to open. Once I caught sight of that lovely parachute opened out like a proud peacock, I could finally enjoy the next ten minutes of tranquility. The second half of my life began as I discovered an amazing new perspective from high above the earth, practicing my newfound ability to fly. Soaring high, I felt the crisp air around me, the heart beating in my chest, and the sure confidence that my feet would eventually touch down. I simply relaxed and enjoyed the ride.

I'm absolutely convinced that nothing—nothing living or dead, today or tomorrow, high or low, thinkable or unthinkable—absolutely nothing can get between us and God's love because of the way that Jesus our Master has embraced us.

Paul's letter to the Romans powerfully describes the split moment in history when the possibilities for human life changed forever. Once Jesus died and was resurrected, our human existence took on an entirely new perspective. We were set free to fly. No matter what altitude life's circumstances take us to, the air of God's Spirit is crisp, the heart of God's power beats strong, and the confidence that we will live with God forever whispers that it's okay to relax and enjoy the ride.

first corinthians

how to live out the faith

The apostle Paul, early missionary of Christianity, traveled widely during his lifetime and planted a number of churches throughout the known world. One was a gathering of believers in the thriving commercial center of Corinth. Corinth, strategically located on a major trade route for both land and sea, was one of the largest and most diverse cities in the Roman world. Greeks, Romans, Jews, and sailors of many different backgrounds all congregated in Corinth to take advantage of its bustling business atmosphere and its smorgasbord of religious and cultural practices.

During the lifetime of Paul, Corinth featured more than twelve temples offering diverse worship opportunities. Most were for Greek god or goddess worship, the largest being the temple of Aphrodite (goddess of love). On the other end of the spectrum, Corinth also had a Jewish synagogue. Even with, and perhaps because of, this broad range of religious practices, Corinth was known for its widespread immorality.

It was within this milieu that the Christian church of Corinth was birthed. On his second missionary journey, Paul spent eighteen months in Corinth, working to establish the community of believers. A few years later, he received word that this young church was struggling. Many new converts were struggling to adjust. The church had developed factions, causing disagreements on practical matters of Christian living. They even lacked a unified understanding of the resurrection of Jesus. Paul wrote the young church the letter we now call 1 Corinthians to instruct and clarify these issues as well as to encourage them in their spiritual growth. Later, Paul wrote them another letter (2 Corinthians), which we'll study next week.

First Corinthians is a heartfelt attempt to show the relevance of Jesus Christ and his lordship to every area of our lives. Paul addressed his concerns about the divisions in the Corinthian church. He also made strong statements about their struggles with sexual immorality and explained God's expectations for living pure lives. Paul provided practical advice on orderly church procedures and on relationships between believers as well as with unbelievers. Of special note is Paul's explicit and detailed description of Christians together composing the "body of Christ," with each one of us having special and unique spiritual gifts to contribute to God's work. Another memorable section of this letter is found in chapter 13, a powerful description of Christ-like love. According to Paul, God's love in and through us can only be truly reflected through our actions.

Though the context of 1 Corinthians is specific to the culture of Corinth at that time, Paul's writing offers timeless truths for all who long to experience transformation in Jesus. As it did for the Corinthian Christians so long ago, may Paul's letter speak God's truth into your heart and life.

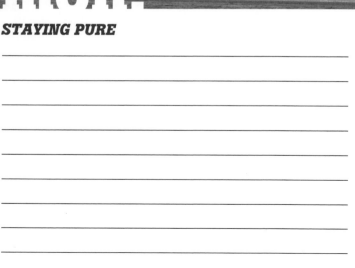

sun.

GOD USES THE WEAK

_____

_____

_____

_____

_____

_____

_____

_____

_____

Paul began his letter to the Corinthian church with an encouraging word for their faith. He then began to deal with the issues he'd heard had become conflicts among them. Paul's deepest desire was for the Corinthian believers to hold primary allegiance to Jesus, not to any human spiritual leader. He emphasized that true wisdom only comes from God, who often uses the weakest and most foolish among us for the greatest purposes.

1 CORINTHIANS 1–2

• According to 2:11-14, why can some people understand God's truth, and to others it makes no sense at all?

• Have you ever felt unworthy or unqualified to be used for God's purposes? From 1:26–2:5, what encouragement do you receive regarding God's intentions for you?

mon.

STAYING PURE

_____

_____

_____

_____

_____

_____

_____

_____

_____

Paul reminded the believers of the solid spiritual foundation he had laid during the time he spent in Corinth. He urgently reminded them that together they formed God's temple (church) and that God's Spirit resided in them. For that reason, it was essential that they work toward purity, faith, and godliness—and that they hold every believer within their fellowship accountable to these standards.

1 CORINTHIANS 3; 5

• What was Paul saying through his example of the yeast and the dough? The bread without yeast?

• Where are you in your spiritual progress?

MORE SCRIPTURE

1 Corinthians 4—Paul describes his servant leader relationship with the Corinthian church

HONORING OTHERS

Paul envisioned the Corinthian church as a close community of believers, bound by the love of Christ, who therefore should be able to resolve any disputes among themselves. Further, he reminded them of God's moral standards both in marriage and in singleness. Paul saw the resolution of the Corinthian church's conflicts and their adherence to relational purity as necessary in order for them to mature and grow in faith.

1 CORINTHIANS 6–7

• Why did Paul say that sexual immorality is a sin? What key points did Paul make about marriage? Singleness?

• Paul advocated finding contentment in every circumstance. Are you content in your current life situation? What could be holding you back?

wed.

RUNNING TO WIN

Paul urged the Corinthian Christians to influence one another through good example rather than cause each other to stumble spiritually. His advice encouraged believers to respect each other's spiritual backgrounds and to do nothing that would offer a relational or spiritual distraction to others. Paul used his own life as an example of how to win all persons to Christ.

1 CORINTHIANS 8–9

• What principle did Paul teach in 9:19-23 about the power of our example to others?

• Reread 9:24-27. What prize did Paul refer to? How can you improve in the race he described?

HONORING THE FAITH

_____
_____
_____
_____
_____
_____
_____
_____
_____

Paul longed for the believers in Corinth to honor God in every way, including in the traditions they practiced. Due to some confusion between Jewish and Greek customs about head coverings, Paul attempted to clarify cultural practices that honored godly intention. He also wrote stern instructions about the powerful Christian practice of sharing the Lord's Supper.

1 CORINTHIANS 10–11

• In 10:13, what encouragement did Paul give about our times of temptation?

• "So whether you eat or drink or whatever you do, do it all for the glory of God" (10:31). Through what practical part of your life can you choose to honor God today?

MORE SCRIPTURE

Numbers 14—Israel's history in the desert

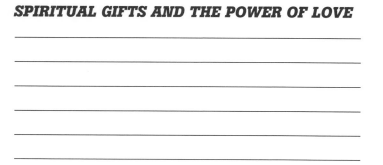

fri.

SPIRITUAL GIFTS AND THE POWER OF LOVE

_____
_____
_____
_____
_____
_____
_____
_____
_____
_____

Paul wanted the Corinthian church to value and appreciate each believer's unique contribution to God's work. His description of spiritual gifts underscores the importance of teamwork within the Christian community. He followed his emphasis on how everyone's spiritual gifts work together with a timeless, beautiful description of the one gift from God we are all called to live out.

1 CORINTHIANS 12–13

• What is clear about the value of each individual believer in the body of Christ? What responsibility is every believer expected to carry out?

• From chapter 13, which truth about Jesus' love do you need to receive fully? To model to others?

ORDER AND TRUTH AMONG BELIEVERS

Paul hoped to help the Corinthian church's gatherings become orderly and effective. His instructions emphasized the need to honor God and one another (as well as new believers) by making sure everything at every meeting was understandable to all. He also clarified the truth of Christ's resurrection.

1 CORINTHIANS 14–15

• "God is not a God of disorder but of peace" (14:33). What key instructions did Paul give for making sure the Corinthian church's gatherings were orderly?

• What does today's reading teach about the resurrection of Christ? In what ways is the truth of Christ's resurrection essential to your faith?

MORE SCRIPTURE

1 Corinthians 16—Paul's personal requests and updates

notes
AND PRAYER NEEDS

transformations

Selling Crazy

Cole and his buddies jump in their refurbished RV and leave the city for their long-awaited entrepreneurial adventure. The young biologists figured out a way to harness the energy that green plants produce via chlorophyll's absorption of sunlight (photosynthesis). Once this energy is "harvested," a fuel-alternative they call Photosyntha-Fuel can be produced. Unfortunately, the small supply of fuel used to power their Airstream is running out. It's time for mass production.

Mass production requires a mass supply of green plants. That's why Cole and the gang are leaving behind their day jobs to find a community of farmers willing to devote their crops to Photosyntha-Fuel. After weeks of research, Cole chose a town of about three thousand people called Shawton.

Cole parks the RV in the center of Shawton and tells his friends to set up the headquarters (an eighth grade science fair project on steroids). As the four biologists hang poster board, Cole walks across the street to the Shawton Diner.

"I'm new to town," Cole announces to three people eating eggs and breakfast meats. Nobody answers. Cole digs into his pockets for the mini-brochures he made explaining his business. "Are any of you guys farmers?"

All three nod. "John thinks he is, but his fields say otherwise." The two laugh at poor John.

"I was hoping I could talk to you about the future of fuel as we know it." Cole gives a two-minute explanation (not a sales pitch) to the farmers. As he finishes, he steps back from the table expecting to be immediately taken to their fields.

Long silence except for sounds of chewing fills the diner.

"Sorry, friend. We're not buying crazy today." All three laugh, even John. Cole turns to walk out of the diner. Pushing the door open, he looks back and tells the amused farmers he'll see them tomorrow.

I would guess (since I wasn't actually there) that the apostle Paul ran into his fair share of "amused farmers" on his missionary trip to Corinth. He left his day job to convince a community of unbelievers to join him in harvesting the power offered through Christ. He went door to door, showed up at board meetings, wrote letters, maybe even waltzed into diners to get Corinth to see that Christianity was the future.

Presenting Christianity is hard work. It's illogical, it's risky, and it requires people to change their way of life. Paul was as "crazy" as Cole to ask a community of people to buy into something so unfounded.

Sometimes I feel like I'm selling crazy. I have one friend who has shot down every persuasive explanation I've given. I have an uncle who can explain the faults of Christianity better than I can explain the strengths. Sometimes I feel like I'm hanging shoddy poster board for a broken down science fair when I try to "show Christ" to my friends.

I learned a little something about science fairs as I read 1 Corinthians. Getting folks to buy into Christianity takes time. Paul spent eighteen months in Corinth. He didn't walk into the first diner he saw and convince the whole town to follow Christ. He set up camp and told his naysayers and the amused farmers that he'd see them tomorrow, and the next day and the next.

I need to set up camp within my friends and family and not quit, even though it may take years. I must trust God that one day, perhaps in a quiet diner over eggs and breakfast meats, they'll finally seek what Jesus is offering.

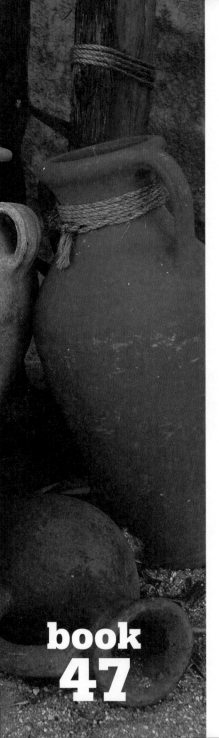

second corinthians

a call to refocus

Paul left a foundational spiritual legacy across the known world of Jesus' time through his passionate preaching and teaching. His instructional, inspiring letters still inform and teach believers today about God's intentions for the church. Paul spent much of his adult life traveling on extended missionary journeys in order to plant communities of Christian believers in key cities. One of his best-known efforts was in the city of Corinth, a well-known center of commerce and culture. The new Corinthian Christians he gathered together as a church came from a variety of backgrounds. After Paul left them to continue his missionary efforts elsewhere, the new believers in Corinth faced ongoing challenges and struggles as a result of their previous diverse spiritual beliefs.

Paul wrote letters to the Corinthian Christians, attempting to address their internal issues. The first, known now as 1 Corinthians, was a challenge to keep Jesus as Lord and to stay focused upon relational purity and orderly worship. Scholars believe Paul also paid the Corinthian church a second visit to attempt to address their continuing issues in person and wrote them a severe letter of reprimand for their contentious behavior (in a letter not preserved). Titus, a missionary colleague of Paul's, visited the Corinthian church afterwards and brought Paul a positive report about the resolution of most of their issues. Happy with this news, Paul wrote the Corinthian Christians one more letter, known as 2 Corinthians, with additional encouragement and instruction.

As do all letters to the early Christian churches, 2 Corinthians addresses specific situations and needs. This is truly a relational letter, full of emotion and advice rather than an orderly and systematic theological defense. The letter's underlying theme is a call to be loyal to Jesus Christ alone, not to any human leader. Having faced criticism by some of the false teachers who had infiltrated the Corinthian church, Paul defended his authority and credibility and also explained his updated plans to make a third visit.

Second Corinthians contains the longest segment in the entire New Testament on God's plan for financial giving. Chapters 8–9 explain what a Christian's practice of giving is to look like. Paul encouraged the believers to demonstrate generosity by resuming the fund drive they had begun the previous year on behalf of poorer Christians in need in Jerusalem. In addition to the theme of financial generosity, this book includes guidance about our call to the "ministry of reconciliation" (reuniting others with God by introducing them to Jesus), what it means to face spiritual warfare, and also the miraculous truth about our weaknesses providing a channel for God's strength to prevail. As it was for the Corinthian believers, may this letter from Paul be a powerful tool for God to use in your spiritual growth.

book 47

sun.

THE COMFORT OF GOD

_____
_____
_____
_____
_____
_____
_____
_____
_____
_____

Paul opened this letter to the Corinthians with a reminder of God's comfort and supernatural power in our lives. Paul's effort to explain the change in his plans to visit them was intended to verify his credibility in ministry and the trustworthiness of his word. Paul longed for the Corinthian Christians to understand and appreciate the triumphant, grace-filled nature of faith in Jesus.

2 CORINTHIANS 1–2

• According to Paul, what is the byproduct of God's comfort to us in times of troubles?

• Paul calls Christians to bring others the "aroma of Christ," which he also described as the "aroma that brings life." To whom can you bring this aroma?

mon.

JARS OF CLAY

_____
_____
_____
_____
_____
_____
_____
_____
_____
_____

In biblical times, people kept valuables in plain clay jars so as not to attract the attention of potential thieves. Paul used the metaphor of clay jars to describe our earthly physical bodies that contain the supernatural life of Jesus. Though our human bodies will not last forever, our life in Christ will span eternity with God. For followers of Jesus, physical health may deteriorate, but spiritual health can always be renewed.

2 CORINTHIANS 3–4

• What did Paul mean by a "letter...written on [human] hearts" (3:1-3)?

• Reread 4:16-18. What "light and momentary troubles" has God used to help you grow and mature in your faith? What encouragement do you find in today's Scripture reading?

"Ministry of reconciliation" describes a crucial, mandatory responsibility of all Christians. If we have received reconciliation with God through the good news of Jesus and have become "new creations in Christ," we have also become ambassadors of this message to others. Our human lives become instruments of a powerful, supernatural message, intended to bring all persons into transforming relationship with God through Christ.

2 CORINTHIANS 5:1–6:2

• What specifically did Paul say was the "message of reconciliation" that believers are to share?

• Verses 5:7-10 remind us that we will be held accountable for our actions on Christ's behalf. Of what would you be confident when standing before God? What would God want you to improve?

The life of a Jesus-follower is often filled with hardships, yet even in difficult circumstances we are called to demonstrate faithfulness. Believers must join together for mutual support and encouragement and must stay away from those who distract or have destructive intent. In today's reading, Paul referred to a confrontational letter he had written to the Corinthian church during a time they had allowed false teachers to infiltrate their leadership.

2 CORINTHIANS 6:3–7:16

• In 6:3-10, what faithful attributes did Paul call us to demonstrate in the midst of hardships?

• Have you yoked (closely connected) yourself mostly with believers, or unbelievers? How have those around you influenced you, and how have you influenced them?

CALL TO GENEROSITY

_____
_____
_____
_____
_____
_____
_____
_____
_____

Second Corinthians offers the most extensive explanation of God's plans for generous giving in the entire New Testament. In 8:5-7, Paul pointed out how necessary it is for believers to give ourselves first to the Lord. Only then is the supernatural grace of giving possible through us. Over and over, Paul confirmed that generous giving is possible because of God's generous gift of grace to us (9:8).

2 CORINTHIANS 8–9

• What does 8:12 teach about God's view of the amount we are capable of giving?

• Make a list of the principles about giving in these two chapters. Which of these are you already demonstrating? Which do you most need to implement?

SPIRITUAL WARFARE

_____
_____
_____
_____
_____
_____
_____
_____
_____

Following Jesus includes faithfulness in our thought life. Paul pointed out that God's power is strong enough to defeat arguments and thoughts that are against the truth of Christ. False teachers had challenged Paul's credibility among the Corinthian Christians, so Paul included in this part of his letter a defense of his own credentials and a clarification of his reputation of servant leadership.

1 CORINTHIANS 10–11

• What kind of "boasting" did Paul say was appropriate?

• In 11:14-15, Paul revealed a shocking truth about the deceptiveness of Satan, the prince of darkness, and those who do not truly serve Jesus as Lord. What do you need to do to stay spiritually alert to these tricks?

STRENGTH THROUGH WEAKNESS

The false teachers who tried to take over the church in Corinth in Paul's absence claimed to have gotten their "truths" from visions and revelations. Paul countered their claim by describing a real vision God had given him years before. With that vision, however, God also gave Paul a revelation about the spiritual purpose of afflictions and weaknesses.

2 CORINTHIANS 12–13

• According to 12:7-10, what was God's explanation for refusing to remove Paul's affliction? What was Paul's response?

• What "thorn in the flesh" do you have that God has not removed? What attitude do you think God desires you to have regarding this? Write a prayer, asking God for help, guidance, and the power to receive God's outcome from this situation.

notes

AND PRAYER NEEDS

Turn the page for this week's Transformations Reflection.

transformations

More Than Enough

Financially speaking, I used to be as tight as spandex on a hippopotamus.

Some people still think I'm tight, but that's just because they only see the surface. I have never spent much money on myself in the past, and I still don't. When I was younger, I didn't like to pay extra just to show off a certain clothing label. I still don't. I didn't like to pay a lot for something that would be worth very little in a short time. I still don't. And I also didn't like giving money to people as an act of charity. That, however, has changed.

What transformed my perspective about generosity toward others? A few chapters from Paul's writings to the Corinthians kicked me into an entirely new mindset. It had never before crossed my mind that in my quest to give myself entirely to God, the entirety of what I have is also included: all my possessions and all my money. If I belong totally to God, then so does all of that. And it's my responsibility, through the supernatural grace given to me, to live out God's spirit of generous grace to others via the tangible means of sharing what I have. It's as simple—and as challenging—as that.

As I've matured in my faith, I've come to realize that the human family is united in God's creation. We are all interconnected. Yet the members of our worldwide family live so differently. Some of us cannot afford shelter, and others own vehicles that are worth more than a house. Some of us cannot afford basic medical care, and others pay people to paint our toenails. Some of us cannot afford to eat every day, and others eat so much that our health is negatively affected. Some of us cannot buy enough necessities, and others cannot buy enough toys. As a believer, I've grown to be embarrassed and ashamed by these contrasts, especially when I know that everything I have belongs to God and that I have much more than enough.

Giving generously to others through self-denial is not a very popular activity. To be honest, I don't deny myself some luxuries, let alone the necessities of life. But I've made a conscious decision to live below my means, which allows me to help others live above their means. If I am blessed financially, then it is my responsibility to help those who need assistance. No, I can't help everyone. But yes, I can help someone. I pray for the strength to loosen my grip on what I think I need to be happy, in order to live generously toward others and cling only to God.

galatians

freedom in Christ

The apostle Paul planted a number of churches in the province of Galatia. These groups of new believers were spread among a number of cities in the part of the world now known as Turkey. The Christian converts came from both Jewish and Gentile (non-Jewish) backgrounds, but in Christ all believers shared eternal life and spiritual freedom. No matter what their individual religious backgrounds had been, all were now "one" in Christ Jesus.

Paul visited the Galatian churches, bringing them further teaching and encouragement. But despite his work to stay connected with them, Paul received word that false teachers were distracting them from the authentic gospel of Christ. Concerned, Paul wrote what some scholars believe was the first of all his letters now included in the New Testament, the one we today know as the Letter to the Galatians. Galatians was written to a group of churches rather than to a specific congregation, which is also what probably happened with letters to the churches in Ephesus and Colossae.

The false teachers had convinced the Galatians that in addition to accepting Christ, they must also obey the entire Old Testament Jewish law, including circumcision, in order to be fully Christian. Paul's primary purpose in writing this letter was to challenge this misunderstanding and to reiterate that the sole requirement to be a Christian is to place faith in Jesus alone. Paul reminded the Galatians of his own Jewish background and his relationship with James, John, Peter, and other early church leaders who were also Jewish. Paul understood and had followed Jewish customs, but God had revealed that they were not necessary for followers of Christ. Paul emphasized what he had originally taught the Galatians at their conversion: Jesus had introduced a new, freeing pathway to God—a relationship that is available to everyone, Jews and Gentiles alike.

With the liberty that comes with new life in Christ, however, comes the responsibility to love and serve others. The final segment of this letter is a strong reminder of what type of behavior pleases God. Paul first recorded the concept of "fruit of the Spirit" in the letter to the Galatians, describing the positive attributes that develop in our lives as a result of consistently obeying God through the power of the Holy Spirit.

Some have compared Paul's letter to the Galatians to his letter to the Romans, since both deal with similar subject matter summed up in the statement, "the righteous shall live by faith"—rather than by works. Throughout his entire missionary career, Paul was tireless in his quest to bring this truly liberating message of Jesus to all people. Freed from the burden of trying to please God by living up to the Law, we can, through Christ, enjoy forgiveness, relationship, and connection with God for all time.

book
48

sun.

CALLED BY GOD

_____

_____

_____

_____

_____

_____

_____

_____

_____

_____

Paul began his letter to the Galatians by making sure they understood he had been called and sent by God, not by humans, as a missionary of the gospel. He felt it was urgent to clarify with them the God-given message of the gospel, not the legalistic version the Galatian church was practicing. Paul gave his testimony, using the dramatic evidence of the authenticity of his conversion to Christ.

GALATIANS 1

• Describe Paul's life before he chose to follow Christ. What did he do after God revealed Christ to him? How did the churches in Judea react to the changes in him?

• Think of your own life before you met Christ. How has your life changed now that you know about the good news of new life through Jesus?

mon.

STANDING UP FOR WHAT IS RIGHT

_____

_____

_____

_____

_____

_____

_____

_____

_____

_____

Paul told the Galatian believers about his challenge of other key leaders of the Christian church concerning their doctrine (a position on or belief about) of the gospel. When Paul noticed the apostle Peter being drawn back to observing the rules of the Jewish faith, he reminded Peter of the freedom we have in Christ. We are brought into relationship with God through faith in Jesus, not by practicing laws.

GALATIANS 2

• According to verse 16, by what are we justified (brought into relationship) with Christ?

• The word "free" is repeated eleven times in this letter. How "free" do you feel to live into your full potential in God? What is holding you back?

Paul urged the Galatian Christians to remember that all humans, both Jews and Gentiles (non-Jews) are descendents of Abraham. Abraham's relationship with God was based on faith alone. Though the Law showed God's people God's priorities and guided them toward godly lifestyles through hundreds of years, it also revealed how insufficient we are as humans to live up to God's perfection. Faith in Christ alone is the path to relationship with God.

GALATIANS 3:1-25

• Paul referred to the Holy Spirit in Galatians 3:1-5 as our resource for living in obedience to God. What did he mean?

• The Galatians wrongly judged some of their fellow believers by whether they obeyed rules and rituals. What struggles with judging others do you have?

Paul used an Old Testament story to illustrate to the Galatian believers the freedom from the Law we have through Christ. He challenged them to understand that the false teachers they had listened to were leading them back into spiritual slavery.

GALATIANS 3:26–4:31; GENESIS 21:1-21

• Paul used the story of Abraham's two sons (one born of a free woman, one born of a slave woman) as an allegory to show how living by freedom and grace is the path to life eternal. Why were the Galatians tempted to enslave themselves once more?

• Galatians 4:6-7 brings the good news that we are children of God, heirs of God's kingdom. What empowerment does this truth provide you?

thurs.

CALLED TO BE FREE

_____

_____

_____

_____

_____

_____

_____

_____

_____

_____

_____

Sometimes believers become distracted from true freedom. Paul encouraged Christians to remember that freedom in Christ is for the purpose of offering love and kindness to others.

GALATIANS 5:1-15; 1 CORINTHIANS 5:6-8

• How would you explain Galatians 5:6, "The only thing that counts is faith expressing itself through love"?

• What "yeast" (sin) do you need to keep out of the "batch of dough" that represents you? What steps can you take to cultivate sincerity and truth?

MORE SCRIPTURE

Leviticus 19:16-18—Old Testament Law on treatment of our neighbors

Matthew 23:34-40—Jesus on loving our neighbors

fri.

IN STEP WITH THE SPIRIT

_____

_____

_____

_____

_____

_____

_____

_____

_____

_____

Today's Scripture describes what happens when believers live in the power of the Holy Spirit. Paul identified a variety of byproducts of this kind of faithful, Spirit-led lifestyle, which he named "fruit of the Spirit." Jesus called himself the vine, with all his followers as the branches. According to Jesus, his greatest desire is for us to bear this "fruit" in his name.

GALATIANS 5:16-25; JOHN 15:1-8

• What "fruit" do we bear when we choose sinful behavior? When we listen and are obedient to God?

• What steps can you take today to stay connected to Jesus through everything that happens? Write a prayer, asking God for the Spirit's wisdom and guidance.

Galatians closes with pastoral advice. Even though most of the letter was about setting the Galatians right in their understanding of the gospel message, Paul's final words were about living out the love of Jesus every day toward others. Jesus himself gave his followers similar instructions, extending their responsibility even to those who were enemies.

GALATIANS 6; MATTHEW 5:38-48

• Reread Galatians 6:7-10. For how long are we to continue to do good? What will eventually be the result?

• List each instruction Paul gave for the treatment of others, and each that Jesus gave. Which do you need to apply right away? Which is most difficult for you?

DOING GOOD TO ALL PEOPLE

notes
AND PRAYER NEEDS

Turn the page for this week's Transformations Reflection.

*t*ransformations

Freedom

Grabbing his shoulder bag as he heads out the door for another chore-filled day in the trenches, Scott wishes he were living someone else's life. He knows it's impossible, so he rests in the memories of simpler times—times when his biggest worry was making sure he ran home as quickly as he could when his mother yelled, "Scotty, dinner is ready!" Those were the good days. Dinner was simply the event marking the transition from daytime fun to a night of catching lightning bugs and campouts behind the house.

Somewhere along life's road, the simple boyhood he cherished had transformed into the bleak existence called adulthood. School days shifted to work days. Playtime shifted to overtime. How did all the important things in life, like friendship and fun, disappear? "Isn't there more to life than this?" he asks himself while driving to work. "I'm a good man. I work hard. I try to do all the right things. So, why do I feel so numb?"

As Scott walks through his office door, he reaches for a book on the corner of his desk. Flipping through the pages, Scott thinks about the time he has spent in this book. He can remember the day he received it. His aunt gave it to him when he started his graduate studies. Life was simpler then, as well. He was busy but seemed to have the energy to tackle just about anything. He was young, ambitious, and ready to save the world.

A lot of life has happened since then. Lost loved ones, a mortgage that doesn't get any smaller, and marriage troubles have drained the joy that once filled his eyes. Now, his eyes are tired and worn from sleepless nights bearing the weight of the world around him. Everything Scott does at work *and* at home feels monotonous, even pointless.

Scott stops flipping through his book. His exhausted eyes catch the heading of the next section on the page in front of him. Freedom in Christ. He reads on. "It is for freedom that Christ has set us free. Stand firm, then, and do not let yourselves be burdened again by a yoke of slavery…The only thing that counts is faith expressing itself through love" (Galatians 5:1, 6). Scott absorbs the idea, and tears gather in his eyes as he realizes his mistake. He remembers Christ has called him to love others. All his religious and life practices are worth nothing without love.

The phone across his desk wakes him to the moment. "Hello, this is Pastor Scott, how can I help you?" On the other end of the line, Emma, one of the saints of Scott's church who recently lost her husband, is calling to talk. A brief pause and deep breath later, Scott welcomes Emma into his day and smiles as he feels the joy of loving someone slowly spread across his face.

ephesians

the faithful in Christ

book 49

After Paul's dramatic confrontation with the resurrected Jesus on the road to Damascus, he became one of the most passionate proponents of Christianity. Traveling from community to community, he ushered thousands of people into a relationship with Christ and organized those converts into churches. Priscilla and Aquila were in Ephesus with a young church (Romans 16:3-5; 1 Corinthians 16:19) when Paul arrived, probably around AD 54-57. Ephesus was a beautiful city and the religious center of Asia Minor. The centerpiece of town was the temple of the goddess Artemis. The local economy was based on the sale of silver charms and images honoring Artemis. After investing three years of ministry in Ephesus, Paul's preaching began to threaten the city's profits. The local guild of silversmiths fueled an angry mob, and the resulting riot sent Paul on to other cities.

Paul's passion for Christ kept him frequently at odds with religious and government leaders. He spent significant amounts of time in prison, often unable to return in person to young churches to encourage them. This letter to the Ephesian believers, traditionally believed to have been written by Paul, is one of the most profound sources of truth about Christ and Christ's church. It was directed to "the faithful in Christ Jesus" in Ephesus and was written against the backdrop of their environment: the highly developed, institutionalized religious system based in the temple of Artemis.

Ephesians has a distinct message for those who know Jesus:

- The church of Jesus Christ is not an institution but a living organism made up of all followers of Jesus and inhabited by the Holy Spirit. Together these followers are one body, one family, fellow citizens, a holy temple, the "ecclesia" who are "called out" to be different from the world. Through relationships within the community of believers, each individual and the community as a whole are formed into the fullness of what God originally had in mind for God's people.

- Those who follow Jesus have a new identity in Christ. Forgiven and accepted through God's grace (undeserved, unconditional love), each one has been intentionally planned, even before Creation, to be God's child. Through Jesus the Son we are offered forgiveness, restoration, wisdom, and understanding. The Holy Spirit, living within each follower, provides the guarantee of God's ongoing presence with us and the hope of God's promising future.

- To truly "be" the church, Jesus' followers must adopt an attitude of submission to one another. Mutual submission comes through the humility that considers others first and does not compete or demand its own way.

This week, hear Paul's challenge for all believers to follow Jesus passionately and be the church to each other, using God's strength, power, and grace that already are at work within us.

sun.

OUR SPIRITUAL BLESSINGS

_____

_____

_____

_____

_____

_____

_____

_____

_____

_____

The opening words are filled with celebration of all the lavish benefits of knowing God through Jesus Christ. Ephesians 1:3-14 is all one sentence in the original Greek—a long litany of praise. How amazing it is that Paul could have written such jubilant words from the difficult prison setting in which he found himself! Paul's hope was to remind the Ephesian church that the spiritual benefits of knowing Christ were more than adequate for all they needed.

EPHESIANS 1:1-14

• Make a list of each spiritual blessing Paul described. What do you notice about the order in which he named them?

• Which of these spiritual blessings do you most need to embrace and take advantage of? Why?

mon.

HOW TO PRAY

_____

_____

_____

_____

_____

_____

_____

_____

_____

_____

Paul outlined for the believers in Ephesus what his prayers for them had been. By naming exactly what he had prayed for, he sought to help them understand more about the spiritual maturity into which God desired them to grow.

EPHESIANS 1:15-23

• In Ephesians 1:18-21, Paul talked about an extraordinary power God makes available to and through us as believers. According to Paul, in what other situation did God also demonstrate this same power?

• The prayer requests Paul offered for the Ephesians are excellent prayers for us to offer on behalf of others. For whom can you pray today?

THE MIRACLE OF THE CHURCH

The letter to the Ephesians clearly reiterates the powerful message of the gospel: we are "saved," or made new in Jesus, by God's grace through faith. Further, it clarifies the bold and exciting reality that through Christ all believers become one church family, with Jesus as the cornerstone. The beautiful metaphor of a congregation of believers from every background uniting to become a "temple" containing the Holy Spirit is an objective for every church.

EPHESIANS 2

• According to verses 13-18, what kind of peace does Jesus bring? What happens as a result?

• Reread verse 10. What do you think God has in mind for you to do next? Write a prayer asking for God's wisdom and guidance in this.

THE POWER AND LOVE OF GOD

Paul felt humbled to think that God had entrusted him to preach the powerful, supernatural message of the gospel to all people. He marveled that God's plan through Jesus was for such a diversity of persons to be united into one family of faith. What a miracle! As he thought about what God had accomplished, his prayers for the Ephesian believers continued to pour out.

EPHESIANS 3

• In what ways is power described? In what different ways does power work?

• Verses 20-21 tell us that God is able to exceed our expectations both in God's work in the world, and in our personal lives. When has God exceeded what you asked or imagined? What happened? What did you learn?

WALKING WORTHY

_____

_____

_____

_____

_____

_____

_____

_____

_____

_____

Paul gave practical instructions about what steps to take to develop spiritual maturity. He reminded the Ephesians that each of them had been equipped with special spiritual gifts. By using these gifts together, all would grow into a life worthy of their calling in Christ. The mark of maturity in Christ would be clearly revealed through their treatment of each other.

EPHESIANS 4

• In our quest toward spiritual maturity, what specifically does Paul say we are to put off? What are we to put on?

• In what area of your life do you still struggle with spiritual immaturity? What steps could you take to grow?

CHILDREN OF THE LIGHT

_____

_____

_____

_____

_____

_____

_____

_____

_____

_____

Not only should our actions honor God, but they should also be visible to others. Paul instructed believers to "submit to one another out of reverence to Christ." Loving servant behavior toward each other in every setting—including the marriage relationship—shows spiritual maturity.

EPHESIANS 5

• In verse 4, what did Paul insist should replace any "obscenity, foolish talk, or coarse joking"? Challenge yourself to follow Paul's instructions today. What blessings might come with this change of attitude and words?

• Paul equally called both husbands and wives to love and submit to one another. How can you show love and submission to your spouse or family members?

Ephesians ends with a reminder that our "enemy" is not human but exists in the spiritual realm. Believers are only able to resist the attacks of evil and prevail against them by putting on what Paul called "the full armor of God." Only by constantly wearing this spiritual armor, plus continually praying, can we live God's best plans for our lives triumphantly and without derailment.

EPHESIANS 6

• Make a list of each piece of the armor named in the text. What purpose does each serve?

• Do a spiritual self-inventory. Are you wearing every piece of God's armor? What are you missing? What piece(s) do you need to put on firmly today?

notes
AND PRAYER NEEDS

transformations
Hypocritical Humility

Frank Lloyd Wright said, "Early in life I had to choose between honest arrogance and hypocritical humility. I chose the former and have seen no reason to change." This quote cracks me up because it is scathingly honest. Wright admitted he was arrogant in a culture where arrogance was, and still is, frowned upon. We humans love stories of humility and love to hate stories of arrogance. We love to see the "little guy" win and the "big guy" fail. But what interests me about Wright's quip is the adjectives he uses: *honest* arrogance and *hypocritical* humility.

At some point in our lives, we all face this crossroad where it's no longer acceptable to be arrogant. When we're kids, arrogance is okay. It's endearing when a toddler puts on her shoes by herself and shouts, "Look what I did, Mom! I'm a big girl!" It's normal to tell kids they're "so smart" when they correctly answer questions like, "What sound does a cow make?" Most kids believe they're geniuses because adults constantly tell them they are.

Once a child gets into grade school, however, honest arrogance loses its cuteness. I doubt if many parents sit their children down and say, "Here's the thing, Sammy. You're not as smart as we said you are. Don't get us wrong, you're a great kid. We weren't lying about loving that macaroni necklace you made, and, who knows, someday you really might be an astronaut. But being the first part-time president, part-time astronaut might be a stretch. So quit telling everyone that, okay?" Yet even if a conversation like that doesn't happen, kids somehow learn that the circle of people they can be honestly arrogant with gets smaller as they get older. By the time we're adults, that circle may contain one or two people. Or, if you're like me, a dog.

Despite the fact that so many humans are arrogant, most of us don't like arrogance. Every one of us deals with pride. But as adults, humility seems to be the way to make friends and influence people, which means either we gain true humility or we create a false persona. So at a party when someone says, "What did you put in this dip? It's so good!" We say, "Oh, just a little bit of this, and little bit of that. It's no big deal," even though we want to say, "That dip is beyond good, it's great! I should get some kind of award here!"

Humility is so appealing that we sometimes fake it. We pretend promotions are no big deal. We shun compliments because receiving them makes us look conceited. Maybe I'm crazy, but I'd like to stop faking humility. I want the real deal. I want to be like Paul when he says (and means), "I am the least of all the saints." Humility is the key to following Christ. But choosing honest humility is unnatural. It goes against our arrogant nature. That is what makes Paul's writing so inspiring. His honest humility can only be explained by a real encounter with Jesus. True humility isn't natural; it's supernatural.

philippians

words of encouragement

book 50

Philippi, a Roman colony located in northeast Greece, was home to some of the apostle Paul's dearest friends and supporters. Philippi was an important city in the province of Macedonia and was located on a major trade route. The majority of its inhabitants were Gentiles—most of whom were Roman citizens. This first church planted on European soil was one of the stops on Paul's second missionary journey, about AD 50.

Along with Ephesians, Colossians, and Philemon, Philippians is one of Paul's "prison letters" because it was written while Paul was living under confinement. Although his location is not identified, he was most probably writing between AD 60–62 from house arrest in Rome. He had been transported to Rome to stand before Nero on charges of inciting a riot in Jerusalem as he proclaimed Jesus Christ (Acts 21:27–28:31). Paul's situation was difficult. Confined and guarded around the clock by Roman soldiers, he faced the lack of assurance of his eventual release, and a death sentence was a very real possibility. He needed financial support to cover his own living expenses, and he dealt with worrisome physical problems (2 Corinthians 12:7-10). Yet in spite of his conditions, joy flowed through the words of this letter—he used the words "joy" and "rejoice" fourteen times.

The informal tone reflects the intimacy of Paul's relationship with the Philippian church and sets it apart from Paul's other letters. The Philippians, most of whom were living in poverty and facing their own problems, had sent an old friend, Epaphroditus, to Paul to assure him of their ongoing prayer support and to deliver a financial gift to help meet Paul's needs. Paul began his response with an outpouring of thanksgiving and an update on his personal situation. But soon he brought the content of his letter around to his deep concern for the Philippian church and the issues threatening them. The church faced problems from within (their unity threatened by two leaders at odds with each other) and from without (false teachers undermining the truth of the gospel). Paul challenged the Philippians to deal with their problems as Christ would.

Paul's words to the Philippians still ring true and provide us with a wealth of wisdom for living:

- how to find joy and peace in the midst of dire circumstances
- how to persevere in living for Christ
- how to be like Christ

Philippians is a devotional book, one to be read repeatedly and meditated upon as you apply its truths. Every chapter contains words of encouragement and concrete instructions to live by. May this powerful book touch your life this week and give you insight into the life of joy offered by Jesus.

PRAYING FOR PARTNERS

_____

_____

_____

_____

_____

_____

_____

_____

_____

_____

Paul followed the form of a typical Greek letter of his time: a greeting, followed by a prayer for his recipients. Paul gave thanks for the long partnership and friendship he had with the Philippians. As he did so, he introduced the primary theme of joy.

PHILIPPIANS 1:1-11

• The word "partnership" comes from the Greek "koinonia" and reflects a community sharing a common focus, with each member contributing what he or she can. Identify the ways Paul thanked and encouraged his partners in Philippi.

• List practical ways a person could love others "with the affection of Christ" (1:8). Choose one of those ways to act upon this week.

MORE SCRIPTURE

Acts 16:11-40—Paul founds the church in Philippi

ADVANCING THE GOSPEL

_____

_____

_____

_____

_____

_____

_____

_____

_____

Paul was incarcerated in a house where he could have visitors and receive mail and gifts. However, he was chained 24/7 to one of the elite members of the Roman army. This provided Paul with a rotating captive audience with whom he could share Christ. Paul not only affected Roman soldiers with the good news of Jesus, but his courageous witness also encouraged other Christians to be bold, and the gospel spread even further.

PHILIPPIANS 1:12-26

• In verses 18-26, what insights do you have into Paul's philosophy of life?

• Paul said, "For to me, to live is Christ." Based on your investment of time, energy, and money, how would you answer, "For to me, to live is _____?" What will you do to make Jesus a greater priority in your life?

Paul shifted from his own circumstances and attitude to the Philippians'. One of the most beautiful statements about Christ in all of Scripture is the centerpiece of these verses. Paul stated the foundational truth of Jesus—who he was and why he came—to motivate the Philippians to proper behavior towards each other.

PHILIPPIANS 1:27–2:18

• In 2:5-8, what did Jesus the Son choose to do in obedience to God the Father? What was the Father's response in verses 9-11?

• When our behavior lines up with God's instructions, our witness for Jesus shines in a dark world (2:14-16). In what ways are you shining brightly? What part of your behavior do you need to line up more closely with God's word?

THE HUMILITY OF CHRIST

wed.

MINISTRY PARTNERS

After teaching the Philippians about honoring the gospel by working together selflessly, Paul gave three examples. He pointed to himself, Timothy (a long time coworker and friend who was with him when he founded the church in Philippi), and Epaphroditus (the representative sent by the Philippian church with a financial gift to support Paul).

PHILIPPIANS 2:19-30;
ECCLESIASTES 4:9-12

• Make three lists: things Paul said about himself, things he said about Timothy, and things he said about Epaphroditus.

• Choose one attitude from your lists to work on this week. What will you do?

MORE SCRIPTURE

1 Corinthians 16:5-24—Some of Paul's ministry partners

FOR CHRIST'S SAKE

_____

_____

_____

_____

_____

_____

_____

_____

_____

_____

Paul turned his attention to the false teachers who were trying to sway the Philippians from the truth. He addressed the false teaching that claimed connection with God comes through strict observance of the Law. Using his own experience, Paul shared his passion simply to know Christ and urged the Philippians to follow his example.

PHILIPPIANS 3:1-15

• Paul challenged the Philippians to pursue daily a relationship with Jesus. What do you think leads followers of Jesus to think and act like we have no further growth to do?

• Paul let go of anything in the past that could hinder his relationship with Jesus. What from your past do you need to let go of in order to be free to press on in your relationship with Christ?

THE PEACE OF GOD

_____

_____

_____

_____

_____

_____

_____

_____

_____

_____

Paul's joy came as a result of being at peace with God in his spirit and in his life situation. In today's verses, Paul addressed how both individuals and the church community could experience God's peace. He challenged them to deal with the issues threatening to divide them and to purposefully develop life attitudes that promote healthy relationships and help in coping with difficult situations.

PHILIPPIANS 3:16–4:9

• Make a list of Paul's instructions from these Scriptures. What attitudes and behaviors can we choose that will help us experience God's peace?

• In what situation do you need to experience God's peace? Which of Paul's instructions can you apply to that situation?

Paul was confident that God would always meet his needs. God used the Philippians, who had faithfully and sacrificially supported Paul in other imprisonments, to come through for him once again. Paul finished his letter to his dear friends with some of his most powerful statements about God's provision. These statements remind us of the confidence we can have in God for ourselves, as well as our responsibility to others.

PHILIPPIANS 4:10-23

• In verses 10-13, what had Paul learned through his many years in prison?

• In verse 19, Paul reassured the Philippians that as they gave sacrificially, God would never let them down. What scares you about letting go and giving sacrificially? What reassurance does Philippians give you?

CONFIDENCE IN THE LORD

notes

AND PRAYER NEEDS

transformations

Stuff Happens

One doesn't have to live very long to realize that despite our best efforts in faith, hope, and love, most days are complicated with various setbacks. The baby spits up, the car won't start, the furnace won't run, the boss won't understand. Or, in those really painful seasons, the tests come back malignantly positive or fertilely negative. Observing no boundaries of age, race, economics, or religious preferences, STUFF happens. It's a fact.

STUFF happens to businesses, too. In the world of economic exchange, however, when the going gets tough, the tough must get going or prepare to go under. There are companies formed just to take care of businesses going through hard times, skilled in the intriguing concept of "turnaround." Turnaround is when a failing business owner, rather than just sitting there and to die, seeks help and takes steps to revamp. The turnaround specialist advises the sinking business owners on where to cut losses, patch up the holes, and set sail for a hope-filled future.

Strangely, turnaround specialists tend to be unsung heroes, even by their satisfied clients. When a specialist attempts to save a troubled business, the owner is usually too upset to praise his or her efforts. After the crisis, when the business is back on track, the business owner wants to forget that he or she almost lost everything. "It's one thing to run a company when things are going well," said Joel Getzler, president of Getzler & Co., a Manhattan, New York, turnaround company. "It takes a totally different mind-set when things aren't going well."

And it's that totally different mind-set that the apostle Paul possessed in a brilliant sort of way. He was so connected to the ultimate Turnaround Specialist that even while sitting in jail he found a way to turn it around. His setbacks became his opportunities. His problems became his pulpit. Paul claimed his biggest dilemma was between life on earth and more life with Jesus in heaven. It was win-win for Paul—all good, all the time. Paul went way past moaning, *"Why me?"* to singing a brand new song, *"For me to live is Christ."*

This made Paul's mission-business failure proof. He turned everything around—saw every issue, every diagnosis, every relational challenge, every need, every sale lost, and every natural disaster encountered as an opportunity for God to show up and for Jesus to become more fully known. Paul's turnaround strategy? One word repeated in myriad circumstances: rejoice. Spoken joy signals to the divine Turnaround Specialist that we trust and relinquish control of Business Plan A and are open and excited to move into Plan B. With God, it's all good, all the time.

So in the business known as Your Life, it's a given that STUFF will happen, every day. And the ultimate Turnaround Specialist is there for you every time STUFF rears its ugly head. You've got every opportunity to cut your losses, patch up the holes, and once again set sail for your hope-filled future, whatever it may bring. And when your life business picks up again, don't forget to thank that Specialist, who is all good, all the time.

In the letter to the Colossians, we discover much about this church—its faith and struggles. Paul had never been to this particular church but had been working closely with its founder and teacher Epaphras, whom Paul spoke of highly throughout the letter. Paul's ministry in the port city of Ephesus had introduced Epaphras to Christ. The church's evangelistic efforts are what sent Epaphras to Colossae.

The city of Colossae was located in the Lycus valley in a region about one hundred miles east of Ephesus, which is in modern day western Turkey. Even though Colossae had been a significant strategic city in ancient days, at the time of this letter it was no longer a place of great importance or commerce. It has, however, become significant to the Christian world because of the value placed on this particular letter and the great Christ-theme that Paul presented in this letter to the Colossian church.

The occasion for the letter is clear. Epaphras had come to Paul with encouraging news about the church's ongoing faith but also wanted clarification concerning certain false teachings that had arisen in the church. Paul persuasively responded with this strong letter of encouragement and instruction. We are not totally informed of the exact content of the false teachings, but we know they included a diminished role for Christ in salvation; worship of angels; and harsh physical disciplines, including specific rules for eating and drinking.

In response, Paul didn't argue the issues point by point. He simply declared that Jesus Christ, being fully God, had fully completed the requirements for saving humanity from sin and death and was sufficient to meet all human needs—both physical and spiritual. He also affirmed that true spiritual renewal occurs through the acceptance of Jesus Christ into one's life. It is by this "Christ in you" that true spiritual discipline takes place and that Christ's followers are empowered to conquer personal sins and put godly characteristics, like love, into practice. Paul was emphatic that any attempt to add extra requirements to what Christ had done and was doing in believers' lives would greatly diminish the gospel message and even Christ himself.

Though it is obvious that the church members in Colossae were struggling with some very destructive teachings, it is also clear that they were still standing firm in their faith in Jesus Christ. Paul, as in most of his letters, praised them for their ongoing faith and encouraged them to continue working to spread the good news of Christ. By listing all the servants of Christ who were ministering with him as well as in the church at Colossae, Paul finished this letter with specific examples of true followers of Christ. The descriptions he used, like "faithful minister," "fellow servant," and "dear brother," showed that many were making an impact with their lives as they showed Christ to the world.

sun.

THE GOSPEL OF FAITH, HOPE, LOVE, AND LIFE

_____
_____
_____
_____
_____
_____
_____
_____
_____
_____
_____

Paul began his letter to the Colossian church with an encouraging word of thanksgiving for them and their evident faith in Christ. This faith was spreading rapidly throughout the whole region, and the Colossians shared in this great movement. He also shared his prayers for them as believers. He prayed they would not only continue growing in faith but also bear much fruit for the kingdom of God.

COLOSSIANS 1:1-14

• List and describe the ways Paul encourages the Colossians to live their lives to please the Lord. Why should believers in Jesus live this way?

• From the list you've created, choose one new way you can please God today. What do you need to do?

mon.

CHRIST IS THE LORD OF ALL

_____
_____
_____
_____
_____
_____
_____
_____
_____
_____

In understanding who it is that the church serves, Paul explicitly described the majesty of Christ. In a thorough yet magnificent way, the supremacy of Christ was spelled out to the Colossians—ultimately stating that Christ is all in all. It is through the sacrifice of Christ's own physical body that we are saved from our sin and reconciled to God.

COLOSSIANS 1:15-23

• Look at the images and descriptions used to describe Jesus Christ in this passage. What information do these give you about Christ's position in the church?

• Because of Christ's supremacy and control over all things, we can trust Christ to reign over our lives. Over what do you need to let Christ have control?

PAUL'S MISSION AND PURPOSE

We receive a clear vision into Paul's mission and why he was actually writing to the church in Colossae and to the neighboring church in Laodicea. His purpose was to encourage and unite them in their faith so they could continue to grow in their understanding and knowledge of God. Obviously Paul wanted them to become mature Christians, but he also wanted them to continue assisting in his ongoing mission: that the whole world would know Jesus Christ.

COLOSSIANS 1:24–2:5

• What is the basic gospel message that Paul wanted all the Gentiles (non-Jews) to know?

• How does knowing that Christ lives in you affect your outlook and motivation to share Christ with others?

LIVING IN FREEDOM IN CHRIST

This letter confronted certain false beliefs that had arisen in the Colossian church and were threatening to destroy their unity and belief in Jesus Christ. To contend with these false beliefs, Paul explained that only faith in Jesus Christ brings new life. Christians are to be judged by their faith in Christ and their growing relationship with him, not on what they eat or drink or how they maintain religious regulations and festivals. Such legalism neither saves nor brings one closer to God.

COLOSSIANS 2:6-23

• What do you think is implied by the words "rooted and built up in him" (2:7)?

• Why does it seem easier to base our belief in Christ on rule-keeping instead of relationship-building? How do you maintain a deep relationship with Jesus?

TAKING OFF OUR SINFUL NATURE

_____
_____
_____
_____
_____
_____
_____
_____
_____
_____

Although we are free in Christ from oppressive rules and regulations, we must take active responsibility in growing closer to him. This is accomplished by setting our hearts and minds on things of God and not on sinful indulgences. Paul was clear: we are to do away with the earthly nature as we put on our new self, which is alive in Christ.

COLOSSIANS 3:1-11

• What are the specific actions Paul wants his readers to take to be free of the sinful nature and its actions?

• What practices do you use to focus your heart and mind on things of God?

PUTTING ON THE GRACE OF CHRIST

_____
_____
_____
_____
_____
_____
_____
_____
_____
_____

Once we have put aside the old self and its sinful ways, we must then allow the new self and its godly ways to be revealed in us. In this new life of freedom given to us by Christ's grace, we are compelled to be people of compassion and love. When we have Christ in our hearts and minds, we really begin to live out the life God wants for us.

COLOSSIANS 3:12–4:1

• What are the ways we literally "put on" new life in Christ?

• With which one of Paul's "holy living" characteristics (3:12-14) are you doing well in your life? Which one needs more of your attention?

Paul's final instructions to the Colossians included praying for his ongoing mission of sharing the gospel. He also encouraged them to be witnesses to non-believers as they made the most of every opportunity God gave them. Illustrating the point, Paul concluded by naming a variety of godly people who were serving in ministry, mission, and prayer.

COLOSSIANS 4:2-18

• What were some of the distinct characteristics of the servants Paul mentioned in his final greetings to the church at Colossae? How were they working in the mission to spread the gospel message?

• From verses 5-6, how can you be a better witness to nonbelievers? In what specific ways can you make your conversation "full of grace"?

FINAL INSTRUCTIONS AND GREETINGS

notes
AND PRAYER NEEDS

Turn the page for this week's Transformations Reflection.

transformations

Sandcastle People

This is painful for me to admit, but I think my dad lied to me when I was four years old, impressionable, and clueless as to what happened in the world after 7:30 p.m. At four, I was crazy about sandcastles. So I believed my dad when he said that little sandcastle people came to life at night and played inside the castle I built that day.

It kind of made sense. After breakfast and a quick lesson with Big Bird, I would go out back to begin my work in the sandbox. The sandcastle people must've been a rowdy bunch because every morning my sandcastle was in shambles. To be honest, I didn't understand the sandcastle people's relentless destruction. If only I could've met them and explained that I didn't mind them playing in my sandcastle; I just didn't appreciate them leaving it worse than they found it.

So with my buckets and shovels I went to work in the damp, morning sand. I thought about the little sandcastle people running around inside. I wondered if they noticed I made windows in the watchtowers so they could effectively keep watch. I built a moat and wondered if at night it filled with real moat monsters and thick moat water. Every day I did my best to rebuild the castle better than yesterday's creation, even though deep down I knew the clumsy sandcastle people were going to mess it up. My relentless desire to rebuild matched their relentless desire to destroy.

As an adult I face a similar situation. Every day Satan would love to leave my life worse than he found it yesterday. He has a relentless desire to destroy any evidence of Christ in my life. Throughout the day he uses pride in a wide variety of ways to convince me the earth was created for me. The resulting selfishness has the sneaky ability to annihilate the selfless qualities built up in me by Christ.

Every morning, I have to wake up and both restore and build further on my relationship with Christ. Paul writes in Colossians that we have to take off our "old self with its practices and put on the new self, which is being renewed in knowledge in the image of its Creator" (Colossians 3:9-10). Spiritual renewal is a daily event. Every morning when I wake up, I may look and feel like me. But spiritually, I'm like a demolished sandcastle. If I don't spend time in devotion with God in the morning, I'll have no defense against Satan's lie that I'm the reason that day exists. Satan has a relentless desire for my destruction, and I must be as relentless about being built into Christ's image as I was about my sandcastle rebuilding.

In the time of the apostle Paul, Thessalonica was the capital of the Roman province of Macedonia and served as a strategically located seaport and commerce center. We learn from Acts 17:1-10 that Paul first visited Thessalonica during his second missionary tour.

Paul's stay attracted the attention of the city's sizeable Jewish population as well as a diverse crowd of Gentile (non-Jewish) residents. His preaching resulted in a substantial number of new believers (primarily Gentile), and he found himself in the role of spiritual parent and mentor. Scholars believe that Paul and his traveling companions stayed in Thessalonica for only a few months, due to a forceful uprising against his gospel message. In AD 50, Paul and friends hastily left Thessalonica, forced to abandon their spiritually young flock of Christians who suffered persecution for their faith. One of Paul's greatest regrets was to have left them before he finished teaching and training them in all aspects of the Christian life.

Out of his deep love for the new Thessalonian church, Paul sent his colleague Timothy to check on them. He was overjoyed to hear Timothy's report that they were doing well (Acts 18:5), but they still struggled with social and moral issues. As Gentiles, these new believers had not grown up with the holiness of the Law of Moses. So the ideas about lifestyle purity that Paul had introduced to them during his brief stay were a stark change from what they had known before. In addition, the Thessalonian believers had become so preoccupied with the hope of Jesus' second coming that some had ceased work, in order to watch and wait.

To address these concerns, Paul wrote two letters to the Thessalonian church. His purpose was to:

- encourage them in their faith
- praise them for their steadfastness through persecution
- affirm his love and affection for them as brothers and sisters in Christ
- remind them of his credibility as their first spiritual mentor and teacher
- teach and train them in practical aspects of living as followers of Jesus
- educate them about the "end times" (Christ's return to earth)

Paul's teaching on the "end times" in these two letters represents some of the most significant explanation in the New Testament about Jesus' return. Most importantly, Paul urged the Thessalonians not to stand around and wait but to work hard. Only through finding his followers demonstrating diligent obedience to God's work, argued Paul, will Jesus be pleased whenever he returns.

May 1 and 2 Thessalonians provide motivation for you as you seek guidance to stay the course in your faith, no matter what.

GODLY MOTIVATION

_____
_____
_____
_____
_____
_____
_____
_____
_____
_____

Paul sought to encourage the believers at Thessalonica by reminding them of the chain reaction of faith. Initiated by their godly obedience and carried out through their lives, the faith of the Thessalonian believers had impact upon many others. Their inspiring example and witness of faithfulness became known everywhere among Christians.

1 THESSALONIANS 1

• What byproducts of the Thessalonian believers' faith, love, and hope did God produce through their diligence? (1 Thessalonians 1:3)

• Consider these byproducts. Which is most strongly evident in your walk of faith? In which do you most need to grow?

WEATHERING CRITICISM

_____
_____
_____
_____
_____
_____
_____
_____
_____
_____

Today's passage refutes a series of criticisms Paul's enemies in Thessalonica had passed along to the believers there. It had become common at that time for imposters to pose as traveling preachers and take advantage of the hospitality (food, housing, and finances) of the churches. Allegation by allegation, Paul corrected the accusations and emphasized his heartfelt commitment as their spiritual mentor.

1 THESSALONIANS 2:1-16

• List the criticisms made against Paul, and his reply to each. What does it take to be a servant leader and mentor to new believers?

• Paul spoke of the word of God at work in those who believe. How do you sense God's word working in you?

STANDING FIRM

A certainty about following Christ is that we will all be tempted and persecuted, just as Jesus was. Paul's concern was that the Thessalonian believers, persecuted by their fellow unbelieving citizens, would succumb to the pressure and be tempted to fall from faith. But even as he wrote his letter, his colleague Timothy brought him an excellent report of their faithfulness.

1 THESSALONIANS 2:17–3:13

• Read about the temptation Jesus faced in Matthew 4:1-11. What kind of temptations might the Thessalonian believers have encountered (1 Thessalonians 3:5)?

• In 3:12-13, Paul prays for the Thessalonian believers. Use this as your prayer to prepare for your day, changing "you/your" to "me/my" to personalize it.

STAYING PURE

For the Thessalonian believers, Paul's concept of sexual purity was new. Apparently, many citizens of Thessalonica lived a promiscuous lifestyle, which was considered normal in their society. Paul's letter taught that they must learn and practice chaste behaviors. Even more, Paul described that Christians must love each other and live a life of respect.

1 THESSALONIANS 4

• Many Thessalonian believers who thought Christ would return immediately had quit their daily work and were idly waiting. In verses 11-12, what instructions did Paul give?

• The last part of today's reading gives some details about believers who have died before Christ's return to earth. What encouragement do you receive from this?

BE READY

_____

_____

_____

_____

_____

_____

_____

_____

_____

_____

When Christ returns someday, believers should be found living lives of faithfulness. Paul summarized practical action steps for them to take, including a warning not to "put out the Spirit's fire" (5:19). When we refuse to obey the Holy Spirit's leading (or ignore the power God provides through the Spirit, and try to do it ourselves), the Spirit can indeed be quenched.

1 THESSALONIANS 5

• According to Paul, what faithful behavior will please Jesus when he returns to earth?

• We see in 5:23-24 a powerful assurance of what God wants to do in and through our lives. For what are you trusting in God's faithfulness to see you through?

MORE SCRIPTURE
Matthew 24:42–25:13—Jesus' teaching on the "end times"

RIGHT FOCUS

_____

_____

_____

_____

_____

_____

_____

_____

_____

_____

The opening statements of Paul's second letter to the Thessalonians contain compliments about the increasing spiritual maturity of the believers there. Paul put forth a perspective concerning how to think about those who were persecuting the Thessalonians for their faith: remember that God will always have the last word.

2 THESSALONIANS 1

• Knowing it was God's responsibility to deal with their persecutors, on what were the Thessalonian believers to focus (verses 11-12)?

• Do you struggle with a critical attitude toward someone who is making your life difficult? Write a prayer today, asking for power to refocus on your own walk of faith.

BE DILIGENT

The last half of this letter covers a number of subjects ranging from the "end times" to advice on practical living. As always, Paul sought to bring an eternal perspective to day-to-day choices. Paul also cautioned believers to be careful of the company they kept.

2 THESSALONIANS 2–3

• Look again at 2:16-17 and 3:3-5. With what specific resources does God desire to provide us for faithful daily living?

• Reread 3:6-15, a reminder that those who are idle provide a negative influence we are to avoid. Think about the persons with whom you spend the most time. To what extent do they motivate you in your faith and service? With whom do you need to spend more time, and with whom less time?

notes

AND PRAYER NEEDS

transformations

A Living, Spirited Dance

6 a.m. and the faint sound of Mix 107.7 interrupts my sleep and confuses my dreams. My drowsy brain struggles to calculate pillow time allotted before pulling up and out for my morning workout. History confers that the gym helps me wake up, so I shift into gear and ease out of the house.

9 a.m. and into the office, the workspace that is now officially my second home. I need a bossy housekeeper for both habitats. Urgent notes litter my chair and desk; e-mails like well-fed hamsters have multiplied since I last logged on. The landline flashes red while the cell phone flashes green. I begin to feel concerned about accomplishing the day's work before the setting sun calls my bluff.

One final word, friends. We ask you—urge is more like it—that you keep on doing what we told you to do to please God, not in a dogged religious plod, but in a living, spirited dance. (I Thessalonians 4:1-2, The Message)

2 p.m. and my stomach is telling me that skipping lunch was not a viable option. I'm making headway plowing through the tasks, trying not to think how beautiful it is outside. Every week isn't like this, I remind myself. It's just a busy season.

…not in a dogged religious plod, but in a living, spirited dance.

6:30 p.m. and the dog is happier to see me than he should be. If I were in his paws, I'd be mad that I'd been left alone for nine hours; but alas, together again. He gets fed, and then I get fed. We patter through our routine, reminding ourselves that no matter what challenges life delivers, the activities of daily living will always be with us.

10:30 p.m. and I've accomplished three clothing changes, four logins, five meals, and six newscasts. Seven projects completed and eighteen hours deleted. It's time to retreat to the pillow so I can get up and do it all over again tomorrow, and then from inside *The Message* on my bedside table I spot these words:

We ask you—urge is more like it—that you keep on doing what we told you to do to please God, not in a dogged religious plod, but in a living, spirited dance.

Paul's urgings smack me upside the head. Life in Jesus was never intended to reflect the drudgery of day in and day out existence. My life, though it embodies all the danger signals of a dogged religious plod, was meant to be infused with Spirit, the same Spirit of God that raised Jesus from the dead. The same Spirit that Jesus bequeathed to his followers and promised would offer more power than he himself had possessed while on the earth. A spirited Dance of Life that prances victoriously all over that dogged religious plod of death.

11 p.m. and my pillow talk with God reveals my problematic sin: I'd plodded through the entire day without acknowledging my partner, the Lord of the Dance. Christianity without the Spirit of Jesus infusing life into every moment is empty religion, and life without spirit is a dogged plod. Forgive me, Jesus. Tomorrow, let's dance.

1 and 2 timothy

pastoral letters

At the end of the letters attributed to Paul are four letters (1 and 2 Timothy, Titus, and Philemon) addressed to individuals rather than churches. Known as pastoral letters, they contain words of wisdom from an older mentor to younger persons in difficult church leadership situations.

The first two letters are addressed to Timothy, a young man converted to Christianity during Paul's first missionary journey. During the time between Paul's first and second visits to Timothy's hometown of Lystra, Timothy was taught by his mother and grandmother and matured enough to become Paul's disciple and traveling companion on subsequent journeys. Timothy was a faithful coworker with Paul: he cowrote six of Paul's letters (1 and 2 Thessalonians, 2 Corinthians, Philippians, Colossians, and Philemon) and served as Paul's emissary on three separate missions to handle church problems in Thessalonica, Corinth, and Philippi. He was Paul's trusted friend and a source of hope to the older apostle for the continuation of his ministry.

The two letters addressed to Timothy are quite different. Some, but not all, scholars think that the first letter was written after Paul's Roman imprisonment, as Paul traveled around the Mediterranean area. After finding the church at Ephesus in trouble, Paul left Timothy there to handle the problems as he continued his journey. From Macedonia, Paul wrote the letter we know as 1 Timothy to advise Timothy on how to handle the negative infiltration of the Ephesian church (which consisted of a network of house churches rather than a single corporate body). Some of the house church leaders were proud and greedy, teaching a combination of Old Testament and Greek beliefs, and having an unhealthy influence on the vulnerable young widows in the community. Addressed to Timothy rather than the Ephesian church leaders (because they were the problem), this book contains one of Paul's clearest teachings on the qualities needed for godly leadership.

Between the two letters (AD 64-67), some scholars suggest that Paul was arrested again for his faith and sent to Rome for a second imprisonment. Sensing the approach of his life's end, he wrote a letter to his longtime friend Timothy, whom he asked to be with him in his final days. This letter commissioned Timothy as Paul's successor in ministry, should Timothy not reach Paul in time to be commissioned in person. Young, shy, retiring, and with health issues, Timothy may not have been the obvious choice to replace Paul at such a precarious point in church history. But Paul trusted Timothy's faithfulness and ability to lead in difficult situations, and continued to coach him about leadership qualities and skills.

May Paul's words to Timothy encourage you this week as you train to be godly, fight the good fight, and finish your race.

sun.

EXPOSING FALSE TEACHERS

_____

_____

_____

_____

_____

_____

_____

_____

_____

_____

The church at Ephesus was being infiltrated with teachers advocating beliefs contrary to the Old Testament Scriptures and Jesus' teachings. Catching wind of this, Paul wrote Timothy to warn him of this heresy and to encourage him in leading the Ephesian church with strength and conviction. Paul challenges us, too, to keep pure hearts, good consciences, and sincere faith, not wandering away from the truth.

1 TIMOTHY 1:1–2:7

• What is the trustworthy statement Paul shared with Timothy? How was Paul an example of the truth of that statement?

• What methods do you use to keep yourself grounded in God's truth, so you are able to discern the truth of the talk at work, in the media, and from your family and friends?

mon.

LEADERSHIP REQUIREMENTS

_____

_____

_____

_____

_____

_____

_____

_____

_____

_____

Paul recommended practices that would help the church maintain order and also demonstrate integrity in the community. Paul emphasized the servant role of church leaders, who were known as overseers (or elders) and deacons. They were to lead by personal example as well as by instruction.

1 TIMOTHY 2:8–3:16

• Paul's list of qualifications for church leaders consists of character traits, not job functions. Why do you think this is what Paul emphasized?

• In our context, Paul's instructions to women seem restrictive. In a first-century context, Paul was influenced by popular moral treatises that established proper behaviors in the household. Have you ever experienced what appeared to be unfair restrictions—but benefited anyway from a positive outcome?

COACHING TIMOTHY

Like any good coach, Paul combined inspiration and information to help Timothy form a training plan that would empower him to persevere in order that he might save both himself and his hearers (4:16).

1 TIMOTHY 4

• According to 4:12, in what areas was Timothy to set an example for the believers? Describe what a godly example would look like for each of these areas.

• From 4:13-14, it appears Timothy had the spiritual gifts of preaching and teaching. Because of his shy and retiring personality, Timothy may have been tempted to avoid practicing these gifts publicly. When are you most likely to be tempted to avoid using your spiritual gifts?

RESPECT YOUR ELDERS

Paul gave practical instruction on the role of the church in caring for its members, especially the widows and elders. The problems within the Ephesian church parallel social issues still present today. Paul is clear in outlining the responsibility of the individual, the family, and the church. He also gives advice on deciding who is truly needy and on preventing individuals from taking advantage of the system.

1 TIMOTHY 5:1–6:2

• What can you glean from 1 Timothy that could be applied to social issues today?

• How is your church addressing the needs of people? How could you become more involved in this effort?

SPIRITUAL WEALTH

_____
_____
_____
_____
_____
_____
_____
_____
_____
_____

The false teachers in Ephesus had no understanding of Jesus' teachings on money (investing in eternal rewards rather than material possessions). Many of these teachers intended to make lots of money by teaching religion, and their contentious attitudes caused many problems in the church. Paul challenged Timothy to stay strong to protect his people from false teaching and to teach the church that "godliness with contentment is great gain."

1 TIMOTHY 6:3-21

• According to verses 10-11, from what is a follower of Jesus to flee? What are we to pursue?

• Reread verse 18. Serving and financial generosity are important practices of Jesus followers. Where are you doing well? Where do you need to do better?

CALL TO FAITHFULNESS

_____
_____
_____
_____
_____
_____
_____
_____
_____
_____

Persecution from the Roman government and infiltration by false teachers created hard times for Paul (in prison in Rome) and Timothy (struggling as he led the church in Ephesus). This personal letter from his mentor encouraged Timothy to persevere and endure hardship for Jesus, our source of hope and comfort.

2 TIMOTHY 1–2

• Reread 2:16-17. When have you observed or been affected by gossip? What could you do to redirect your conversations?

• In 2:20-21, Paul drew on his knowledge of Jewish law concerning ritually clean and unclean containers. From what do we need to cleanse ourselves to be a utensil suitable for the high, excellent purposes of God?

One of the best explanations of the purpose of Scripture lies in 2 Timothy 3:16-17. God's inspired word, which Paul knew as the Old Testament, teaches us how to be righteous and ready for faith in Jesus. As we spend time in God's word and submit ourselves to the transforming power of the Holy Spirit, we go beyond a "form of godliness" to true relationship with God.

2 TIMOTHY 3–4

• Paul reminded Timothy to preach the truth, not what people wanted to hear. How could that have been a problem? What advice does Paul offer?

• How do you stay faithful in representing Jesus, especially when it would be easier to say what people want to hear?

FIGHT THE GOOD FIGHT

notes

AND PRAYER NEEDS

Turn the page for this week's Transformations Reflection.

transformations

Wise Role Models

"I just don't see myself as a role model," stated a controversial professional athlete. He started a firestorm of conversation around the country with his comment. Can we choose not to be role models? Does being in the public eye make it mandatory to be a good example?

These questions exist for me as a Christian as well. If I profess Christ, what are the requirements of living in front of others? If I live in the freedom Christ gives, will my decisions cause another who is not yet freed to make sinful choices? How do I balance appearances (guilt by association) with living in the freedom Christ gives? Where do I land on drinking, gambling, smoking, myspace.com, recreational drugs, prayer in restaurants, Santa Claus, speeding, premarital sex, dating, public school, Halloween, politics, motorcycle riding, spanking, Harry Potter, and so forth? So many big and small influences in our society challenge my choices. I often feel like I need some guidance from a Christian who is further along the path of experience and wisdom than me, someone who models what faithfulness best looks like in the realm of daily choices such as these.

From Paul's letters to Timothy, I have learned that early Christians also struggled with their own set of societal influences and faced the same balancing act. They discussed, prayed, and waited for a word from God to help them find their way. In the end, they relied on both the Holy Spirit and wise role models to set the standard for their behavior. Paul's influence upon young Timothy was a prime example.

All of us also have role models who influence us to think differently and act intentionally, for better or for worse. A role model might be someone we observe from afar, or a person with whom we interact every day. I see that Timothy intentionally aligned himself with Paul's mentorship in order to make sure he stayed on track. We, too, can intentionally choose our role models; we can also choose to be one.

I'm convinced that great Christian role models embody certain characteristics. First, they live their lives with authenticity and joy. Rather than being rule-bound law enforcers, they exude contagious energy and confidence about their faith-filled lifestyle choices. They organically integrate their faith into every minute of their lives. Second, role models show genuine interest in others. They aren't sequestered in their prayer closets all the time, privately perfecting the inner disciplines of the Christian life. They're active in the community and extend hospitality and friendship to those around them. Third, role models challenge others to move beyond comfort and to become their best selves. They are willing to have difficult conversations to hold others accountable, because they know helping others grow is more important than being liked all the time.

How can I make choices today to follow wise role models? And how can I serve as a role model to draw others into an intimate love relationship with Jesus?

titus and philemon

encouragement and forgiveness

The apostle Paul lived under house arrest in Rome from AD 59-62. As a Roman citizen, Paul filed an appeal to the emperor and was released following its approval. Leaving Rome, Paul and his coworkers Timothy and Titus traveled through the Mediterranean area, preaching in local churches. Titus was left behind on the island of Crete to establish the church there while Paul and Timothy continued on to Ephesus. Later, Paul wrote Timothy and Titus very similar letters (known today as 1 Timothy and Titus) to encourage them and instruct them in ministry.

Titus was a Greek (a Gentile) who likely converted to Christianity under Paul. Mentioned thirteen times in Paul's letters, Titus was an important colleague who frequently played the role of "troubleshooter." While helping organize and lead churches in the eastern half of the Roman Empire, Titus was sent to Corinth twice to bring order to the church there. He delivered Paul's confrontational letter to them (the missing letter referred to in 2 Corinthians) and was in charge of their collection of money for the poor in Jerusalem. One of Titus' most significant trips was with Paul to the Council of Jerusalem (Galatians 2:1-10), where the important decision to equally embrace Gentiles in the faith was decided.

At the time of writing the letter to Titus, Paul was an old man and relying more and more on Titus, whom he called, "My true son in our common faith." His letter served as a training manual and provided structure in developing this new church. This letter laid down basic lessons and requirements for a church being established in a land of immature Christians.

Philemon was a friend of Paul and a wealthy Christian living in Colossae. This personal letter is the only one of Paul's letters included in the New Testament that deals with a private issue and not ministry matters, though in our day we would consider slavery a ministry issue. Paul interceded on behalf of Onesimus, a runaway slave owned by Philemon, who was converted under Paul in Rome, possibly as a prison cellmate. Rather than approach Philemon as a slave owner (who had the right, under the harsh laws of the Roman Empire, to severely punish, execute, or brand Onesimus' forehead with a symbol indicating that he was a fugitive), Paul appealed to Philemon as a Christian brother and asked that Philemon receive Onesimus back with as much kindness as he would Paul.

The book of Philemon teaches much about the power of asking for and offering forgiveness. It also emphasizes the importance of intercession and advocacy for each other within the church, no matter how awkward and uncomfortable the situation. We don't know the end of the story—but it is said that fifty years later the name of the bishop of Ephesus was Onesimus. As we take to heart the importance of forgiveness and advocacy, lives and churches can be forever changed.

HOLD FAST TO SOUND DOCTRINE

_____

_____

_____

_____

_____

_____

_____

_____

_____

_____

Titus' responsibility was to straighten out the church on Crete and establish leadership that honored God. Paul urged Titus to choose as leaders only those who upheld sound doctrine (living and teaching what is taught in Scripture and brings honor to God).

TITUS 1

• What are the qualifications for church leadership? What would disqualify someone from church leadership?

• What qualities are important to you in a spiritual leader? How evident are those qualities in your own life?

mon.

GRACE THAT BRINGS SALVATION

_____

_____

_____

_____

_____

_____

_____

_____

_____

_____

God's grace (the unconditional love, acceptance, and reconnection with God [salvation] provided through Jesus) has been poured out to all people. God's ongoing supply of grace is meant to be experienced every day as we grow into the fullness of what it means to follow Christ. Old and young, men and women, no matter their life situation, can live freely and fully because of God's grace.

TITUS 2

• What does "the grace of God that offers salvation" teach us (2:11-14)?

• Consider your life stage and situation, and carefully look at what Paul tells Timothy to teach to different groups. Which of these teachings is most applicable to you? What will you do to apply it to your life?

POWER TO LIVE GODLY LIVES

In Titus 2, Paul admonished followers of Jesus, "Say 'no' to ungodliness and worldly passions, and live self-controlled, upright and godly lives." We jump over to Galatians for advice on how to do that. All of God's power lives within each follower of Jesus in the form of the Holy Spirit, who provides us with the strength to make and follow through on godly choices.

GALATIANS 5:13-26

• As a follower of Christ, it can be extremely frustrating and discouraging to still be struggling with our old way of life. According to Paul, why do we still struggle with sin?

• What does it mean to you for your sin nature (your inclination to act separate from God) to be "crucified"? What does it mean for you to "keep in step with the Spirit"?

SPIRITUAL CLEANSING

Paul used the term "justification" in many of his writings to assure all followers of Jesus that Christ's death and resurrection bring us the "washing of rebirth and renewal by the Holy Spirit" (3:5-7). Through God's grace and mercy we are forgiven, cleansed from sin, and set free from guilt. Justification means that God sees me "just-as-if-I'd" never sinned.

TITUS 3

• In 3:3-8, how does Paul describe life before knowing Jesus and life after knowing Jesus?

• Describe your life before and after knowing Jesus. What is the biggest difference?

GOD'S WORKMANSHIP

_____

_____

_____

_____

_____

_____

_____

_____

_____

One of Paul's primary teachings emphasized that our connection with Jesus (and the eternal life we receive) comes not through "works" (rituals, rule-keeping, or trying to be pure through our own efforts in following the law) but through God's grace. But Paul also taught that believers who faithfully follow Jesus "do good works" (Titus 3:8; Ephesians 2:10) as a result of our love for God and our desire to serve and please God.

EPHESIANS 2:1-10

• According to Ephesians, why is grace important?

• Knowing that we are accepted through the good work God prepared in advance for Jesus to complete on the cross, we are free to focus on the good works God has prepared in advance for each of us. What are you currently working on to fulfill God's plan for you?

fri.

A REQUEST FOR A FRIEND

_____

_____

_____

_____

_____

_____

_____

_____

_____

Just as we experience the overwhelming, undeserved grace of God, we are called to pass that grace on to others. Paul's letter challenged Philemon, a wealthy Christian from Colossae, to forgive and restore the slave Onesimus, who had sinned against him. Though we may have the desire (and maybe even the legal right) to treat someone harshly, Paul reminds us that forgiveness is the better and more Christ-like choice.

PHILEMON

• Why do you think Paul had Onesimus return to Philemon's household, rather than declaring him free?

• True repentance may require facing your past and asking for forgiveness. Is there something you need to make right with another person? What do you need to do?

ACCOUNTABILITY AND FORGIVENESS

Jesus is serious about relationships between members of his "body." God has treated us gently and lovingly, and we are to act in the same way toward one another. Paul challenged Philemon to treat Onesimus as God treats us, asking him to forgive and receive Onesimus as a brother. Through our brothers and sisters in Christ and the Spirit within us, God holds us accountable for the way we treat each other.

MATTHEW 18:15-35

• According to Matthew, is it enough to forgive someone internally without dealing with him or her directly? Why or why not?

• Have you ever experienced the relational, emotional, spiritual, or physical fallout of withholding forgiveness? How could you use verses 15-17 to move forward in any situation you face now?

notes

AND PRAYER NEEDS

Turn the page for this week's Transformations Reflection.

transformations

Shaken

I sat surrounded by strangers in the back seat of a Honda Civic. Two Korean students sat silently to my right. "Hello," was the only word we had in common. A guy with thick sideburns sat staring at the dashboard in the passenger seat. He spoke English. Just not to me. The driver, Mark, was the only person I knew. I had met him earlier that week. He told me my parents were "probably" going to hell. Exact words. But let me back up and tell this story from the start.

I had arrived early to my history class, so I sat outside on one of the benches. Mark, a guy with the swagger of an upperclassman came up to me and said, "Hey man. Would you be interested in a Bible study?" Weird—not because a complete stranger asked me that question but because just that morning I'd told myself I needed to find some kind of campus ministry to plug into. I was walking back from the bathroom to my dorm room, dodging the ramen noodles, beer cans, and trash that littered our hallway. A Bible study seemed like a good idea.

I met Mark and his friend Eric at the library the next day. Things started off all right. They asked about my life and for a quick summary of my Christianity. It quickly went from surface level niceties to them spending the next hour explaining why everything I believed was wrong. They said my baptism didn't count. My mom was a sinner for giving me spiritual direction. Mark told me I was a horrible sinner who deserved to go to hell. "You yourself said things were pretty bad in your dorm. Admit you're a sinner!" That took the weirdness to another level.

But what's scary is that the twisted logic worked. He used the Bible to back up almost all his points. He was able to make me feel horrible about myself, my family, and everything in my life. I left that little room with a paralyzing sense of confusion.

The next day was when I got in Mark's Civic with the Koreans and sideburns guy. They took me to their church. Even more weirdness. I was reminded again how desperately I needed to be a part of their church. Not "a" church, but specifically theirs. Again, they were able to back it up with Scripture, so I was uncertain what I believed. My faith was shaken.

I called my parents and explained what had happened. They calmed me down, answered my questions, and then got off the phone to call our pastor. My pastor and his wife called me. They explained how Mark had used Scripture out of context.

Deep down I knew all along that something was "off" about Mark and his church. But it was hard to argue when he used the Bible—the very thing I believe in—against my beliefs. Paul wrote in Titus, "There are a lot of rebels out there, full of loose, confusing and deceiving talk . . . They're disrupting entire families with their teaching" (1:10-11, The Message).

This is happening right now. It's not some weird thing that only happened in biblical times. It's real, and it's dangerous. And if I didn't have a truth-centered community to retreat to, who knows where I'd be now. I could be hanging out with sideburns guy, telling college freshmen they're going to hell. That, friend, is a weird and scary thought.

hebrews

the superiority of Jesus

book 58

The book of Hebrews carries with it a few mysteries. The first of these is the identity of its author. Though in early centuries of the Christian church the writer was believed to be the apostle Paul, in later times it has been speculated that this book might have come from the pen of Luke, Philip, Barnabas, Apollos, or even Priscilla. This book was most likely written between AD 60-70, to an audience of Jews who had been converted to the Christian faith. But details of where it was written and to what specific church (if it was even intended to be a letter) have been lost with the passage of time.

Hebrews is a logical, bold, literary masterpiece intended to help early Jewish believers stick to their Christian way of life, rather than default to their former religious practices in order to avoid persecution. The writer assumed the readers understood the history and rituals of Old Testament Jewish traditions. Throughout this book, believers were encouraged to stay spiritually sharp and to be diligent in faithfully following Jesus.

The book of Hebrews was designed to show the superiority of Jesus—the new covenant that is the fulfillment of the old. Step by step, Jesus is compared and proclaimed to be:

- better than angels (who because of their roles in God's Old Testament history, were sometimes worshiped—but God called Jesus his Son)
- better than Moses (who was honored as a great historic servant in God's house—but Jesus is over God's house)
- better than the Temple priests (who mediated the people's relationship with God—but Jesus as our ultimate high priest is sinless and perfect)
- better than an Old Testament sacrifice (which needed to be offered every time a sin took place—but Jesus' sacrifice on the cross was once, for all time)
- better than the old covenant given through God's Law (Jesus provided an eternal inheritance in the new covenant given through his blood in the heavenly places, rather than in an earthly temple)

The book of Hebrews is well known for what is often called the "Hall of Faith." Chapter 11 includes a long list of Old Testament leaders who persevered in their faith, even without knowing of Jesus' eventual provision for forgiveness and eternal life with God. The purpose of this chapter is contained in its opening verse, "Now faith is being sure of what we hope for and certain of what we do not see." Surely, if these ancient followers of God could persevere without knowing of God's provision through Jesus, how much more can we persevere through trials!

Then as now, the book of Hebrews offers its readers a systematic understanding of why Jesus is the ultimate provision from God for our spiritual relationship with God. As the author intended for believers so long ago, may you also be encouraged to stay diligent in your pursuit of spiritual maturity.

sun.

BETTER THAN THE ANGELS

_____
_____
_____
_____
_____
_____
_____
_____
_____
_____

In ancient times, the Israelites often resorted to angel worship in acknowledgment of the angels' role in God's plan as reflected in Old Testament history. The writer of Hebrews, however, makes clear that Jesus is superior to any of God's angels by citing a variety of Scripture verses that show the difference between angels and God's Son.

HEBREWS 1–2

• According to the Scripture quoted in chapters 1–2, what are the characteristics and roles of angels? What are the characteristics and roles of Jesus?

• Reread 2:14-18. Why did God make Jesus fully human, like us? How does this encourage you to trust Jesus to guide you?

mon.

BETTER THAN MOSES

_____
_____
_____
_____
_____
_____
_____
_____
_____
_____
_____

Moses was God's leader to guide the Israelites into the Promised Land of Canaan. But Jesus is God's chosen leader to guide all people into spiritual reconciliation with God and into eternal rest in God. The wayward example of the Israelites who followed Moses serves as a warning to Christian believers about staying faithful.

HEBREWS 3:1–4:13

• What was the consequence of the Israelites' disobedience while following Moses? The consequence of Christian believers' disobedience while following Jesus?

• Which part of chapters 3–4 penetrates your soul and spirit and calls you to change what you're doing?

MORE SCRIPTURE
Numbers 13:1–14:38—The Israelites' disobedience when following Moses

BETTER THAN A HIGH PRIEST

The author explains how Jesus is superior to any Jewish high priest who ever lived. The high priest's role was to facilitate the offerings of sacrifices for sins the people brought to the Temple (as well as offer sacrifices for his own sins). Because Jesus suffered on earth yet demonstrated perfect obedience to God, he was without sin and so became the ultimate "high priest" on our behalf.

HEBREWS 4:14–5:10

• According to 4:14-16, what about Jesus allows us to "receive mercy and find grace to help us in our time of need"?

• Verse 5:8 says that Jesus learned obedience to God through what he suffered on earth. Through what sufferings does or has God desired you to learn obedience? How are you doing?

GROWTH TOWARDS MATURITY

The author instructed Christian believers to grow past the "basics" of their faith and into true spiritual maturity. The result of such diligent obedience is a life that produces godly fruit, which pleases God.

HEBREWS 5:11–6:20

• In 6:10-12, what are the qualities and behaviors of obedience that please God? How long does God desire us to practice these?

• Are you a Christian who still lives on spiritual "milk," or have you grown through obedience into "solid food"? What changes do you need to make in order to grow?

MORE SCRIPTURE

John 15:1-8—Jesus urged his disciples to produce godly fruit by abiding in him

BETTER THAN MELCHIZEDEK

_____
_____
_____
_____
_____
_____
_____
_____
_____
_____
_____

Melchizedek, a priest during the time of Abraham, became known as the ultimate Jewish high priest, of a special order that preceded even Aaron (the first "official" priest during the time of Moses). Yet Jesus exceeds Melchizedek as the ultimate high priest, reuniting us into eternal relationship with God.

HEBREWS 6:19–7:28; 9:11–28

• As explained in 7:23-28, why is Jesus the perfect priest, once and for all? The perfect sacrifice (9:11-15)?

• What does it mean to you that Jesus sacrificed his life for your sins? How does this affect your relationship with God? Reread verse 9:14.

MORE SCRIPTURE

Hebrews 8–9—Christ exceeds Melchizedek as priest

Genesis 14:17-20—Abraham receives the blessing of Melchizedek

PERSEVERANCE

_____
_____
_____
_____
_____
_____
_____
_____
_____

Having carefully explained how Jesus has ushered in an incredible means by which to live out an eternal relationship with God, the author of Hebrews shifted to a focus on persevering in the faith. The author not only reminded the readers of their own faithful perseverance but also identified a long list of God's faithful from Old Testament Scriptures. The ultimate example of perseverance is Jesus our Lord.

HEBREWS 10:19–12:3

• Hebrews 11 is often called the "Hall of Faith." Which person named inspires you the most, and why?

• Look again at 10:19-39. Make a list of what we are encouraged to do and what we are warned to avoid. What from these lists do you need to put into action in your own life?

THE VALUE OF DISCIPLINE

God sometimes disciplines us in order to help us grow. This discipline may come through difficult situations, unexpected challenges, unavoidable misfortune, or even as a consequence of our own poor decisions. When we submit ourselves to this discipline and learn from it, it provides enormous spiritual benefits. The final chapters of Hebrews describe the behavior of those who have grown as faithful followers.

HEBREWS 12:2–13:25

• Identify behaviors believers should demonstrate (chapter 13). Rank them in order of importance. Which did you list as most important, and why?

• Think of a time in which you underwent a season of God's "discipline." What triggered it? What did you allow it to teach you spiritually? (See 12:11 for God's hoped-for results.)

notes

AND PRAYER NEEDS

transformations

A Few Questions...

Who are your heroes? The book of Hebrews devotes an entire chapter to the stories of great persons of faith. Along with those biblical heroes, each of us has individuals we've known intimately—influential persons we aspire to emulate in our day-to-day lives.

One of my heroes from my childhood was Dorothy. She was the age of my grandmothers but gave me something unique for a girl from a large family: her focused attention. I spent many Friday nights with Dorothy and her husband Red. It somehow soothed me to watch her arthritic hands methodically wash dishes while we talked, laughed, and sang together.

She shared my joy at reading my first book and gave me a gold star for the inside cover. By the time I was confident enough to move on to other books, the entire inside of that first book was covered with gold stars. Each of those stars was a physical representation of time and love invested.

Dorothy and Red always fascinated me because they were about the only people I knew with no children of their own. From an early age, I knew viscerally that they needed me in their lives, that that my presence helped assuage a hole that could have been filled by grandchildren if they had been so blessed. Now I can see how easy it would have been for Dorothy and Red to be busy with their own lives and not to have taken the time with me. Dorothy worked full time in their family business (really my first example of a woman working outside the home) and was very involved in community and church activities. But she gave herself to me, from taking me out to dinner every Friday night to memorizing the state capitols. From giving me a desk to do my "work" in her office to giving me a safe place to stay in Florida during my college spring breaks. She gave me her example of quiet faith, giving back to her community and being amazed by each child, regardless of color or background.

Those in the list in Hebrews, those we often consider to be superheroes, were simply obedient human beings with faith that motivated them to invest themselves in obedient service to God and to the people around them. They are part of a long list of faithful God-followers that includes my friend Dorothy. For all of this and so much more, I'm glad we gave our daughter the middle name Dorothy. It reminds me to take time with my daughter to know her, to laugh about the little things, to pass along that which is good, to extend the legacy of faith to the next generation.

books 59-61

james and 1 and 2 peter

living out the faith

The letters written by James, Peter, John, and Jude are known as the General Epistles. These letters were written to all followers of Christ rather than to one person or church.

James (Jesus' biological half-brother, and not the apostle) was the leader of the church in Jerusalem. James presided over the Jerusalem Council, which decided the issue of equally accepting Gentiles into the faith. He was also part of the group that confirmed Paul's call to the Gentiles. Written around AD 40-50, James' letter was among the first New Testament writings and was intended to be circulated among Christians living throughout the Roman Empire. James' letter consists of practical instructions on how to live as a Christian.

James' primary theme is that "faith without deeds is dead" (2:26). James affirmed that the path to become a Christian is solely through the grace of God. But he also wrote that good works are the necessary outward evidence of our internal faith in Christ. Naming many challenges that faced the early Christian believers (favoritism, control of the tongue, hypocrisy, materialism, and pride), James emphasized that life in Christ goes beyond believing right to living right. Now as then, our bottom-line question as Christians is the same as the one James held out to his first readers: how are you making your faith alive and visible to others?

Peter, one of Jesus' closest friends, was one of his original disciples. Late in his life (AD 60-68), Peter wrote the two letters in the New Testament that bear his name. His first letter was a response to the persecution that followers of Jesus were experiencing as tolerance for Christianity within the Roman Empire faded. Peter addressed what it meant to live as followers of Christ in a hostile world. Peter's growth from an impulsive denier of Christ to a solid leader of the Christian movement was evident through his encouragement to rejoice in suffering. Persecution is an expected part of life for those sincere in faith, and God can use it to strengthen us and our witness for Christ.

Peter's second letter was also to those scattered over northern Asia Minor by Roman persecution, but this time it addressed the enemy within the church. Peter was close to death, and this letter served as his farewell speech as he laid out how to stay true to Jesus in the face of false teaching. Jesus' followers must live in a way that pleases God and hold firmly onto truth; we are empowered to do so through regular study and application of God's Word. Peter's challenge to all followers of Christ is to "be on your guard so you may not be carried away by the error of the lawless…but grow in the grace and knowledge of our Lord" (2 Peter 3:17-18). May you grow in that grace and knowledge with James and Peter this week.

PERSEVERING THROUGH TRIALS

_____
_____
_____
_____
_____
_____
_____
_____
_____
_____

James, one of the pastors/leaders of the Jerusalem church, knew that living out faith in Jesus would bring changes personally and corporately. For centuries, followers of Jesus have wrestled with outward persecution as well as their inward response to the lifestyle and attitude changes needed to act out their faith. James pointed out the need to go beyond merely hearing the word, to doing what it says.

JAMES 1:1–2:13

• From chapters 1–2, list at least three things we are to do as we go beyond hearing the word to acting on the word.

• Based on 1:27, how are you measuring up in practicing "pure and faultless religion"? What could you do better?

FAITH AND ACTIONS WORKING TOGETHER

_____
_____
_____
_____
_____
_____
_____
_____
_____
_____

James explored "genuine" faith, as demonstrated by Abraham and Rahab in the Old Testament. He focused on the relationship between good deeds and faith in the lives of those who have chosen to follow Christ. His premise: genuine faith goes beyond right thinking (an intellectual belief system) into the demonstration of right living.

JAMES 2:14–4:12

• What is the main reason for hypocrisy? What actions does James say to take in order to change (4:7-10)?

• Which of these actions do you need to take?

MORE SCRIPTURE

Genesis 22:1-19—The story of Abraham and Isaac

Joshua 2—The story of Rahab

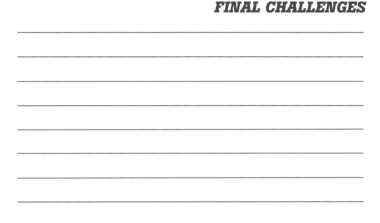

James made some confrontational statements yet showed sensitivity to those who were suffering. James explained how God can ultimately use suffering for good (compare Romans 8:28), even though it may be beyond our understanding at the time. James ended his book with statements of hope through the power of prayer and God's healing.

JAMES 4:13–5:20

• What did James say to the rich? What encouragement did he give the suffering poor?

• How are these statements applicable to the situations of suffering around the world today? How can you be part of the solution for the poor?

MORE SCRIPTURE

1 Kings 17:1-6; 18:16-46—Elijah and the withholding of rain

During Nero's reign as emperor of Rome, the church (made up of both Jewish and Gentile believers) was considered a threat because its beliefs and values conflicted with those of Rome. The resulting persecution brought suffering, discrimination, ridicule, and in many cases, death. In the midst of this situation, Peter called the church to "live such good lives among the pagans that, though they accuse you of doing wrong, they may see your good deeds and glorify God."

1 PETER 1:1–2:12

• In 1:13-23, Peter described the actions that define holiness (being set apart for God). What are they?

• Give a specific example of how you could demonstrate one of these actions at work, at home, in your community, or in the church.

GRACE UNDER FIRE

_____
_____
_____
_____
_____
_____
_____
_____
_____

Peter warned that followers of Christ will participate in Christ's suffering. He encouraged us to approach our painful situations with the same attitude as Jesus Christ, who humbled himself, submitted to the will of God, and went to the cross. As we demonstrate humility and submission, the Spirit can and will transform us into the image of Christ.

1 PETER 4:12–5:14

• In 5:1-11, what role do humility and submission play in overcoming anxiety? In resisting the devil?

• In what area of life are you experiencing anxiety and suffering? How can today's passage help you overcome?

MORE SCRIPTURE
1 Peter 2:13–4:11—Service, a household code, and discipline

EVERYTHING WE NEED

_____
_____
_____
_____
_____
_____
_____
_____
_____

Peter's second letter warned about false teachers and called believers to practice spiritual disciplines to keep from being ineffective. Peter reminded his audience that we have everything we need in Jesus. We discern the truth of a teaching by seeing how it lines up with the whole of Scripture and with what the church has historically held to be true.

2 PETER 1

• According to verses 3-11, what do Jesus' promises provide for us? What are we to make an effort to do? Why?

• Why is the validity of Scripture so important? What steps are you taking to know and apply the Scriptures to your life?

MORE SCRIPTURE
Matthew 17:1-13—The Transfiguration referred to in 2 Peter 1:16-18

As the first-century Christians waited for Christ's return, some of their neighbors scoffed and made fun of them. Peter's letter has reminded followers through all centuries that Christ will return—but the time will be determined by God, who is patiently waiting and longing for all to come to repentance. The instruction is clear for all believers: stay faithful and productive as the time draws near.

2 PETER 3

• How are Christ's followers to act as they await his return (verses 14-18)?

• Peter charged all followers of Christ to "grow in the grace and knowledge of our Lord and Savior Jesus Christ" in order to live godly lives. As we anticipate Jesus' return, what will you do to grow deeper in this grace and knowledge?

notes

AND PRAYER NEEDS

transformations

The Power of the Tongue

There's not much space in the Bible devoted to body part talk. Oh, an occasional description about hair (Samson, John the Baptist) and physical disabilities (Mephibosheth, Paul) but more often than not, parts is parts! That is, until you get to the book of James. For some reason, James feels compelled to give a sizable portion of this very practical letter to a certain physical feature—a body part he claims has the same fire-blazing potential as a spark landing in a forest on a crisp fall day. He's talkin' The Power of the Tongue.

James claims that the tongue has the power to create the most insidious of evil and the greatest of good. It can wag either way, which makes this muscle imperative to tame. Thinking back over my own life, words spoken to me have gone both ways, leading my spirit towards new life or pronouncing pain, depending on the wag.

Mama whispered in my six-year-old ear, "You're a special little girl." Now, Mama wasn't the kind of woman who was known for her positive statements, and thus I chose to believe her words. In fact, I didn't just believe her; I worked hard to live into that prophecy. I was determined to prove her right! Mama kindled a great fire that day.

"You just think you're little miss perfect!" Painful words spoken by a slightly younger sister in preteen turmoil. I turned her words over in my mind for years afterward, my adult brain asking what prompted my teenaged-self to criticize her and risk ruining everything between us. Her reply sparked a fire that singed my spirit.

Two decades and three kids later, my young family had just received news that we'd be moving out of state and away from the home of our dreams, a house we'd designed and built with our own hands. Distraught, I remember hearing my mother's voice, warm and encouraging, speak out truth and love. "You built one home, honey, you can build another." She was absolutely right, and at that moment her words became my hope and named our next steps. We moved forward to design and build our best dream home a state away, a beautiful fulfillment of that spark of blazing potential.

I've noticed that tongues still "wag me towards" life. On many occasions, times when I doubt myself right down to the carpet, my husband will speak words of life to spark light into my dark soul. "You are different, and different is good." I can feel the warmth of new life blaze every time I hear that encouragement.

Now, the Power of the Tongue is wagging into the next generation. Recently I asked my grown son if he remembered any words spoken his way that had made a difference in his life. He remembered as a teen bringing home a less-than-great report card and trying to convince me that the other kids in his class had done worse than him. I told him that was absolutely no excuse. "You are different, and different is good." Familiar words passed down, sparking a blaze of potential in his brain—and fueling his present career success.

Train and tame the tongue, for each one of us has the power to lead our listeners downward towards insidious evil or upward towards great, godly good. Tongues, like fires, can passionately warm hearts or violently destroy spirits. It all depends on the wag.

books
62-65

The apostle John, Jesus' closest friend, wrote his Gospel late in his life, somewhere in the AD 80s, and penned three letters soon afterward. The first persecution of the Christian church under Nero, during which Peter and Paul were martyred, had come and gone. John, the last surviving apostle, wrote to encourage and strengthen Jesus' followers in the area around Ephesus.

A loose organization of Christian churches had developed among the communities springing up throughout the Roman Empire. These churches were influenced by heresy spread by false teachers, primarily from the group known as Gnostics. The Gnostics believed that all physical matter was evil; in their belief system a pure, perfect God would never inhabit a sinful, human body, so they denied Jesus was God in the flesh. They also believed that increasing knowledge would lift them to a higher plane spiritually. The offshoot of this thinking was the belief that pure spirits could not be contaminated by earthly sin, so they were free to act any way they wanted. John's letters warned of the danger of these faulty beliefs and defined the characteristics of a true follower of Christ: right belief, righteous (moral) living, and demonstration of love for others.

John's second and third letters were written as personal notes to expose false teachers and warn against connecting with them. He encouraged followers of Jesus to stay alert and disassociate from those teachers. His letters reflected the tension within the church between the need to protect it from heresy yet offer hospitality to true teachers of the faith.

Jude was the half brother of Jesus and the full brother of James (author of the New Testament book of James and leader of the church in Jerusalem). Jude was most likely not involved in Jesus' earthly ministry (John 7:1-10). He became one of Jesus' followers after the resurrection (Acts 1:14) and provided leadership among the churches in Palestine. Jude stated his reason for writing in verses 3-4, "I urge you to contend for the faith…for certain individuals whose condemnation was written about long ago have secretly slipped in among you. They are ungodly people, who pervert the grace of our God into a license for immorality and deny Jesus Christ our only Sovereign and Lord." Using examples from the Old Testament, Jude's fiery words attacked the false teacher's behavior (hypocrisy, divisiveness, and loose morals) rather than their teachings, and called for true believers to resist their example and hang on to those who were wavering from truth.

May Jude's encouragement, offered to all followers of Jesus, strengthen your walk in truth this week: "To him who is able to keep you from stumbling and to present you before his glorious presence without fault and with great joy—to the only God our Savior be glory, majesty, power and authority, through Jesus Christ our Lord, before all ages, now and forevermore! Amen" (Jude 24-25).

sun.

LIGHT AND DARKNESS

_____

_____

_____

_____

_____

_____

_____

_____

_____

_____

John extends an invitation to fellowship (intimate relationship) with God through God's Son, Jesus Christ. To have this relationship on an ongoing basis, Jesus' followers must walk in the light. Our values, behavior, attitudes, and commitments must line up with God's character. Everyone is in need of forgiveness because at any time we are capable of choosing darkness over light. God provides forgiveness and restoration as we confess our sins.

1 JOHN 1:1–2:14

• According to 2:3-11, what characterizes the person who walks in the light?

• An old bumper sticker reads, "Christians aren't perfect… just forgiven." How does confirmation of this in 1:8–2:6 encourage you?

mon.

LIVING AS CHILDREN OF GOD

_____

_____

_____

_____

_____

_____

_____

_____

_____

_____

John wrote to ordinary people who struggled with sin just as we do today. Expecting something totally new as a result of their relationship with Christ, they became frustrated with what remained of the old sinful habits that were patterned into them before they came to know Jesus. John's advice: keep following Jesus, and deal with each incident of sin through confession, repentance, and the filling of the Spirit. As old patterns are broken, Jesus' life will emerge and "we shall be like him" (3:2).

1 JOHN 2:15–3:10

• From 2:28–3:10, make a list of statements John made about sin.

• From your list, write a paragraph about sin and its implications for you personally.

LOVE ONE ANOTHER

The biblical understanding of love goes far beyond the emotion commonly associated with the word. God is the definition of love, and those who are in relationship with God will demonstrate God's character of proactive, serving, selfless love. Biblically, love is a verb; it is an action, not a feeling. We show our love for God by the way we treat people. Love for God and love for people are so intricately connected that John declared, "If we say we love God yet hate a brother or sister, we are liars."

1 JOHN 3:11–4:21

• According to 4:13-21, we are to live in love. What does it look like to live in love in everyday life?

• To whom do you need to show the proactive, serving, selfless love of God in a greater way?

WHOEVER HAS THE SON HAS LIFE

Many people turn to the last chapter of 1 John in times of doubt. Can Christians ever be completely sure of their salvation? Through God's word, we see the love of God; we are chosen by God and held in the palm of God's hand. Because of God's word, we can *know* that we have eternal life, not because of who we are or what we have done, but because of who Jesus is and what he has done on our behalf.

1 JOHN 5

• Why did John write this letter (verses 13-16)? What is the testimony of God about God's Son, Jesus (verses 9-12)?

• Choose one verse from 1 John that has been especially meaningful for you. Write a prayer asking God to help you apply this verse to make a difference in your life.

thurs.

WATCH OUT FOR DECEIVERS

_____

_____

_____

_____

_____

_____

_____

_____

_____

_____

_____

_____

During the first century, teachers of the faith traveled across the Roman Empire, spreading the good news about Jesus. They depended on the hospitality of followers of Jesus for their food and lodging. False teachers (such as the Gnostics) began to travel as well, promoting their own version of the gospel. John warned followers of Christ to test the message of teachers before opening their homes to them.

2 JOHN

• According to verses 4-9, what identifies a teacher of truth? What identifies a false teacher?

• On what basis do you decide the truth of a teaching? How do you guard against false teaching?

MORE SCRIPTURE
Romans 16:17-20—Paul's warning about false teachers

fri.

HOSPITALITY

_____

_____

_____

_____

_____

_____

_____

_____

_____

_____

_____

In his third letter, John challenged followers of Christ who were withholding hospitality for genuine teachers of the gospel. He addressed two members of the same church. One was warmly providing for the Lord's workers, while the other not only refused to offer hospitality but also was encouraging others to follow his pattern. Hospitality is a principle reinforced throughout Scripture.

3 JOHN

• Why are we to show hospitality?

• What would you need to change in order to offer hospitality more frequently?

MORE SCRIPTURE
Romans 12:9-13—Paul's instruction on hospitality

HOLD ON TO THE FAITH

Jude's concern was the same as John's: false teachers, who prostituted God's grace by using it to justify every manner of immoral behavior, had infiltrated the church and were being supported by Jesus' followers. Jude warned the church to hold on to the true faith in the face of false teaching, a warning equally applicable today.

JUDE

• From the readings in Jude, how has God handled teachings that stray from the truth? How serious is God about truth?

• How are you cooperating with God as God "keeps you from stumbling and presents you...without fault" (verses 24-25)?

MORE SCRIPTURE

2 Peter 2:1-10—False teachers and their coming punishment

notes

AND PRAYER NEEDS

Turn the page for this week's Transformations Reflection.

transformations

Motorcycle Obsessions

My best friend lives in New York City. Actually, he just made a financially sound move by moving to Brooklyn. In Manhattan he had been paying over $1,300 for an apartment that had as much floor space as my Jeep Cherokee and a daredevil squirrel that regularly bombed through his window at inopportune times (candlelit dates and REM sleep).

So with his rent nearly cut in half, my friend did what any "normal" person would do. He bought a motorcycle. But of course he couldn't go about this in a "normal" way. Not my friend. He had to do it in the most romantic way possible. He bought vintage leather boots that a war general supposedly used to rescue a distressed damsel. He also found vintage goggles that make him the coolest 6'7" rider his Honda Nighthawk has ever seen. And last but not least, he took his motorcycle courses on the banks of Coney Island. I don't know why, but learning how to shift gears with that rusty old amusement park in the background just seems right.

Now that my friend is licensed, I get messages from him like, "I just rode up to the Hamptons and fell asleep on the beach for two hours." Or (I've gotten this message a number of times), "Brad, you wouldn't believe the cool reactions I get when I'm on my bike."

What's interesting is that my friend's obsessions never last more than a few months. Before the motorcycle, he ran a marathon. He trained like America's freedom depended on his running twenty-six consecutive miles. After the marathon running grew old, he took a two-week trip to South America. He saved birds or something. After that he tried Internet dating. Twice a week he met different women until he got bored and bought an old school typewriter. Now he's writing letters the old fashioned way while drinking wine and listening to classical music. And once again I feel like the most boring person alive.

It's easy for me to get caught up in my friend's big city adventures. All it takes is one phone conversation about him riding over the Brooklyn Bridge on his motorbike, and I'm convinced he's living

The Dream while I'm just sleeping. This week, however, the end of 1 John sort of woke me up.

The Message says it this way: "Jesus is both True God and Real Life. Dear children, be on guard against all clever facsimiles." The NKJV says it this way, "Little children, keep yourselves from idols." It's easy to get fooled by clever facsimiles. Old-fashioned motorcycles and typewriters can trick us into thinking they provide Real Life. Adventure-envy has the sneaky ability to rob us of the Real Adventure Jesus provides.

So I've been racking my brain to figure out a way to make my friend feel some kind of Jesus envy. I'm pretty sure it's going to take years of me obsessing over Jesus while he goes through countless clever facsimiles like saving whales and learning Russian. I'm confident, however, that someday my friend will notice the difference between our obsessions and choose the one providing Real Life.

revelation

a new heaven and earth

book 66

The book of Revelation was written near the end of the first century, AD 90 to 95. The setting for this writing is the island of Patmos, off the coast of modern day Turkey, where some think that the apostle John was living in exile, though the author did not claim to be an apostle.

Revelation addressed two issues especially important during the time in which it was written. One was the growing persecution of Christians throughout the world by both the Roman government and the Jews. The letter encouraged followers of Christ to stand firm. The early Christians lived in expectation of Christ's return, but it had been sixty years since Jesus' death, resurrection, and ascension. Revelation offered hope and urged them to hold fast to their faith. The second issue was a perspective on the "end times." The author communicated that in all situations, no matter how things look, God is still in control and Christ will come again not only to execute judgment but also to deliver the saints.

The book itself is written in a different style from most of the Bible. It makes use of highly symbolic language and contains many descriptions of visions and creatures of various characteristics. It belongs to a particular style of ancient writing called apocalyptic literature, where symbolism, strange images, visions, dreams, and journeys are carefully crafted and conveyed into a message that makes sense to the intended readers but is usually meaningless to oppressive authorities who might use it against them. The book of Daniel is another example of this type of writing.

Generally there have been two extreme attitudes toward the reading and study of Revelation. The first group would say that the book is too difficult to comprehend or understand and would completely ignore its words, whereas the second group believes Revelation to be the only New Testament book that should be studied. This second group spends most of its time coming up with specific times, dates, and other predictions that the author and the literature itself never intended. The proper attitude is somewhere in between. Revelation is an important and profitable book, but it must be read and studied in the greater context of other books in the Bible.

As you go through this week's study, you may find some of your questions unanswered and many aspects of Jesus' second coming still unclear. Be encouraged, however, by the overall theme that God is still in control. Christ will have the ultimate victory over sin, Satan, evil, and death—and by his grace we will reign with him forever and ever.

sun.

GOD'S REVELATION TO THE CHURCHES

_____

_____

_____

_____

_____

_____

_____

_____

_____

_____

Revelation starts with Christ's words of encouragement and warning to seven particular churches in the Asia Minor area. In this dialogue, Jesus described each church's strengths and faithfulness, if any, as well as the correction that needed to take place. Each message, whether harsh or uplifting, ended with a strong word of eternal promise in heaven to those churches that overcome.

REVELATION 1:1–2:11; 3:14-22

• What were the characteristics of the churches that God deemed good versus the characteristics of those that were condemned?

• What things in your life vie for your love? How will you make God your first love each day?

mon.

THE THRONE OF GOD AND THE LAMB

_____

_____

_____

_____

_____

_____

_____

_____

_____

_____

John was taken in spirit to heaven and to the throne of God. As heaven opened up, John saw God on the throne surrounded by people, angels, and other beings, all in worship and praise. The scene changed slightly as a scroll was produced that could only be opened by the Lamb who was slain for all humanity. Christ then appeared, opened the scroll, and received praise and worship from all around the throne.

REVELATION 4–5

• What attributes of God and the Lamb most grab your attention? What detail about this image of heaven helps you realize God's awesomeness?

• What do you think it will be like to stand in the presence of God's throne and to worship Jesus our Savior? How does knowing this shape your day as God's servant?

JUDGMENT OF THE SEALS AND THE RIGHTEOUS MULTITUDE

According to John's vision, the righteous judgment of the earth had begun. As Christ opened each of seven seals, a different judgment was cast upon the earth. In the midst of the judgments, an uncountable multitude of people appeared before the throne of God singing God's praises. An angel described the multitude as those who have had their sins forgiven by Christ's blood and over whom God will forever watch and bless.

REVELATION 6:1-17; 7:9–8:5

• In 7:9-10, what was the response of the multitude to God and the Lamb? What were God's promises to them (7:15-17)?

• How can you apply this picture of eternity to your everyday struggles of life? Which of God's promises speaks to your life the most?

BATTLE BETWEEN GOD AND SATAN

As judgment on earth continued, John saw the ongoing battle between God and Satan. In the initial battle, Satan and his angels lost their place in heaven as the archangel Michael defeated them and hurled them to the earth. So Satan made war on God's people by raising up the antichrist and the false prophet to lead the world away from God. These two rulers proceeded to deceive the world.

REVELATION 12–13

• What deceptions did Satan and his associates use to deceive the world into worshiping and following him?

• Name some of the worldly deceptions you face on a daily basis. How do you keep yourself from being deceived?

MORE SCRIPTURE
Revelation 14:6-14—The three angels

thurs.

JUDGMENT OF THE BOWLS

_____

_____

_____

_____

_____

_____

_____

_____

_____

_____

The judgment of the seven trumpets and seven bowls increased in intensity as God continued to judge those who rejected God's sovereignty. And yet the stubbornness of those on earth also increased, and they continually refused to repent. Once the last bowl was poured out, a loud voice from the throne claimed the judgment time had come to an end.

REVELATION 16

• How did the severity of the judgments demonstrate God's power? Why do you think God chose to judge the earth in such a harsh manner?

• How has pride kept you from worshiping God? What area of pride do you need to surrender to God?

MORE SCRIPTURE
Revelation 8:6–9:21; 11:15-19—The trumpet judgments

fri.

JESUS RETURNS, HUMANITY JUDGED

_____

_____

_____

_____

_____

_____

_____

_____

_____

_____

Once Satan was doomed to the lake of fire, John saw the final judgment of humanity. Two sets of books were opened: one set was filled with the deeds of all people and the other was the book of life. Only those whose names were found in the book of life were allowed to enter heaven. Everyone else was condemned to the lake of fire.

REVELATION 19:11–20:15

• Putting these chapters with 1 John 5:11-13, how is God's grace revealed amidst this final act of judgment?

• Write a prayer expressing to God how you feel about his saving grace, offered to you through Jesus.

MORE SCRIPTURE
1 John 5:11-13—God's provision for your name to be written in the book of life

Once the final judgment of humanity was complete, John saw the new heaven and new earth created for God's people. This dwelling place was not only new but eternal in all its features and magnitude. The holy city itself was resplendent with the presence and light of God, and everyone saw and served God forever and ever. God now dwelt with humanity and humanity with God.

REVELATION 21:1–22:5

• Write down the characteristics of the new heaven and earth. Which characteristic holds the most promise for you?

• How does the hope of heaven keep you from being enslaved by sin in your everyday life? What steps will you take to keep eternity always on your mind as you live in this temporary and dying world?

GOD CREATES A NEW HEAVEN AND EARTH

_____

_____

_____

_____

_____

_____

_____

_____

_____

_____

notes
AND PRAYER NEEDS

_____

_____

_____

_____

_____

_____

_____

_____

_____

_____

_____

Turn the page for this week's Transformations Reflection.

transformations

What's at the End of the Road?

One of my favorite poems is "The Road Less Traveled," by Robert Frost. It makes a comfortable analogy of life being about the road we choose to travel and the curiosity many people have about the road they didn't take.

Two roads diverged in a yellow wood

And sorry I could not travel both

And be one traveler, long I stood

And looked down one as far as I could

To where it bent in the undergrowth

My senior year in high school was full of crossroads. I was faced with the choice of entering the military, college, or the workforce. I chose the Navy. But I often wonder what life would be like had I gone straight to college.

We all face crossroads. They may be decisions about marriage, buying a house, or which job we take. Most crossroads in our life have no guaranteed outcome. We make a decision and do the best we can to produce the desired outcome. Some crossroads are more important than others. The decision I made about breakfast this morning will more than likely not have eternal consequences. However, certain crossroads do have eternal consequences. In Matthew 7, we read Jesus' explanation of how each of us has a crossroad choice to make. We can either take the broad road to destruction, or we can take the narrow road to life. This crossroad has defined outcomes—see Revelation.

Revelation is a message to us about the eternal consequences of our choice at the crossroads. John paints a picture with mystery and symbolism, but the message is clear: we're going to be held accountable for the road we choose. Of all our crossroad choices in life, our choice to serve God rather than ourselves is paramount. It is the one crossroad that affects everything. In the Old Testament, Joshua put it this way, "Choose for yourselves this day whom you will serve…but as for me and my household, we will serve the LORD" (Joshua 24:15). Joshua knew that life is found in following God's commands.

Choosing the road less traveled is not easy. The distractions of the world cloud our thinking, and many people choose the path to destruction. So what is the answer to today's question: what is at the end of the road? Well, John described it. And today—right now—I need to make sure which road I am on. I need to ensure my destination and know in which book my name will be found. I don't know about you, but for me, when it comes to that day, I won't wonder about the road most traveled. I'll be thankful for the road less traveled, the narrow road, the road that leads to life.